electronic
MUSIC
PRESENTS

THE
RECORDING
SECRETS
BEHIND
50
GREAT
ALBUMS

PRESENTS

THE
RECORDING
SECRETS
BEHIND
50
GREAT
ALBUMS

EDITED BY KYLEE SWENSON GORDON

Backbeat Books

An Imprint of Hal Leonard Corporation

Portions of this book are adapted from articles that originally appeared in the magazines *Electronic Musician*, *Remix*, and *EQ*.

Published in cooperation with Music Player Network, New Bay Media, LLC, and magazines *Electronic Musician*, *Remix*, and *EQ*. *Electronic Musician*, *Remix*, and *EQ* are registered trademarks of New Bay Media, LLC.

Published in 2012 by Backbeat Books
An Imprint of Hal Leonard Corporation
7777 West Bluemound Road
Milwaukee, WI 53213

Trade Book Division Editorial Offices
33 Plymouth Street, Suite 302, Montclair, NJ 07042

All text content courtesy of New Bay Media, LLC, except articles by J. J. Blair, Blair Jackson, Heather Johnson, Ken Micallef, Bill Murphy, Bud Scoppa, Patrick Sisson, Richard Thomas, Jeff Touzeau, Rich Tozzoli, and Tony Ware, used by permission.

Photos of the Doors, Nick Drake, M83, Pink Floyd, ?uestlove, Billy Corgan, Pete Townshend, and the Yeah Yeah Yeahs are from Getty Images. Photos of Fleetwood Mac and Ali Shaheed Muhammad are from Retna, Ltd. Photo of Andre 3000 © Ian Mcfarlane. Photo of Dr. Dre © Mr. Bonzai. All other photos appear courtesy of New Bay Media, LLC.

Printed in the United States of America

Book design by Damien Castaneda

Library of Congress Cataloging-in-Publication Data is available upon request.

ISBN 978-1-61713-041-0

www.backbeatbooks.com

Contents

Introduction

There's quite a bit of subjectivity in what constitutes a "great" album. Who says an album has to be popular or even critically acclaimed to be great? Some wonderful albums have sold merely hundreds of copies and were virtually ignored by the press, whereas others sold millions and were showered with praise from music journalists across the globe. Meanwhile, some talented— and very fortunate—artists released albums that would go on to become "classics" after they stood the test of time through the passing decades.

To create truly great music, a musician or band doesn't need an enormous recording budget, cutting-edge technology, ultra-rare and expensive vintage equipment, or the most sought-after producers and engineers. Having those luxuries can ensure that the sonic quality is professional and radio-ready, but a truly great album can't exist without memorable songs, beautiful sounds, and excellent performances. (Although considering the capabilities of today's digital audio workstations, it could be argued that even rock-solid performances aren't required anymore.) Sometimes all it takes to create an album that inspires fans and influences musicians is one person with some motivation, ideas, and a laptop. But there are two key ingredients that artists really must have as a starting point: passion and inspiration. From there, every great artist has a different story.

The circumstances of each record discussed in the following pages run the gamut of genre, era, geography, popularity, and recording methodology. For example, while he was alive, none of British songwriter Nick Drake's albums—released from 1969 to 1972—sold more than 5,000 copies. It wasn't until more than a quarter century later that his music became popular. Meanwhile, following Outkast's hit album *Stankonia*, Andre 3000 claims he was "terrified" about how the follow-up, *Speakerboxxx/The Love Below*, would be received. But the Atlanta, Georgia–based rapper needn't have worried, as the album hit number one on the *Billboard* 200 chart shortly after it was released, in 2004.

The 30 interviews in *Electronic Musician Presents the Recording Secrets Behind 50 Great Albums* convey a common thread of each artist's enthusiastic—sometimes obsessive—creative drive. Struggles, successes, writer's block, and artistic epiphanies are revealed in honest detail throughout. These stories are culled from the last 10 years of *Electronic Musician*, *Remix*, and *EQ* magazines (the later two of which folded into *Electronic Musician* in 2009 and 2011, respectively), with albums ranging from 1967 to 2011.

Naturally, there are numerous fantastic albums made in the last half century (and before that) that don't appear in the pages of *Recording Secrets Behind 50 Great Albums*. Some of those may be unearthed in future issues of *Electronic Musician* magazine or future Backbeat books. But while this book is not a comprehensive be-all, end-all collection of the best albums in *history*, it is rather a sampling of many great ones and the inspirational, sometimes surprising stories behind them.

Focusing on the songwriting, production, and mixing process, each chapter demystifies the creation and construction of many innovative works of music, with genres ranging from hip-hop, R&B, electronic, and pop to hard rock, country, folk, Latin music, and many permutations in between (such as Nortec Collective's fusion of norteño and techno).

In addition to a range of musical genres, there are also many methods of recording. Some producers and musicians, such as Sharon Jones & the Dap-Kings and TV on the Radio, eschew software technology almost completely. Others embrace it fully, as with Imogen Heap and Massive Attack. Some artists believe in prioritizing performance, recording hundreds of takes in the studio (Tegan and Sara), while others piece together sounds and samples bit by bit (A Tribe Called Quest). And some artists have faced technological limitations based on the recording era, having no other option than to splice together analog tape, while artists in the new millennium have unlimited digital trickery and minute editing capabilities at their disposal.

Whichever paths the artists, producers, and engineers interviewed in this book have taken—whether they dealt with the frustration of their restrictions or, sometimes worse, option anxiety—they all ended with the same result: great, sometimes brilliant, music.

Here, you'll read about the studios, gear, techniques, songwriting, and personal stories behind 50 great albums. If you're looking for ideas in the pursuit of your own musical mission, the following chapters have plenty of fodder for inspiration.

Kylee Swenson Gordon
San Francisco, 2012

electronic
MUSICIAN
PRESENTS

THE
RECORDING
SECRETS
BEHIND
50
GREAT
ALBUMS

Classics

Aerosmith

TRACKING TECHNIQUES AND MIXING METHODS OF *TOYS IN THE ATTIC* AND *ROCKS*

By Rich Tozzoli

This chapter features an abridged version of the Aerosmith article in the May 2008 issue of *EQ* magazine.

The year was 1975, and a five-piece band from Boston known as Aerosmith had just wrapped up a lengthy tour to promote its sophomore release, *Get Your Wings*. Both that album and the band's self-titled debut had charted gold, but the members were still hungry—ravenous, even—for breakout success. Little did they know that the next 24 months would propel them from an opening act to full-fledged arena-rock superstars and forge a legacy that, three decades later, would remain strong as ever.

But the band didn't get there alone. When studio mastermind Jack Douglas and engineer Jay Messina stepped on board for the *Get Your Wings* sessions in 1973–74, they established the beginnings of a production team that would help provide the "bad boys from Boston" with the sounds, songs, and swagger to dominate the airwaves. Fully in charge for the next album—co-producer Ray Colcord and engineer Rod O'Brien helped with *Wings*—the duo channeled Aerosmith's raw, reckless brilliance into the 1974 smash *Toys in the Attic* and its 1976 platinum follow-up album, *Rocks*. Those ground-breaking and influential records secured Aerosmith's status as rulers of the mid-'70s hard-rock scene.

Now, 30-plus years after *Toys in the Attic* and *Rocks* first hit the shelves, Messina broke out the albums and sat down with EQ to reveal the studio techniques used to create two rockin' masterpieces.

It was while working at the Record Plant that you got hooked up with Jack Douglas, right?

Yes. Jack was assisting at that time, and he got on a few of my dates. We clicked as friends, and we also liked the way we worked together. It was a real natural partnership. Then Jack got a couple of good opportunities to advance his production skills. I guess the first big one was when Bob Ezrin gave him the chance to co-produce *Get Your Wings*. Aerosmith was up-and-coming, and Columbia recognized them as a band that was going to happen. So that's when we met the guys, and Jack and I ended up working on *Get Your Wings* together. Well, that record didn't take off, but Columbia was still impressed with the band, and they also felt Jack and I were a good match for them. So we started *Toys in the Attic*.

Did the band write a lot of *Toys in the Attic* in the studio?

Yes, and also during pre-production with Jack. Certainly, a lot of [vocalist] Steven Tyler's lyrics were written in the studio. For instance, we all went to the movies one night and saw *Young Frankenstein*. The "walk this way" line in the film is what inspired Steven to write "Walk This Way." The band was in a very creative place.

What did you record *Toys* on?

The deck was an MCI two-inch 16-track that was running Ampex tape. We used the Spectrasonics console in Studio A, and we had some really cool outboard pieces such as Roger Mayer limiters, and an old Altec compressor that gave the guitars a cool, subtle squash.

How did you track the guitars on that album?

Typically, I would use the combination of a Shure SM57, a Sennheiser 421, and a Sony C37. I would place all three mics close to the grille and mix the

Jack Douglas (far left), Jay Messina, Steven Tyler (in background), and Joe Perry. (Courtesy of *EQ* magazine)

signals down to one track. The "edge" would come from the 57 and the 421, while the C37 would provide the "weight." Sometimes we would add a little bit of phasing to get some extra edge. We had an Eventide flanger that we used occasionally, as well, and if it sounded really good, we would just print the effect to tape. In the mix, we would usually pan Brad Whitford's guitar to the left and Joe Perry's guitar to the right. They had some great old Fenders, and Joe used a small Gibson stereo amp that just sounded amazing. Most of the time, it was just one or two amps per player being tracked. Once we experimented with assigning one guitar to 13 amps, and miking them up. That's when we discovered that having 13 amps doesn't make the guitar sound 13 times better than one amp!

What about Joey Kramer's drums?

We set the drums on a wood floor. I would get a Sennheiser MKH 415 shotgun mic up as high as I could, point it straight down at the snare, and then put a Universal Audio 1176 on it, squashing it at around a 20:1 ratio. Generally, I would just add some of that channel under the dry track in the mix. On the snare, I sometimes used an Altec 633A "salt shaker" in place of a Shure SM57. I only miked the top head, and I used a Pultec EQ to boost slightly at around 10kHz and 100Hz. The hi-hat mic would be a Neumann KM 84, and for the toms and overheads I used Neumann U87s. With the overheads, I would position the mics so I had a good shot at all the cymbals, but I always tried to maintain the snare in the center of the image. For the kick, we used an Electro-Voice 666. We also added some board EQ on the kick to boost the low end at 50Hz and the attack at around 3kHz.

Toys in the Attic had drums assigned to five tracks: kick on one, snare on two, everything else on three and four, and the shotgun mic on five. The exception was "Sweet Emotion," where the shotgun mic was multed to two preamps. One was limited with a UREI 1176, and the other with a Universal Audio 175. Each signal was printed on a separate track. I rarely adhered to traditional miking techniques back then. I was all about experimentation.

You also played some percussion on the album.

I played bass marimba on "Sweet Emotion." We felt the bass part was missing a little edge to it, and Jack knew I played vibes, so I gave it a shot and doubled the bass part. It worked great with the bass sound. It's in the intro, and the re-intro after the first chorus.

Was Tom Hamilton's bass sound all direct, or a mix of amp and DI?

It was a mix of both amp and DI, which were submixed to a single channel. Tom used an Ampeg B15 amp, and we would take the direct line off the amp head. The mic would have been an Electro-Voice RE20. We also used an old Flickinger tube limiter—a monstrous bass compressor that had its own special sound. If you applied it moderately, it kept the low end from getting muddy, and it added lots of punch in the mids. We would occasionally use a Lang Program EQ to boost the 2kHz range for some added edge.

I heard Steven didn't use headphones for most of the album. How did you record his lead and background vocals?

When Steven didn't hear headphones, I would record him with the shot-gun mic because of its narrow polar pattern. I would set him up with a couple of monitors in the live room, and send a mono feed. We'd place the monitors out of phase and then position Steven in the sweet spot where the two signals almost completely canceled each other out. If he was hearing headphones—which he did on occasion to sing background vocals and other parts—I'd use a U 87. While the backgrounds are mostly Steven, Joe would sing occasionally, too. You can hear him on there if you listen.

Was *Toys* mixed right there at the Record Plant?

Yes, and it wasn't that difficult. Jack and I would both get our hands in there on the mix, and if we needed other hands, we would just ask. You couldn't be shy about asking for help, because there was no automation. You had to manually ride the faders. The mixes were often a combination of using extra hands, or mixing songs in pieces, and then editing sections together. We would cut and assemble the order on 1/4-inch tape running at 15 ips. The whole record took around four months to finish.

What reverbs did you have at the time?

They had some really cool EMT plates and a spring reverb. Most of the reverb you hear—like on "Sweet Emotion"—was the EMTs. If we had a cool reverb sound going, we just printed it to tape.

Did you rely on a lot of compression for the mixes?

We didn't use much. We would hit the tape hard enough to get some natural compression and then add just a little to the guitars and bass to even things out. The exception was the shotgun mic above Joey's snare. I'd really squash that one.

Later on, when we recorded *Rocks*, I'd take the drum mix—mostly kick and snare with a little bit of the overheads—and route it from an aux send to an 1176. I would really squash that signal at 20:1, and I'd have the input level up to the point where you think it's too much. The 1176's release function would almost enable you to put the compression in time with the song. What I mean is, based on how quick or slow the release was set, I could try to have

5

the 1176 back to zero compression by the time of the next snare hit. That way, you always hear the crack of that next snare fully. Also, if you were hearing

JACK'S TALES FROM THE ATTIC

Often referred to as the "sixth member of Aerosmith," Jack Douglas was instrumental in helping shape the band's early sound. With a long track record that includes the likes of John Lennon and the Who, Douglas is certainly no stranger to making hit records. Here, he reflects on working behind the scenes with "the bad boys from Boston" for *Toys in the Attic*.

What were some of the challenges in making the album?

At that time, their performances could be dodgy. They would get a few moments of brilliance, and then fall on their asses, but I wouldn't want to stop the take. I would just go for whatever I could get. Sometimes I would be banging a cowbell in a booth just so the tempo would stay straight. That way, I could edit all the takes together when it was done, because the brilliant parts would just be incredible.

The band has often called you their "sixth member." Explain the specifics of that role.

That "sixth member" phrase is because of the situations that went down in preproduction, when I would basically move in with them. We would create songs from the ground up, and, because of their touring schedule, they would just show up and ask, "Got any songs?" We would develop stuff from the ground up—such as the riff on "Walk This Way," or the bass part to "Sweet Emotion." The major contributors were Steven, Joe, and myself, but everyone certainly pitched in.

You mixed *Toys* with flying fingers.

That's right! We would mark fader levels with pencils and razor blades down to block faders from being moved past a certain point, and then it would be all hands on deck. Sometimes you would just do a verse, then reset for the chorus, and make all your pre-planned moves. There would be stop points set for the drum fills and so on. I miss that process, because things happened by accident on those records that were just really cool.

Did you realize how great *Toys* was when you were working on it?

No. I was too close to it. When Bruce Lundvall [president, Columbia Records] came in to listen to the whole album, I was thinking, "Oh, my God, it's just terrible." I thought it must have sounded like this mushy big mess flying at him. After it was over, Bruce said, "I think I can take a breath now." And I thought, "Wow, he really hates it." But then he said, "It's brilliant. There's gotta be four singles on there that are amazing." And there are only nine songs on that record!
—Rich Tozzoli

too much of the cymbals, you could slow up the release, and it wouldn't pull up a lot of cymbal bleed. When mixing, I would add the compressed signal in parallel to the other drums to get an apparent loudness to the kick and snare without adding much meter level. This is how we got that "hit you in the chest sound" for Joey's drums.

How many tracks did you use?

When we remixed *Toys in the Attic* for 5.1 surround a few years ago, I had it transferred from the 16-track master to Pro Tools. When I looked at the track sheets, I noticed that there was at least one track open on all the songs. We basically used only 15 tracks for the whole record.

What did you print the mixes to?

The final master was a 1/4-inch Ampex tape. We were very conscious of the low end and any out-of-phase material, because we didn't want the vinyl records to skip. Doug Sax did a great job mastering the record. He sonically brought it up another notch.

Let's move on to *Rocks*. What's the story there?

The guys were rehearsing in a warehouse in Waltham, Massachusetts, and they were getting really comfortable up there. It turned out that everything sounded really good in the room, so we just parked the Record Plant mobile truck in the warehouse.

So you just miked everybody up where they were in the room as if they were practicing?

Yes, even to the point of using this huge speaker cabinet Joey had set up behind his drums for the rehearsals. He had a mic just lying in his bass drum, and we ran the signal through a little MXR equalizer with everything from 125Hz and up rolled off, and everything below 125Hz boosted all the way up. A big woof of air would come out of that cabinet, and he'd feel it every time he hit the bass drum. It made for a really cool bass-drum sound, although it bled through everything except the guitar mics that were positioned right on the speaker grilles.

How were the band members positioned in the warehouse?

They were set up in corners. As you walked in, the drums were just to the right. There was a guitar amp in the far right corner, a guitar amp in the far left corner, and Tom's bass rig was in another corner. It was so loud that they would easily hear each other no matter where they stood. That was the point. We isolated amps and the drum kit a bit with blankets, but, of course, that only worked so well.

Was everyone miked up the same way as on *Toys*?

Yes, although we did try a pair of binaural mics on Joey. Those mics have their applications, but they weren't an overwhelming success, in my opinion. We also miked this big cement room off the loading bay to get some ambience. It sounded huge. We got some great tracks up there, and we went back to the Record Plant for overdubs—mostly vocals, but some added percussion and guitar parts, as well—and mixing.

Here's a funny story: At that time, CBS had to have their union engineers on the session, so we always had these two guys hanging around the warehouse. Right at the end of one tune, we heard a door creak open. It was one of the guys coming back from coffee. In the mix, we had to make the creak louder, because we couldn't get rid of it. You can hear it at the beginning of "Nobody's Fault."

What console was in the mobile truck?

It was a De Mideo board that was super straight-ahead and clean. It had minimal EQ, so it was just used to get the sound on tape.

How did the limitations of the board affect your approach to recording the album?

It was a matter of just finding the right mic, putting it in the right place, and getting it on tape as clean as possible. In that sense, it made the album easy to record.

When you listen to *Toys in the Attic* and *Rocks* now, what are your thoughts on them?

I didn't realize at the time that these would be big releases, or that they would go down in history as classic rock records. Who knew that "Walk This Way" and "Sweet Emotion" would become the radio staples they did? But I do remember being excited about the sessions. These albums were fun to work on, and fun to mix, and it's nice to be driving in the car and still hear them playing on the radio.

HEWITT'S ROCKING MOBILE RIG

David Hewitt—the Grammy-winning president/chief engineer of Remote Recording—was on the scene when Aerosmith recorded *Rocks*. Leaving the hustle and bustle of New York, the band and production team set up shop in an empty warehouse in Massachusetts, not far from Aerosmith's hometown of Boston. To track the sessions, Hewitt rolled up an entire mobile studio, and here he tells us about some of the gear he brought in to keep the sessions running smoothly.

What was the setup for *Rocks*?

The band had a rehearsal room called the Where-house—a big, insulated industrial space with unusually high ceilings. We brought the Record Plant's truck up there, which had a De Mideo console loaded with UREI 1108 modules. These were basically solid-state discrete versions of the old tube circuits UREI had made, so they sounded really good.

How many inputs did the console have?

It only had 24 inputs and eight mix busses, and tracking was a little difficult due to the limited inputs. To get around that, we also used some Ampex AM10 submixers, which were six by two. We brought the submixers in on line positions, because, even then, we started using up to 35 or 40 inputs for the band, Joey had tons of drums, Jay had room mics up, and Brad and Joe had a bunch of guitar amps all around. Every time they would add something, I'd be scrambling to find another preamp somewhere and another way to get it in.

What tape machines did you use?

We were still doing 16 tracks at that point, and we had a pair of Ampex MM1000s—the first 16-track recorders ever produced. Those things were big and clunky, but they sounded great.

Where did you put the truck?

We actually pulled the truck right inside the Where-house from the loading dock. Everything stayed in the truck. We ran the cables out into the room and set things up just like a live date. We had great big honking Westlake monitors that were just awful. They reached compression at like 9 o'clock, but the guys knew them so well that we used them. The whole point was to make the band feel like they were just rehearsing—to catch them in their element, and that's what we did. —Rich Tozzoli

What comes across is the energy of the songs and the mixes, which is what we always wanted to put into the records in the first place. Listening back, it's not about asking, "Is there enough 10kHz on this or that," or focusing on specific technical points in the mix. It's more about reflecting on the album in the context of "Does it feel good, and do you get excited when you hear it?"

The answer, in these cases, is "Yes." I guess the magic was there when we put the records together, and that magic still comes across in the mixes 30 years down the road.

2

Erykah Badu

THE ANALOG/DIGITAL FUSIONS OF
NEW AMERYKAH PART TWO:
RETURN OF THE ANKH

By Bill Murphy

This chapter features an abridged version of the Erykah Badu article in the April 2010 issue of *EQ* magazine.

On a chilly December night in New York City, a gaggle of journalists is being crowded into one of the live rooms at Chung King Studios in Soho. Not your typical album preview, everyone from Britpop soulstress Corinne Bailey Rae to legendary label exec Sylvia Rhone is rumored to be on hand, while in the small reception area on the penthouse floor, cell phones are being collected, bagged, and numbered to avoid "Internet leakage" of the night's proceedings.

Some are grumbling about the over-the-top security measures, but when Erykah Badu makes her entrance, all is quickly forgiven. Relaxed and regal to the core, she explains to her hushed audience that some unsavory type has already uploaded a bootlegged track from the previous night's session. That song, "Jump in the Air (Stay There)," with spotlights from Lil Wayne and Bilal, has since been leaked officially, and given Ms. Badu's unwavering commitment to creative control of her music, she can't be too happy about it.

Even on this night, she seems almost uneasy about drawing back the curtain on her fifth studio effort—maybe because some of the songs are not yet in the final stages of mixing. But she needn't have worried. *New Amerykah Part Two: Return of the Ankh* (Universal/Motown, 2010) delivers on multiple levels, one of the most prominent being a return to form that recalls the honey-soaked revelations of Badu's groundbreaking "neo-soul" debut *Baduizm* (Universal/Motown, 1997). Deeper still, *Part Two* is a meticulously crafted concept album, both in the vintage sense of Music of My Mind–era Stevie Wonder and in the alt-underground hip-hop vein repped by such artists as Madlib, J Dilla, Karriem Riggins, Georgia Anne Muldrow, Shafiq Husayn, and 9th Wonder—all of whom, it so happens, lend their production cuts (posthumously for Dilla) to the finished gem.

"I wanted the themes on this album to have a very warm and sometimes familiar feeling to them," Badu says. "Sonically, most of the first album jelled together because of the digital sound, but this time I wanted to feel it in more of an analog way. Some of the samples we used might sound very familiar, too, but it's fun for me to revisit things like that and put a melody over it that has never been heard before. That's really what the art of hip-hop is about, and what makes it exciting. It doesn't have to be something totally new. It can be something redone or recycled that has a new twist, or a new feel to it."

Devout fans will also recognize shades of the slightly off-kilter, almost psychedelic jazz overtones and tape-saturated lushness that were the main ingredients in Badu's sophomore release, *Mama's Gun* (Universal/Motown, 2000). Some of the key personnel from that outing, who have worked consistently with Badu over the years, reprise their collaborative roles here—including, in particular, Roots drummer Ahmir "?uestlove" Thompson and keyboardist/producer James Poyser.

"We definitely share a similar-mindedness," Poyser offers. "Erykah can go from the beatnik thing to the hip-hop hardcore thing to the jazz thing, but in the end what she really loves is music. She has taken in a lot of different styles and influences, and she's grabbed them and made her own niche. When you're working with somebody like that, it just makes everything easier."

Regardless of the hat she's wearing—producer, composer, musician, performer—Badu is constantly exploring the range of her voice and delights in the

Erykah Badu at Merriweather Post Pavilion, Columbia, Maryland, in 2009. (Candice/Footprint Fotos)

experimentation that modern technology affords her. When a song first begins to take shape, she'll record a demo vocal straight into GarageBand, and then manipulate it until it begins to line up with the sound she has in her head.

"I just keep turning knobs until I hear the right match for the song and how my voice should sound," she explains. "Each song has its own woman—its own character. I playfully call it 'she' when we're mixing or doing a sub-mix or a rough mix, so I might say, 'She needs some more of this.' Chav [Mike Chavarria, engineer/producer] will listen to what I've concocted and try his best to make it match."

Chavarria takes the lead vocal from "Don't Be Long," co-produced by Detroit-bred beatsmith Ta'Raach, as an example; the song immediately conjures up Stevie Wonder's classic "Girl Blue," where his voice is squeezed through an undulating, kaleidoscopic tape flange. "For her demo of that song, Erykah used one of GarageBand's phasers," Chav explains. "It tends to have a harsh quality to it, so I used several instances of a Waves MetaFlanger to get the sound she wanted. The vocal is feeding itself—really the flanger is feeding another flanger, and then it's sent to another flanger as if it were a reverb. The way it's set up on the console ends up being pretty complex, but it was the only thing that was able to make it move like that and have the right blend of effects."

Understandably, Badu is a perfectionist when it comes to her vocal perfor- mance and how it fits the final version of a song, so there's no telling when she'll scrap a take, even during mixing. "That's what's very unique about working with Erykah," says Tom Soares, whose tenure with Badu as recording and mixing en- gineer goes back to *Mama's Gun.* "I'm in mix mode all the time—if I'm not in Pro Tools, I'm in the computer on the SSL console. She likes to hear the progression of how the song is coming together, so at any given point in the process I have to recall the record that she's gotten used to hearing. Sometimes I'll be ready to print, and all of a sudden she'll ask for a couple of new vocal tracks, and it'll be a brilliant performance. She has really good ears and she knows what she wants."

Finding the right microphone to get the job done has been a Grail-like quest over the years, but Badu feels she has finally found the right one, thanks to Soares, in the Shure KSM9. "Tom was telling us that James Taylor uses that mic to record with, so I tried it out," she says. "Now I religiously use it all the time, no matter how much they try to force these other mics on me. I even carry it with me in my purse. [*Laughs.*] Tom knows how much midrange I have in my voice, and how I hate to hear it coming back at me because it sounds too nasally, so this is the one I use now, for my live shows and in the studio."

It's already pretty well known among producers, engineers, and gear geeks that Badu rarely, if ever, records in a vocal booth, preferring instead to sing in the control room with a live monitor mix. "As long as she's facing the speakers straight on, I can turn them up significantly and not have a problem with leakage [into the mic]," Soares explains. "But Erykah is not easy to record, because her voice is so dynamic. She has a heavy range from 2.2 to 2.6k, so when she goes up there and really belts it out, you need a signal path that can take it. Lately I've been using the Little Labs Lmnopre—it's clear and big sounding, with tons of headroom. I run that into an Amek 9098 mic pre, but I just use the EQ end of it. I filter a little bit on the bottom and a little up around the high ess area, around 12 or 13k. Then from that, we go into a Summit TLA-100 compressor, with 2dB of leveling at the most. I'm not a big fan of compression on vocals, but the tubes help, especially when you're using Pro Tools."

For that matter, so does recording to tape. Soares acknowledges the speed and efficiency in editing that Pro Tools offers, but he remains skeptical of the digital platform's ability as a tape machine, especially when it comes to recording vocals. "All the music is coming out of Pro Tools," he admits, "but most of Erykah's vocals are coming off of two-inch tape." It's a nod to how records used to be made, and really to how Badu continues to work; her vocals for *New Amerykah Part One* were tracked to tape, and she'll likely stick with it in the future. "I've even tried to fly a vocal take back into Pro Tools, but it just sounds different," Soares continues. "Even with a great converter, the difference is huge, so for us the best way to get around it is to lock up the two-inch with Pro Tools."

From the start, *Return of the Ankh* swells with the velvety atmospherics that define the best tape-based analog recordings from the '70s: thick low end, warm limpid mids, and punchy highs, with close attention paid to the stereo spread and panning techniques. It's really the only way to transmit the hypnotic mood of the album, which shifts gears effortlessly from dreamlike (in the opening echo-drenched sequence of "20 Feet Tall," co-produced with 9th Wonder) to get-down funky ("Don't Be Long") to groove-introspective (in the closing epic "Out My Mind, Just in Time," with James Poyser and Georgia Anne Muldrow).

"Window Seat," the album's first single, is a prime vehicle for Badu to channel all her creative strengths, as well as her penchant for analog warmth. The song has its origins in an informal session at her Dallas home with Poyser. "Erykah has this old lime-green, ridiculously out-of-tune piano," he quips. "She refuses to get it tuned because it has character—it's a sight to see and hear. We were just sitting there playing some things, and she started singing and that's how the idea came about."

Badu had a vocal melody, but no words. Like most of the songs she writes, she follows the path perfected by Marvin Gaye, allowing the lyrics to emerge from the rhythm of the melody. "I write on beat, very much like an MC," she says. "I'll keep listening back to it, and once the rhythm starts to sound like syllables of words, I just say whatever word fits. Sometimes that becomes what the song will be, then I fine-tune it so it makes sense, or sometimes I just leave it as is."

Using her own home 4-track, she laid down a drum pattern from her Korg Triton, and the demo began to take shape. From there, recording engineer Chris Bell, who first joined the Badu camp with *Mama's Gun*, went in to prep Luminous Sound in Dallas—Badu's de facto home away from home when she's working on an album—to track a session with Poyser on Fender Rhodes and ?uestlove on drums.

"When they came in to work, I was instantly ready to pull up a two-inch machine," Bell says, recalling how *Mama's Gun* was recorded entirely to tape. "I had a vintage drum kit delivered because I thought Ahmir would want that old-school sound. He's very particular about what mics he wants on the kit— no [Shure] SM57s allowed—so I used Royer R-121 and R-122 ribbons on him, along with some Coles 4038s. It's a real smooth sound. We basically came in and knocked it out in an afternoon, but Ahmir wanted to add some percussion parts, and pretty soon working with the two-inch was getting cumbersome, so we dumped it into the computer."

What emerged was a fat, loping groove with a minimalist arrangement of claps and conga hits, all punctuated with ?uestlove's signature snap on the snare drum. "Initially, I played the bass parts on the Rhodes," Poyser says, "and I over-dubbed a bass sound out of Logic. I had it controlled by a Motif [Yamaha MIDI controller keyboard], and I'm sure it was a sound from [Spectrasonics] Trilogy. The bass sound from that just married well with the track. Usually I scroll through and try playing a few things, and whatever marries well with the track is what I use."

Badu lived with that version of the "Window Seat" demo for months afterward, working diligently until she had two verses and a bridge recorded. "One of the things I'm accused of is demo love," she jokes. "I want it to sound just like that, forever. We hadn't put a real bass on it—James was playing that on keyboards, and it was just perfect. There was nothing more to be done to it . . . until Thundercat came in."

As bassist with Sa-Ra Creative Partners and Bilal, Stephen "Thunder-cat" Bruner is a known entity on the hip-hop underground. "He put a funky-ass bass line on it—very simple, just three or four notes—and that was all it needed," Badu recalls. "I guess you could say that songs are crafted the way Subway sandwiches are made. You start with the bread, then a little bit of lettuce, then we point to the pickles and so on, and the bass line was the oil and vinegar. That's how it happens."

In the mix, Soares called on some key pieces of outboard gear to thicken the bass sound even further. "I've got a Moog 3-Band Parametric Equalizer that works really well on bass," he says, "and I'll also use the Drawmer 1969 [Mercenary Edition] tube compressor, usually across the mix bus. There's a little switch in the stereo link section, and when you move it to the 'BIG' position, all the bass comes through so it only compresses the midrange and treble." The effect makes Poyser's Rhodes sound almost bass-like, and Bruner's bass sound almost synth-like.

Like the first installment of *New Amerykah, Return of the Ankh* swells with the contributions of some key figures in experimental hip-hop. Drummer and producer Karriem Riggins is one of them, having worked closely with J Dilla on what would turn out to be his last solo project (2006's *The Shining*); his musical connection with Badu goes back to 1998, when she joined Dilla at his studio in Detroit for sessions that led to the Grammy-nominated "Didn't Cha Know?" from *Mama's Gun*.

"Erykah had a batch of songs that were inspiring to her, and she burned a CD for me and James [Poyser] to listen to," Riggins begins, referring to the events that led to the making of "Get Money"—a smoldering soul groove based on the Sylvia Striplin classic "Can't Turn Me Away" and one of several standouts on *Return of the Ankh*. "She didn't actually say she wanted to remake these songs—it was more to spark some creativity. So when we finally booked the studio time [at Chick Corea's Mad Hatter Studios in L.A.], we started to re-create that break."

Riggins soon came across another inspirational break during a session at Sa-Ra's studio. "I brought my [Akai] MPC3000 in, and I think I had about 50 records with me, and I stumbled on this Eddie Kendricks loop ['Intimate Friends']," he says. "I knew that a lot of people had used it, so I thought about how I could do something different. I just stretched it out into a long form on the 3000, and then added some clavinet and Rhodes when we dropped everything to Pro Tools. Erykah was incredible. She let the beat roll for at least half an hour and basically recorded a freestyle reference; then she pulled ideas from that." The song became "Fall in Love," which pays tribute to the stutter-step rhythmic explorations of Dilla but also serves as a test case to the challenges Soares had to meet in the mixing phase. Riggins points to the song "Umm Hmm," a sample-stacked workout co-produced by Madlib, as another example. "We got Madlib's music in the form of a stereo MP3," he explains, "and I've developed a method of working with that format so it fits with the overall sound Erykah wants.

"Basically, I duplicate the track about six or seven times, and then I go in with some heavy-duty EQ plug-ins and literally destroy the 2-track and then rebuild it. I use the Massenburg EQ plug-in a lot for this. It allows you to separate the bandwidths, so it plays only the bandwidth that you're highlighting. I'll usually start with the kick drum; if it's slightly out of phase, I'll fix that and then pan it up in the middle. Then I'll just keep isolating different parts of the two-track, each time panning it out a little bit more, until I've re-created a stereo image from a whole bunch of small snippets. How it works depends on the density of the 2-track. You're gonna get phasing, so you have to keep adjusting until it makes sense, but at this point it's almost like I can go in there and [pull out individual] instruments."

With yet another album already nearly in the can—*Lowdown Loretta Brown*, named after one of her many aliases and described as a character "from the '50s who acts like she's from the '40s . . . the 2040s"—Erykah Badu continues to push soul and hip-hop music into entirely uncharted waters.

"Georgia [Anne Muldrow] and I have very similar worldviews, and we're very serious about the vitality of our families," she says. "Making ["Out my Mind, Just in Time"] with her—and in fact making this album—has been a liberating time for me because we're defining ourselves through our relationships as women. It woke me up to really acknowledge my part in my own heartache, and what I'm doing wrong. I wasn't in any particular situation at the time, but the music has so many elements of liberation in it, and that's all I could think of to talk about. It's a diary entry of what's inside of my mind, and a way for the whole deal to come out."

3

Beastie Boys

BUILDING A VINTAGE SOUND COLLAGE IN A DIGITAL REALM FOR *TO THE 5 BOROUGHS*

By Ken Micallef

This chapter features an abridged version of the
Beastie Boys article in the September 2004 issue of
Remix magazine.

Swallowing snacks while previewing the in-flight entertainment lineup aboard a New York–to–L.A. flight, two
Beastie Boys are suddenly surrounded by the jet's cabin
crew. No strangers to adulation, the Beasties welcome
the perks that come with million-selling-record status
and recognizable pop-culture faces.

"Nice to meet you," says Captain David Ricketts as
he introduces himself. "We appreciate your being onboard, and we appreciate your music. How long are you
in L.A.?" Adam Yauch (aka MCA) and Adam Horowitz (Ad
Rock) extend their hands, smile amiably, and chew the
airline fat. Mike Diamond (Mike D) has already landed in
L.A., his newborn baby making his life even more hectic.

"This is actually my personal plane that I am letting
Adam Horowitz fly on," MCA claims. "Normally, Adam
doesn't let me fly on his plane, but I am letting him ride
on my plane."

Private jets, first-class travel, a personal introduc-
tion from the captain—it all sounds like a scene from a

Beastie Boys video. Each Beastie Boy has his own personal jet? "Nah," MCA says with a laugh over the phone. "I am just kidding. This is a commercial United flight."

The ability to fly high with the beautiful people while maintaining supreme street credibility illustrates why, six years after their last album, *Hello Nasty* (Capitol, 1998), the Beastie Boys' *To the 5 Boroughs* (Capitol, 2004) is one of the year's best-selling albums—debuting at number one on the *Billboard* 200 chart—and a call to arms for hip-hop's old-school faithful.

SOUND ECONOMY

Still enamored of raw samples and old-school hip-hop, the Beasties trawled their record collection for sound bites and inspiration from a decades-span-ning cache as far-flung as the Sugarhill Gang, Marley Marl, the Partridge Fam-ily, the Flaming Lips, Peggy Lee, and the Dead Boys. With recording techniques that had transformed since the more laborious *Hello Nasty* sessions, the Beas-ties went whole hog importing sound files on Apple iPods and CD-Rs to their Tribeca-based New York City Oscilloscope Studios. At Oscilloscope, the Pro Tools HD and Apple Mac G4 system ran dutifully alongside an analog Neve and Studer rig. And though the dozens of outboard effects occasionally met with the mild consternation of the album's studio overlord, Super Engineer Duro—who performed final mixdown on a Pro Tools|24 Mixplus system and a G4—the Beasties gained a new kind of recording efficiency this time around.

"The way that we interacted with each other using computers at home and bringing stuff in on iPods was like nothing that we had done before," Mike D recalls. "*Hello Nasty* was done on Pro Tools at Oscilloscope, but it was prohibitively expensive for everyone to have that in their home. In the four years since, the technology changed completely. It was very nice having that freedom where each of us could work on things in our own environment and bring them in from home. In my home studio, I am using [Propellerhead] Rea-son and [Digidesign] Pro Tools HD on a Mac G4; I also have a PowerBook and a Digidesign Mbox. The Adams have similar setups, though Horowitz still likes the E-mu SP-1200 for beats."

With everyone home-brewing 2-tracks, the Beasties reunited at Oscillo-

Beastie Boys: MCA (far left), Mike D, and Ad Rock. (Phil Andelman)

scope to play the results of their labors. Soon, they were cracking heads and writing rhymes. "We'd take our 2-track demos into Pro Tools and plug some handheld mics into a PreSonus Digimax setup," Mike D explains. "We throw rough vocals onto that and see how it comes together. Then we will hone in on a track that appeals to all of us, loop 8 or 12 bars of a section, and literally sit there with our notebooks open and try to write raps and ideas. If the song starts to sound good, we will reinforce the music at a higher quality, separate all the instruments when we reimport it, work on the arrangements, and recut the vocals with AKG 414 mics running Neve EQs and compressors coming into the Neve console. We work fast: Whatever sounds good, we refine it."

Rife with old-school vibes—as well as TV commercial impressions ("It's fressssssh"), inside jokes ("your Grandma's kugel!"), and excellent smart-ass rhymes—*To the 5 Boroughs* is unabashedly nostalgic for an era when hip-hop was at its most fertile and techno was just beginning to introduce its catalog

21

of blips, bleeps, and tweaked-out flourishes. "The album is old-school but old-school-meets-the-future," Ad Rock says. "We were trying to do new stuff, but we were also unable to get away from our hip-hop influences. And there is a fine line between old school and techno."

"In terms of an old-school direction, that was never planned or even talked about," Mike D adds. "When we are making hip-hop, we've got this mid-'80s thing stuck in the hard drive of our brains, and it is impossible for that not to be an influence. So it was not as much a conscious decision to draw on that as much as it is impossible for us to get away from it."

WHAT'S IT ALL ABOUT?

Album opener "Ch-Check It Out" is classic Beastie Boys, with silly lyrics charging over ear-splitting brass shouts and a bell-driven, ultrafunky beat that pulls and punches rhythmic sleight of hand with all the madness of a *Looney Tunes* chase scene. With its stuttering vocals and warbling effects, "Ch-Check It Out" is as cool as "Riunite on ice." It all began with Ad Rock's beats.

"On 'Check It Out,' we did the beat and the whole track in Pro Tools," Ad Rock says. "The song has two beats, both from Peggy Lee's *Is That All There Is?*, a record I bought 15 years ago. One beat is from 'Sitting on the Dock of the Bay'; the other is from another song on the same record. I added extra kicks and snares from Reason. It took a minute to sync all the stuff up. The Time Compression/Expansion plug-in in Pro Tools lets you get the beat in the ballpark of the tempo, then stretch it to exactly where you want it. I would never even think to have done that before; all I would have done is chop it and make a whole new beat.

"What I brought in originally for 'Check It Out' sounded terrible," he adds. "So I brought my Peggy Lee record back in so we could resample it. Yauch got the CD, but the old, shitty record sounded better than the new CD. The CD didn't capture as much of the dynamics, and it was almost too bright. The cymbals and the beat became this wash whereas the vinyl actually had greater high-end definition, which is surprising."

MCA handled the Pro Tools maneuvers, letting Ad Rock function as the eyes and ears to decide what the track needed. He also cut the track's brass hits. "We exported the beats into Pro Tools and time-compressed one of them to make them both the same tempo," MCA says. "Then we decided to make one the chorus beat and the other the verse beat. The chorus beat had this horn hit on the one, so we left it. Then there was this other horn sound in the other drum sample, so we chopped it up and came up with a horn pattern for it in the verse. Then we took the second half of the beat and played it first; we flipped them. There is no bass line—we programmed an 808 kick pattern underneath so there is some low end."

Both "Ch-Check It Out" beats are so flowing and hyperactive, you have to wonder how much was played in real time by Ad Rock (using Reason's instruments) and how much was quantized to fit. MCA explains: "We don't always quantize, but that song is pretty on the grid. We just made the loop work. The snares don't hit right on the two and the four; they float a little. But the horn stabs are right on the grid. Sometimes it is easy to work on the grid because you can move things around real fast. If it doesn't work, you can slip it a little bit."

"Ch-Check It Out" also has what sounds like a mystery vocal, or at least ghost notes. Way, way back in the chorus is the soprano aura of a grade school girl's choir—or is it? "That is some leftover reverb from the bar before the Peggy Lee vocal sample," Ad Rock says. "She is singing the chorus; then there is a breakdown in the song, but right before the breakdown, the horns climax, then stop. So what you are hearing is the carryover note. That is why sampling is so cool, because you get sounds and shit that you would never, ever think of making that just sort of happen accidentally."

THREE'S COMPANY

Although many vocalists choose to do their parts solo, the Beastie Boys work best with a three-mic, three-booth vocal setup. Using movable gobos (a type of baffle) and three AKG 414s, Ad Rock, Mike D, and MCA record their vocals simultaneously in full view of one another.

"There is something about the energy of the three of us in the room at the same time," MCA says. "The main take for any given song will always come from that setting. You could go individually and really scrutinize and do a million punches, but somehow the master take always comes from the three of us to-gether. We don't do as many fixes as compared to how most records are made."

Although the approach to recording vocals sounds straightforward, effects are more experimental. MCA spills the beans, challa bread and all. "Some-times we would create delays for the vocals just editing within Pro Tools," he says. "Years ago, on an analog console, we would set up a throw and throw the vocal to a delay. But with Pro Tools, we will duplicate the vocal on another track and then go through and delete whatever part of the vocal we don't want and throw to a delay, leaving little bits of the vocal you do want to hit the delay."

"The Beastie Boys are unique in their three-mic, three-booth setup, though EPMD used to do it that way, too," says studio guru Super Engineer Duro. "Usually, each person does their part individually, but it works for the Beastie Boys because their chemistry is really good and they bounce off each other's energy. They are all hilarious in their own way, but MCA is more the studio guy, Mike D is the business guy, and Ad Rock is strictly about the music. It was a really relaxed environment, and there was no pressure, so I spent more time on each song than I usually do. The hours we worked were like banker's hours—it was a ghost town by 7 o'clock."

SUPER DURO CHARGED

Receiving top billing after the Beastie Boys in the album credits for his mixing efforts, Super Engineer Duro previously handled the board for Fabolous, Jay-Z, and DMX; he has also produced Mariah Carey, DJ Clue, and Jay-Z. And despite the Beasties' studio intentions, Duro had a plan of his own for *To the 5 Boroughs*.

"Mixing is not really a technical science—I listen to the record and the way it makes me feel, and I react to the sounds," he says. "The Beastie Boys wanted me to mix on their old Neve console, but I convinced them to do it all in Pro Tools HD. The album has an old hip-hop feel, but, sonically, it is up-to-date. I look at mixing like a collage: I try to carve the sounds and place them accord-ing to priority, which sounds I think will affect people the most and what people will gravitate toward. I did some crazy panning, delay effects, warped stuff. It is a headphone album. I manipulated vocals and sounds with a Lexicon 960 reverb, dbx 902 de-essers, and a couple of old Tapco spring delays. But it was mostly Pro Tools plug-ins like Echo Farm, Focusrite EQ plug-ins, Bomb Factory compressors."

MIKE'S MIDI BRIDGE

Fortunately, working 9-to-5 hours didn't hinder the group's creativity. And the Beasties found themselves mixing their old methods with the new technology that they were previously hesitant to jump on. "We were late on the whole computer thing," Ad Rock admits. "I was always like, 'Who needs a computer?' But it really changed how we made this record. There are things that get lost. Working a drum machine, you can smack it around and feel like you are making a pizza. The old days of punch-ins and everybody standing there putting different fingers on different buttons to get the song right in the mix are gone. But I am sure we will be going back to that. The computer thing is cool, but I don't think we are going to do everything the same way on the next one."

Nevertheless, the group was definitely into the new process. For Mike D's techno-addled, politically charged "Time to Build," he mixed vinyl with software when he sampled an Indian string instrument and then used MIDI to match it with an EPMD vocal sample. "That began with a combination of a beat I did in Reason and a sample I took—and completely changed—of a Punjabi instrument called a *tumbi*," he says. "I put that into Reason's Dr.Rex sample player and mapped it out in MIDI using ReCycle; then I chopped it up just taking individual notes and basically replayed the line. So I had a programmed beat and this MIDI-mapped-out sample, if you will, then brought that into the studio, and we somehow ended up with the EPMD sample, which is in the chorus. It is hard to say who thought of the EPMD sample, 'cause we really collaborate on everything."

But even after more than 20 years working together, Ad Rock, MCA, and Mike D still don't have all the answers when it comes to making records. Nothing is that simple for this triple-trouble trio. "I don't have any advice!" says Ad Rock with a laugh. "We take a long time. We are never happy, so we end up going back and tweaking things. That is why we always take so long to make a record. Sometimes you got to work. If it sounds good, just be happy with it and know that it sounds good."

4

Cee Lo

TALES OF *THE LADY KILLER'S*
GLOBE-TROTTING ADVENTURES

By Tony Ware

This chapter appeared in the January 2011 issue of *EQ* magazine.

The eccentric soul known as Cee Lo Green was born Thomas Callaway to ministers of the Baptist church, but he came into his own within a far more flamboyant congregation. As part of the Dungeon Family musical collective (including Outkast, Goodie Mob, Sleepy Brown, and Organized Noize), Green helped put the closet freaks of Atlanta, Georgia's mid-'90s hip-hop/R&B scene into the national consciousness.

After several albums of Dirty South slang and social commentary, Green broke off to explore his Perfect Imperfections, a throaty hybrid of crooning and MCing as captured on the 2002 solo album bearing that phrase. In 2004, he further consolidated his avant-garde approach to urban formats with the Soul Machine, working with stellar New South producers such as Timbaland, the Neptunes, and Jazze Pha before getting caught in label shutterings and personal frustrations. It was the next year, however, when Green would see his most high-profile and, in a way, indirect, recognition.

Green would produce the song "Don't Cha," a massive hit for the Pussycat Dolls, and would record an independent album under the playful guise of Gnarls Barkley. Providing vocals for the ruddy funk shui of producer Danger Mouse, finding lyrics came quickly, "like some kind of hieroglyphics," he says, "like writing on the wall . . . something already there just waiting 'til the right music helped reveal it." Green co-scored the international Internet sensation and hit single "Crazy."

Finding it hard to maintain a shroud of mystique, Gnarls Barkley would release one more "sobering" album, 2008's *The Odd Couple*. But it was definitely the transatlantic success of that neo-soul, '60s-soundtrack-influenced project that set the stage for the 2010 return of Cee Lo Green as *The Lady Killer*. Releasing in a market primed by Motown-through-a-British-filter artists such as Amy Winehouse and Mark Ronson, *The Lady Killer* flips the formula, embodying a theoretical world where Barry White's Love Unlimited Orchestra collaborates with Burt Bacharach and John Barry in a concept that Green himself sums up in four words: big, black James Bond.

Soliciting contributors to compose with that persona in mind, Green assembled tracks from a list of producers including Fraser T. Smith, Jack Splash, Paul Epworth, and the Smeezingtons. When asked if he has an overriding aesthetic song approach, Green holds true to motifs he says he has long preferred, both physically and emotionally: "Flow and curve . . . sure, those are still the physics, those are the laws that don't change."

The first indication of how all of the influences of the past coalesced into a direction for the future was "F**k You," a viral single released to YouTube in August 2010. Produced by production trio the Smeezingtons, featuring Green's fellow Atlantic/Elektra recording artist Bruno Mars, "F**k You" [and its alternate, PC version, "Forget You"] is a retro-modern groove that maintains subtle grit, a song about the complex pursuit of pleasure that thrives on the interplay of authoritative percussion and creative spatial manipulation. The widespread embrace of "F**k You" resulted in *The Lady Killer*'s release date being bumped up from 2011 to November 2010. But this adversity-has-its-smooth-silver-lining pop tune is actually one of the last pieces that was seated in a work that was more than two years in the making.

Cee Lo. (Kai Regan)

Green's dozens of tracks, ultimately about the frustration/salvation in chasing the ladies, were conceived throughout studio sessions in Atlanta, Los Angeles, Miami, New York, London, Paris, a tour bus, and a Georgia country ranch, according to Green's longtime engineer, Graham Marsh. Many initial, improvisational home sessions began on a Pro Tools HD3 rig, playing with everything from a Yamaha Motif workstation and an Akai MPC to Native Instruments' Komplete software suite. Scrolling through sounds, Green and Marsh might veer a track from an urban to a more country feel. Halfway through the creative process, Green set out to reboot under a more proactive, nigh-neurotic work ethic and sat down with Rick Nowels for a few weeks to generate several tracks, including "Satisfied" and "Cry Baby."

Contributions came from many directions, but with their sensitive-with-a-sense-of-humor, International Man of Mystery vibe, the 14 final tracks selected for *The Lady Killer* certainly drew plenty from an obvious UK sensibility. It's another city, however, that provides a key to understanding Green's aspirations here. "It can sound like vintage Las Vegas for me," Green says. "What I mean is, what I wanted from this album is not to offer a tour [of styles]; instead, it's like a residency, piecing together a performance with a consistency throughout."

At the heart of this coherence is Green's voice, of course, and to reproduce it with consistency, Marsh set up a customized chain that accompanied them throughout the album's tracking. "Cee Lo can be very nasal when singing—which is his signature—and is extremely dynamic," says the engineer, who performed vocal production, mixing, and additional programming duties on *The Lady Killer*. "The Telefunken ELA M 251 reissue [cardioid] smoothed out a lot of that 2k, midrange harshness and stood up to the loudest scream he could muster, while still sounding present, warm, crisp."

"I find the John Hardy M-1 pre to be very present and transparent," Marsh continues. "I get more 'vibe' out of [running it into] the Universal Audio 1176. As a rule, I don't compress Cee Lo's vocals hard to tape, doing -5dB of compression at the most, but I have in certain instances when I wanted a particular sound [by setting four fingers in 'nuke' mode on the 1176]. And I use the Manley Pultec EQ at the end [of the chain] just to bump a very small amount of 10k 'air' to tape. I find this EQ gives me the sparkle I'm looking for."

A relaxed but involved delivery is indeed one of the vocal strengths on *The Lady Killer*, which Green says was conceptualized to showcase his sensitive, sexy, and sociable sides, and this balance of out-and-about and intimate energy was captured by whatever means necessary. One standout, "Satisfied," was tracked within the control room on headphones and with monitors muted, as the vocal booth felt too isolating. When describing the immediacy he intended to achieve, Green visually leans forward, gesturing as if singing to a Shure 55S cupped in his hand (what he describes as a "curl on the forehead . . . Dewey Cox mic"). The mic actually used was a Heil PR 40 (to avoid the nightmares of manhandling a 251, among other reasons), but the anticipated effect, to deliver a dynamic country-soul croon, is fully achieved.

Another successful era-bridging, soul-bolstering technique applied throughout *The Lady Killer* is the use of delay/reverb trails at the end of vocal phrases, applied on top of a good deal of spring reverb already on the lead vocal. "I would automate a send in Pro Tools to a delay on the last word of a particular phrase," says Marsh. "Nine-tenths of the time, I would be using [SoundToys] EchoBoy for an analog delay emulator—usually a fast, 16th-note delay, with a pretty high frequency, so that the delay is long. I would then automate a send on the delay track back to a reverb, so that with every delay hit, the reverb of the delay grows larger, as if it is descending down a large hall. Sometimes I will automate the room size parameter on [Digidesign's] ReVibe to make the room grow larger as the delay gets longer."

While most instruments were treated either at the source while tracking or later in the box, Marsh says reamping experiments were applied to vocals cut throughout the process. "I would run sessions later through a vintage Victoria amp, or this little Orange toy amp," he says. "You can hear this on the girl vocals on 'Bodies,' 'Red Hot Lover,' and 'It's OK.'" Additional studio routing for these tracks included Apogee Rosetta 200/800 and AD-16 DA-16 converters, UA 610s, Distressors, Tube Tech CL-1B, Neve 1079/1073/33114 pres/EQs, and Manley Pultec-style EQ.

The final thread that secures the seams, and a "Live at the Sands" vibe, on *The Lady Killer* is the presence of strings (as well as horns) on the lion's share of tracks—produced with the help of Salaam Remi, known for his work on the Fugees' *The Score*, Amy Winehouse's *Back to Black*, and releases by Nas, among many other productions. "I'm an album specialist . . . the whole idea was for me to score [*The Lady Killer*], and really make it feel like the movie that it is," Remi says.

To achieve this vision, Remi, who also co-wrote the album track "Bodies," called on his relationship with the Czech Film Orchestra, a partnership originally developed during scoring duties alongside composer Lalo Schifrin for *Rush Hour 3*. Putting together scratch tracks in Logic Pro, Remi collaborated with arrangers Stephen Coleman, Tim Davies, and Nicholas Dodd for "getting whatever was necessary . . . and steering it back in the pocket." Working over Skype and Source-Connect, Remi monitored the Prague sessions, which were recorded at 96kHz and returned via Digidelivery to the States. Once back in Remi's hands, compression and plug-ins, as well as hits of tonally competitive panning, were applied in order to balance high fidelity with intentional edge. Once the ratio of rub-to-ride was achieved, the orchestration was comped to the tracks, where sometimes synths would have to be dropped an octave, or even removed, to cede some necessary sonic real estate.

"Strings, that sophistication, it insinuates the 'scenic route,'" says Green on the quest for consistency without complacency. "So much of today's music can sound so local, dedicated to where it's made at. It hasn't been anywhere, and often doesn't want to go new places. At the heart of the best music will always be pots and pans, making something out of nothing. But it should be a success story, not stories about success. Those just all start sounding the same. That's why for *The Lady Killer*, we had to tear down walls . . . make tangible a savvy, grand production that was as much '60s personality as '80s English pop as an independent spirit where modern music can go again, and bringing it all together so it's very palatable. These songs are traveled!"

The Lady Killer embodies a quest to recapture Holland-Dozier-Holland Motown and Gamble & Huff Philadelphia International, to craft something that could have sat compellingly among the Four Seasons, Stevie Wonder, Prince, and Solomon Burke on episodes of *Soul Train* or Burt Sugarman's *The Midnight Special* variety show. But it also adds the club-friendly, 808 low-end of roughened hip-hop to soul, bringing in the nicely choppy, negative-space-rich influence of drum programming like that of Gorillaz, and it makes recognition of and concessions to modern reproduction.

For instance, Marsh discusses the use of light "distortion" on certain bass parts, such as those on the song "Cry Baby," to give tracks more presence on computer speakers. "I run the bass through two concurrent Neve 1079s [mic pres/EQs], turning the gain all of the way up on the first channel, achieving some tasty analog distortion, then using the second channel to control my level to Pro Tools. I will do this with my amp channel and blend it with my DI signal."

Ben H. Allen is a longtime Green associate who engineered Gnarls Barkley sessions, helped assemble Green's Solitaire Studios, and produced "Bright Lights, Bigger City," the most synth-heavy track on *The Lady Killer*. He also mentions using Neve mic pres on live drums for a distinct crunchiness, as well as Eventide's H3000 Factory plug-ins on bassist Tony Reyes' "Billie Jean"–like strut to give a "percussion sizzle."

"What I try to generate, which worked great for this album, is a lift and a pull, some resistance, rather than the energy being linear," Allen says. "It isn't Logic fairy dust that makes the tracks great, it's the arrangements. Cee Lo had ['Bright Lights, Bigger City'] for over a year, and added vocals, horns, and strings, when the label called to ask if I could take it and finish it. I printed stereo stems of all the parts and on my way to California, on a plane, did a new version of the song on my laptop, half mixing and half adding some [soft-synth] production, but mostly taking things out. I did it all on $150 Altec-Lansing earbuds, because you don't have to worry about the tools as much when you can establish flow."

Ultimately, all this activity—not just vocals and strings, but snares, claps, shakers, casabas, and even vinyl crackles on the album's cover of Band of Horses' "No One's Gonna Love You"—resulted in an album of punchy, clustered midrange. This was an area that many involved agree was constantly being carved and compartmentalized to maintain both timeless groove and contemporary pressure. For Marsh, it was the melodic phase shifts of Dave Fridmann on MGMT's *Oracular Spectacular* and the restless edges of Tchad Blake on Los Lobos' *Colossal Head* that stood as an inspiration for how to wrangle textural shifts. Marsh would maintain 4dB to 5dB of headroom on 48kHz/24-bit files, in order to give the mastering engineers room to augment the dynamics.

For Grammy-winning Manny Marroquin, who helmed a vast majority of the post-production mix engineering duties at his Los Angeles board, it was a conversation with Green about the spacing, depth, and crinkled reverbs of Portishead that gave the green light to playfully fray the fringes. Marroquin said he used "a lot of [Universal Audio] 1176 compression going to an RCA BA-6A, while EQwise, it was mainly a [K-series 9000XL 'Super Analogue' SSL console] and some Pultec EQs to warm it up, with a lot of Fairchild parallel compression on the drums." Spreading out the stems and using those EQs with spring, tape, and Bricasti Design reverbs to apply the last wash of continuity, Marroquin maintained Green's cool in a world of albums printing hot.

Even with so many hands pushing faders, *The Lady Killer* comes across as an album that resonates with dapper confidence, through tracks aimed at both the back row and the bedroom. "I never had to share creative space until Gnarls," reflects Green. "And with this album everyone had an opinion on how it could or should go, so this was an opportunity for me to have a theme but not be overly insistent on anything. If my approach didn't nail it, I could give a second thought and ask people their take, see if I could feel it, if the logic would come to life for me. And we all came together on the way it should play out, without resorting to one formula. I have a very analog approach to my own music. I like it live, I like it lush, and I like it to have a mystique, even if it has to bend a rule or two. People cannot live off standard pop alone. I'm an album artist, and with Lady Killer I have an entire album at a time that I feel it's possible to turn people's ears and make this sincere sound commercially viable again."

5

Danger Mouse and Daniele Luppi

CLASSIC ITALIAN FILM MEETS MODERN TECHNOLOGY ON *ROME*

By Blair Jackson

This chapter appeared in the July 2011 issue of *Electronic Musician* magazine.

It is a union that, on paper at least, probably should not work: Danger Mouse (aka Brian Burton), superstar producer and songwriter of eclectic acts including Gnarls Barkley, the Black Keys, Gorillaz, and Broken Bells; Daniele Luppi, Italy-born soundtrack composer and producer; Jack White, chameleon-like musician and producer behind diverse acts such as White Stripes, the Raconteurs, and the Dead Weather; and Norah Jones, multi-million-selling jazz/country/pop singer and songwriter. The "band" on their remarkable new collaboration, *Rome*, consists entirely of Italian studio musicians in their 60s and 70s. The music is a fascinating mélange of classic Italian movie soundtrack sonics and thoroughly modern pop songwriting, vocals, and mixing. Five years in the making, *Rome* is completely unlike any other album on the popular music landscape—which was the point from the beginning.

The story starts with Daniele Luppi, who created a modern cult favorite with an instrumental album called *An Italian Story* in the early 2000s. For that project, Luppi, who grew up admiring Sergio Leone's late-'60s "spaghetti westerns," Dario Argento's violent horror thrillers, and the strange and sometimes whimsical work of Federico Fellini, sought to re-create some of the eclectic sounds that made the soundtracks for Italian films of the '60s and '70s so distinctive and unusual. Reverence for the stark and lonely music of Leone's primary film composer, Ennio Morricone, has been widespread in America for many years, but on *An Italian Story*, Luppi tapped more into strains of Italian film music that had more jazz and bubbly pop elements, from twangy late-'60s guitar stylings, to breezy conga-driven party melodies. To capture the authentic vibe of the soundtracks he so loved, Luppi tracked down many of the musicians—most of them retired—who had played on sessions for Morricone, Nino Rota, Nicola Piovani, and other composers, and had them interpret his tunes in a loving (and fun!) homage to the sound they had created. The disc was cut at Telecine Studios in Rome in 2001 and released in 2004 by Rhino Records. Around the time the album came out, Luppi moved from Italy to L.A. and started landing soundtrack work there.

One of the many admirers of *An Italian Story* was Brian Burton, who, as Danger Mouse, was emerging from the remix underground and making waves in 2004 with a viral sensation called *The Grey Album*, an inventive (and controversial) mash-up of vocal tracks from Jay-Z's *The Black Album* and instrumental samples from the Beatles' "White Album." That year Danger Mouse also produced Gorillaz' *Demon Days* album. Burton, it turns out, was also a huge fan of Italian film music, so he and Luppi hit it off immediately.

"I saw a lot of those classic Italian movies when I was in film classes in college," Burton says during a break from working on U2's long-awaited next album. "They had this great mixture of dramatic, melancholy music with strings, mixed with these psychedelic electric guitars. And the way the drums were played had a lot of interesting rhythms—a little bit jazzy, but some of the drums almost sounded like it was coming from R&B or some James Brown stuff. There were also some avant-garde things in there, as well. It was a great mixture of things with a lot going on."

Daniele Luppi (far left), Norah Jones, Danger Mouse, and Jack White. (Frank Ockenfels)

It wasn't long after they met that Burton and Luppi began working to-gether: Luppi contributed some bass, organ, and synth parts to the mega-suc-cessful 2006 *St. Elsewhere* album by the duo known as Gnarls Barkley—Cee Lo Green and Danger Mouse. The smash hit single from that disc, "Crazy," con-tained elements from a piece by Italian film composer Gianfranco Riverberi, and other tunes of the album borrowed from Nicholas Flagello and Armando Trovaioli. The logical next step in Burton and Luppi's friendship was writing music together—and it was that partnership that evolved into the *Rome* album, which would both pay tribute to and expand upon their mutual love of Italian film music.

"At first we worked independently," Luppi says. "I have a piano and a Ham-mond organ, so I mainly worked on those. We wrote sketches and played them to each other and found we were on the same page and we both liked each other's material." Burton adds, "I would be writing ideas on piano and guitar, putting melodies together and working on instrumental song structures, and he was doing the same thing, and we would kind of pull them together and add to each other's songs, or mix them together."

Once they had a number of pieces written, in October 2006 the action shifted to Forum Studios in Rome, where Luppi once again assembled the cream of veteran Italian soundtrack musicians, including a few who had worked on *An Italian Story*—guitarist Luciano Ciccaglione, bassist Dario Roscaglione, and keyboardist Antonello Vannucchi—plus stalwarts such as drummer Gege Munari and keyboardist Gilda Buttá. The day before the first instrumental tracking sessions found Luppi scrambling around *Rome* in a van digging up period instruments for the players—a couple turned up in the collection of a Vespa mechanic, who was paid in wine for the brief rentals; how Italian!

For more than 40 years, Forum Studios has been a center for recording Italian film music. Built underneath an old church in the Parioli section of *Rome*, and initially known as Ortophonic Studios, the facility opened in 1970 specifically to do soundtrack work—the original owners were composers Morricone, Piero Piccioni, Luis Bacalov, and Armando Trovaioli. Through the years, all sorts of projects have been recorded there, including classical, pop, rock, and jazz albums (Clapton, Quincy, Eno, Chili Peppers, et al.), but it is still the go-to studio for soundtracks—Oscar winners *Cinema Paradiso*, *Life Is Beautiful*, and *Il Postino* were all scored there.

The heart of the three-studio complex is an enormous live tracking room (Studio A) that can fit 80 musicians and has a high ceiling, several support columns, parquet wood floors, and acoustical treatment on some of the upper walls and ceiling. The control room is equipped with Neve VR Legend 60-channel console with Flying Faders; Genelec 1039A and PMC IB1S main monitors; scads of outboard gear, including Teletronix LA 2A, Urei limiters and EQ, and a wide range of Lexicon digital reverbs; and for this project, the studio's Studer A820 two-inch 24-track. "Brian and I decided from the beginning we had to record to analog tape," Luppi comments. "It goes with the sound we were looking for."

Engineering the sessions was Fabio Patrignani, son of the man who designed the studio for Morricone and company, Franco Patrignani, himself a noted engineer who later ran the studio with his wife. Franco was also a colleague of Morricone's principal engineer Sergio Marcotulli, whom Fabio assisted while still a teenager. Though Marcotulli is long retired, Luppi brought him into Forum for a day at the beginning of the *Rome* sessions, "partly to show him respect," Luppi says, "but also because I wanted him to take a look at what we were doing with the mics. He could say, 'This is how we did it,' and 'You know, the drums sound a little better in that corner over there.' He knew the studio so well."

To Luppi, it was important to record *Rome* at Forum because "I wanted it to have a big sound. When you record in a big space, you hear the air, you hear the sound of the place. Also, I knew I wanted to have an orchestra and the choir, which that room [at Forum] is perfect for. But even when you record a single instrument—a harpsichord or an acoustic guitar—I wanted it to be close-miked but also have a mic up in the air to capture the room. Doing that let us add less reverb later at the mix stage."

Though Luppi and Burton arrived in Rome with charts fully written for the basic tracking group, "a lot of times the players took it further themselves and made it better," Burton says. "Sometimes we would start a song and the whole feel of the song would be wrong, but it wasn't their fault, because for us it was like, why tell them exactly what you're looking for? Why not let them try it based on what you've put in front of them and see what they do with it? I've always found it's a lot better to let people do whatever it is they're instinctively going to do even if you have an idea in your head. If you don't, you might miss out on some really good ideas."

Early on, both producers fell in love with the thick and snappy bass sound that engineer Patrignani was getting out of Dario Roscaglione's Fender VI six-string bass and Bassman amplifier with an Electro-Voice RE20 mic and a "wet" EMT plate reverb. That bass is the foundation of most of the songs on *Rome*, along with Gege Munari's minimally miked mid-'60s Gretsch drum kit. The studio also has its own echo chamber, and that was utilized on a couple of guitar parts for that extra-echo-y '60s sound. Burton liked the bass sound so much he brought a Fender VI onto a Black Keys album he worked on shortly after these first sessions.

39

While Luppi and Danger Mouse tended to other projects during the early part of 2007, the vocal component of *Rome* was just starting to take shape. Luppi says that having some time off from the project allowed him and Burton to gain some perspective on where to go next: "If we only had a few months to do this, once we did the [basic] tracks, you might think, 'All right, this is sounding pretty retro, so maybe we should get an older singer like ['60s pop and rock vocalist] Mina to match the music and finish the record that way.' But because we had time, we could say, 'Let's have a twist—let's turn in a direction you would not normally go. Let's not do what's obvious—let's do something else.' So we went more modern, and that's how we ended up with Norah Jones and Jack White on the record."

Burton had played some of the basics to White, and White liked what he heard so much he volunteered to pen lyrics to three of the "themes" and then he cut his own lead vocals at Blackbird Studios in Nashville (where he lives). A famously versatile and expressive vocalist, White brilliantly uses both his higher and lower registers on his tunes, harmonizing with himself to powerful effect. Burton notes, "We didn't know which way we wanted to go—higher or lower for the lead vocal—and they ended up sounding really good together, so we left both in."

Luppi and Burton wanted a female vocalist to contrast with White's tunes and were excited when Norah Jones agreed to sing three songs for which Burton wrote the lyrics. Her tracks were cut at Glenwood Place in Los Angeles, where Burton has worked often during the past five years. Her vocals, too, are doubled and tripled and compressed and slightly distorted to give them a more mysterious edge. The song "Black," which she sings, is good example of the album's eclectic elements coming together to create an unusual and emotional song: It features some funky wah-wah guitar, "a musical theme that's like a Serge Gainsbourg thing," Burton says, referring to the French pop icon, "and then I thought it would be cool to have the lead vocal be a little Dylan-y, but then you have Norah Jones sing it and it turns into this other thing. It's amazing that it works as well as it does," he laughs.

With the lead vocals in place for the album's six songs, Burton and Luppi returned to Forum Studios in the fall of 2007 and added other vocal parts for some of the other nine mainly instrumental pieces—backgrounds by the Cantori Moderni, octogenarian Alessandro Alessandroni's legendary four-man, four-woman "choir" which added (usually) wordless vocal passages to so many Italian film soundtracks and pop songs in the '60s and '70s. (Alessandroni was also the moody whistler on those famous Morricone soundtracks.) Patrignani says he captured the Cantori with three overhead Neumann U 87s spaced evenly above them about three or four feet. Adding haunting vocalizations to a couple of tunes, too, was 72-year-old soundtrack warbler Edda dell'Orso.

A whole 'nother year went by before Burton and Luppi went back to Forum a third time, this time to cut strings with the *Rome*-based B.I.M. Orchestra, whom Patrignani again recorded with a large complement of U 87s, both for sections and as elevated room mics. Though some of the string parts had been conceived during the initial writing sessions, other arrangements were developed to fit with the finished vocal parts—another luxury of the album being stretched out over a long period.

Originally, Burton says, "We thought of mixing it in Rome, but we decided it would be much less expensive to fly Fabio over here and mix at Glenwood Place [to half-inch analog] rather than having Daniele and me and my mixing engineer Kennie Takahashi go all the way over there. Glenwood has a great board [a Neve 8068], too. But it was really important that Fabio was part of it. He knows how that music is 'supposed' to sound, but at the same time we all had our opinions, and we tried out a lot of different approaches, and in the end the album sounds quite a bit different than when we came back from Rome and mixed the backing tracks."

Indeed, it was at the mixing stage that the album really took on its modern sheen. Even when the backing tracks have that deep '60s sound, and the strings their languorous majesty, the vocals are 21st-century all the way, panned and effected in interesting ways. Two of Jones' tracks also clearly owe a debt to contemporary hip-hop, which is definitely Danger Mouse territory. So, though the press coverage of this album has portrayed it as some glorious throwback to an earlier musical universe—and there *are* the reverb-drenched guitars, wheedling Farfisa organ, spooky celesta parts (played by Gilda Buttá), and prominent strings from that world—the overall feel of the album is quite fresh and contemporary, as you'd expect from a restless creative spirit like Danger Mouse.

"This was never supposed to be a kitschy, nostalgia kind of thing," Burton concludes. "It was more like, 'Let's make a record that has a great mood to it, and a great sound as the background to it, and then do modern songs over the top of it, but not make it seem too out of place. I had great confidence that it would work out."

Adds Luppi, "We wanted to do something creative and unique, make a different kind of pop record for today, rather than just a replica of a nonexistent movie soundtrack."

6

Classics

The Doors

FROM ORIGINAL SESSION LIMITATIONS
TO THE MODERN 5.1 MIXES OF
*THE DOORS, STRANGE DAYS, WAITING
FOR THE SUN,* AND *L.A. WOMAN*

By Jeff Touzeau

This chapter appeared in the October 2007 issue of *EQ* magazine.

Summer 1966, Los Angeles—a young Bruce Botnick is living his dream in a 10 x 20–foot room, jam-packed with recording equipment, and, at most hours of the night, slightly disheveled band members. Life is good, because life is all about recording music. The long hours don't really faze anyone.

A voice calls: "There's a band called the Doors coming in. They have a guitar, drums, vocals, and an organ, and the organ player plays a piano bass."

Forty-one years later, Botnick is back in the same place. Not literally, but certainly figuratively. The studio legend—who engineered *The Doors* (1967), *Strange Days* (1967), *Waiting for the Sun* (1968), *The Soft Parade* (1969), *Absolutely Live* (1970), and *Morrison Hotel* (1970), and co-produced *L.A. Woman* (1971)—is tasked with revisiting his classic Doors sessions and using today's tools to usher the band's tracks into a new sonic era, as well as into the 5.1 format. The ceremony is about to begin. Is everybody in?

So you're finishing up work on the remixed and remastered versions of all the Doors' studio albums. What will be the final medium for the masters?

Vinyl. Why? First, the fans have been clamoring for it. Second, the state of the art for vinyl today is much better than it once was. The technology is more effective, and the pressings are quieter and cleaner. They don't degenerate as fast. It's interesting, because we are going back to the original master tapes—from 1967 to '70—and they are all in various states of disintegration. Some play perfectly, others don't play well at all.

What have you found in particular that's funky about the originals?

I retrieved the tapes—including the original stereo and mono masters, safety copies, EQ copies, and anything that was a complete master—from a climate-controlled vault in Hollywood. And, interestingly, I found that the first Doors album never ran at the right speed. When the Scully 4-track machine it was mixed on [at Elektra Studios, New York] neared the end of a full roll of tape, it would slow down because of the tension. As a consequence, the speed was pretty much normal at the beginning, but everything could be flat by the end. In fact, "Light My Fire" [from *The Doors*] is a quarter-tone off by the end of the song. It's just unbelievable.

So, for these new high-resolution stereo remixes, I was finally able to get everything on pitch by playing the 4-track master back at the proper speed when I transferred it into my Pro Tools 7.3 rig at 24-bit/96kHz. Some people complained we were not being true to these classic records by taking them into the digital world. But doing this saved us from the speed issues and from the deterioration of the originals.

Would you say this is an instance where digital tools made a truly positive impact on the end result?

Absolutely. In the case of *Strange Days*, there is one song where somebody had taken the tape out of the vault, and there was a big stretch in it. I had to go to another safety copy to access and replace the one and a half bars that were damaged. I couldn't have cut this in analog, because it wouldn't have

The Doors. (Michael Ochs Archives/Getty Images)

matched. Now, I couldn't assume the tape was running at the same speed. Therefore, I had to A/B it against the original to see what would happen.

What other elements needed sonic adjustments?

Over time, the tapes have lost some high end. Also, there are level changes that need to be addressed so that each song is the same volume as the

45

ones that precede and follow it. And some of the songs are brighter than others—which is the nature of the beast—so there needs to be some global EQ.

Are you EQing in the digital domain?

Yeah. I'm really into George Massenberg's digital EQ, and the Sony Oxford EQ plug-ins. They impart a pleasing character. I'm more into doing subtractive equalization than additive. Something I heard from [mastering engineer] Bernie Grundman has been really sticking with me lately: If you listen, there is usually something "clouding up" your sound. If you have a really good microphone placed in the right spot running into a really good preamp, and so on down the chain, you're going to increase your chances of realizing a great sound from the start. But sometimes the room itself can introduce problems that you don't catch until the mix. And when you find them, your tendency may be to push something up. Where you might feel like you need to add some high end, you may just need to cut at 200Hz to clear the sound up. Then you can add a dB or two at the top end, and it will sound as open as adding 6dB or 8dB of high-frequency EQ and never cutting at 200Hz.

These are your original recordings. You're not just some new-jack mixing engineer trying to spice up a classic album, so you have real perspective on these sessions. Given that, when you pulled the tapes and started looking at them as soon-to-be 5.1 mixes, did you rediscover anything about the recordings that floored you?

Given the limited tools we had to work with, there were actually quite a few things that impressed me. And I was also incredibly depressed by other things. I'm proud these recordings still impart a certain beauty. To me, they sound pretty and sweet. It could get raw and rocking, but this sweetness still came across and held true. There were so many variables that made it all work, and you can never, ever go back. I'm not 19 anymore. I hear differently. I was eating different food, breathing different air, and recording differently.

In what ways were you recording differently?

One noteworthy technique was that I came up with a different way of tape delaying the Sunset Sound echo chamber. I had a three-track Ampex 200 machine that could handle 14-inch reels. It was able to provide separate record and playback equalization from the input to the output, so you could basically

EQ the machine for your sound. There were NAB, CCIR, and AME equalization curves. It was a type of noise reduction, if you will. I remember using the AME EQ on the record side to put in more highs, then playing it back with the NAB curve to take out highs and reduce tape hiss. This would put a rise in the EQ curve in the chamber. Then I would delay the output of the chamber—not the input. Nobody else was doing this that I know of, and it's a special sound.

Tell us how you recorded John Densmore's drums.

There were only three mics on the drums at any one time: a Sony C37 overhead at just about forehead level; another C37, flipped out of phase, underneath the snare drum; and an Altec Salt Shaker dynamic mic—the kind they used to use for announcements in airports—for the kick. And we didn't record with an outer drum head—which was why the kick had that real "pop" to it. That was it. Sometimes I would put a Telefunken U 47 about six to eight feet back from the kit in the room and add some heavy compression to open up the sound. I also set up the drums against the far brick wall, because I liked the reflection of the drums coming back into the overhead mic—it added a real liveness to his sound.

What was the room like?

The room at Sunset Sound had concrete floors with asphalt tile, brick walls, and plasterboard ceilings that were three or four inches thick. That place was hard. It sounded hard. You could hurt yourself in there, and you can hear that come through in the recordings. The room influenced the sound enormously. I remember being at the old Record Plant, and doing a session in Studio B, where Stevie Wonder had done "Living in the City." I set up the drums in there, set up my mics, and when the track came over the monitors I said, "My God, that's the same sound!" Even though I was using my choice of mics, that studio had a very distinct sound to it. It blew me away.

What did you use for Jim Morrison's vocals?

A Neumann U 47—which has pretty much always been my favorite vocal mic. And yes, for *Strange Days* we didn't use any pop filters. I hate them, because I can hear them. Jim was very controlled, so a light compression when he screamed into the mic was all it took to keep him sounding even. In those days, it was very common to have technical recording information on the back of the albums. They would list, "Trumpets: U 47" and the like. So I would listen to the records, hear those sounds, and then when I got back to the studio I'd try out the mics. I'd say to myself, "Wow, it does have that sound character. That's cool. I'm going to use it!"

How did you mic Robby Krieger's guitar?

I used the U 47 right up on the grille of his amp. I didn't know any better! Same for Ray Manzarek's organ—a Vox Continental—though we always ran the piano bass through a direct box. [Editor's note: The bass was a Fender Rhodes keyboard bass, which, according to Manzarek, sounded too "blown out" on record. So, starting with *Strange Days*, the Doors used various electric bass-ists, including Doug Lubahn, Ray Neapolitan, Harvey Brooks, Jerry Scheff, and guitarist Lonnie Mack.] For the acoustic-guitar tracks, we would just put one of the C37s back a foot or so from the body of his acoustic, which just sounded huge. He absolutely loved the sound of them.

What was it like mixing those albums the first time around?

You have to understand that most of these albums were done in a week! If you only have four tracks to work with—or eight tracks—there are only so many things you can do. Now you have so many tracks to work with that you can virtually do anything, and you don't have to make a commitment at every step of the process. But having to make decisions quickly added to the feel of those records. We recorded with reverb live, we compressed and limited live, and we added equalization live. What we heard when we were recording was the mix that you heard in the end.

But didn't the Doors' dramatic spatial elements lend themselves well to the 5.1 remixes of the albums?

Some of it really did. For example, when we did the original mix for "Riders on the Storm" [from *L.A. Woman*] and added the rain and thunder, I just had a tape machine running in the back, and, by serendipity, the thunder came in at the right place. It wasn't planned. That speaks to the notion that recording somewhat recklessly can end in moments of perfection. But when it came time to remix in 5.1—which I did in Sonic Solutions—I rebuilt the mix, put the thunder in the place it had always lived, and then panned the rain, and added a delay to the thunder track to create a 360-degree environment. It ended up working really well.

What about "The Unknown Soldier" from *Waiting for the Sun*?

Well, there is that whole sequence where the prisoner is being marched to a stockade to be shot. So it marches all around the room. Jim is doing the cadence. The gun cocks and fires. Then the crowd starts screaming, and the church bells are ringing. There's a great deal of movement going on. There were other places where I'd just put a nice piano in the rear, or maybe the background vocals. I would have Jim's vocal in the center speaker—just as we recorded it. In the beginning—up until *The Soft Parade*—we always had three Altec Lansing 604e monitors in front of us, because we recorded three tracks. It was normal to hear Jim in the center, so when I got a chance to remix these into surround, I got him back in his own environment. He's in his own place now, and it really makes a difference.

You clearly believe equally in classic techniques and modern tools. What have you held on to—despite the passing of the years—in terms of recording techniques?

HOME COOKING

When Bruce Botnick talks about using EQ before and after reverb—and changing the position of delay with respect to reverb—he's recalling the days when you had to physically move patch cords around and match levels (often with preamps and attenuators). But with today's software, you can try the same types of experiments in minutes—just by moving plug-ins around in track inserts.

Does pre-delay before reverb sound different than delaying the reverb signal? Try it yourself, but remember that, in those days, tape was providing the delay so it affected the sound. Also, plate and room reverbs had a very different character compared to modern digital reverbs.

Set up the following plug-in chain: EQ1 (high boost) > Delay > Reverb > Delay > EQ2 (high cut), and start by setting both delays to a specific delay time, like 70–100ms. Bypass them individually to hear how each one affects the sound, then enable both and vary the delay times—delay before and after reverb is a whole other sound entirely. Also try boosting the high frequencies going into the chain, and cutting the highs coming out to simulate the effect Botnick describes. Even though you won't be cutting tape hiss, the result will often be a "rounder" reverb sound. —Craig Anderton

Many things are the same as they ever were. You still decide what it is that you are going to record, and what your goals are. You still have to pick your instruments, your mics, and your room—partially on faith, and partially from past experience. You still have to set up your instruments. You still have to play well. You still have to really listen to what you've tracked before you start with the adjustments. When you look at it that way, not that much has changed. The reality of a good recording is still capturing good sources.

But if you're looking for advice, the best I can give you is this: Get everybody who is playing on the track in the same room, open up all the mics, assign them to their channels, and try to balance it all live. Learn to hear it all together, and make your decisions then. By focusing on one element at a time, you'll never get the perspective you need to tackle the recording of an album. The album is the whole thing—not just the sum of its parts.

7

Dr. Dre

THE RECORDING ETHOS BEHIND
SNOOP DOGG'S *DOGGYSTYLE*, EMINEM'S
THE SLIM SHADY LP AND *THE MARSHALL
MATHERS LP*, AND DRE'S *THE CHRONIC*

By Lisa Roy

This chapter features an abridged version of the Dr. Dre
article in the June 2001 issue of *EQ* magazine.

Recently, the *Los Angeles Times* did a survey among 22
record company executives to name the artists they believe will sell the most records over the next seven years.
Dr. Dre was at the top of that list. One executive said that
Dre, who won a Grammy in February for Producer of the
Year, might be the greatest talent in the music business
right now. "Hip-hop is the most dynamic sound in pop,
and he's the king of hip-hop."

It came as no surprise that catching up with Dr. Dre
for this interview was a bit of a challenge. After all, he's
been busy putting final touches on a mix for Eminem's
side group, D12, making beats with Busta Rhymes,
working on a new single with Eve and Gwen Stefani,
and producing a soundtrack for a major film, *The Wash*,
which he also stars in with Snoop Dogg. He manages to
accomplish this mindboggling schedule with the aide of
his production manager, Larry Chatman.

As I walk into Record One in Studio City, Chatman is

in between juggling phone calls and greets me with a warm smile, informing me that Dre is on his way. He invites me into the control room, where Dr. Dre's Dream Team is already warming up. Ensconced in Studio B, engineer "Yelo" (aka Mauricio Iragorri) is tinkering on the SSL 8000, while Mike Elizondo, bass player, and Scott Storch, the expert on keys, file into the studio. The activity seems normal, even mundane, until Dr. Dre walks into the room. The vibe in the control room shifts up a level of energy. During a lunch break, the conversation turned to a VH1 documentary on the Doors that Dre had seen the previous night, and, after commenting on how much he liked the keyboard sound, Scott Storch immediately launched into what was a near-perfect rendition of the classic Doors sound. Soon Mike Elizondo had joined in on bass, Dre added a beat at the turntable, and, before you knew it, a song was born!

Contrary to media reports that his recording sessions are filled with drugs, alcohol, and gang warfare, all I saw was positive energy, professional vibe, creativity, and solid business. After completing a call with his protégé Eminem (aka Marshall Mathers), where he was advising the young rapper on some crucial business decisions, Dre turned his attention to the interview at hand.

Dr. Dre can be described as many things—a catalyst, an astute businessman, an innovator—but perhaps the most interesting description of the man, born 35 years ago as Andre Young, is his description of himself as "a motivator." "I direct well," he shares. "I'm a person that will spend three or four hours working on one line of a song to get it correct. I have to be able to work with artists who are ready to go through that torture."

Some of the artists that have signed up for his unique brand of "torture" are Snoop Dogg, Eminem, and the hardcore rap group N.W.A., which Dre founded in the mid-'80s with fellow rapper Ice Cube and signed to Eazy-E's Ruthless Records. Although Dr. Dre had been rapping and DJing since his early years growing up in one of L.A.'s rougher neighborhoods, Compton, he's surprisingly realistic about where his truest talents lie, and that's in production. In addition to being credited with inventing gangsta rap, he's responsible for creating his own musical style—G-funk. This patented, often imitated style of music immediately became the defining characteristic of the entire generation of music. There are few people who would argue that from the introduc-

Dr. Dre at Record One in Studio City, Los Angeles. (Mr. Bonzai)

tion of G-funk, Dre's sounds and rhythms shaped the future of rap music, while impacting its history at every turn.

One of the key moments in Dr. Dre's career came in 1992, when he founded Death Row Records with his friend Suge Knight. This became a platform for Dre's obvious production talents. He released only one solo record for Death Row, the critically acclaimed *The Chronic*. While the production values behind G-funk dominated the hip-hop world for the next four years, collaborations with stepbrother Warren G and the immense success of Snoop Dogg's 1993 debut *Doggystyle* cemented Dre's name on the list of the most powerful and influential men in the music industry. Unfortunately, all of this success did not prevent the eventual collapse of the record label in 1996 amid financial difficulties and creative differences—not to mention a lengthy murder trial for the label's star, Snoop Doggy Dog.

The businessman in Dr. Dre had matured through all the challenges and obstacles of the '80s and early '90s. His instincts served him well when he made the decision to bail from Death Row Records almost a year before its ultimate demise. Eventually, he formed Aftermath Records and turned his production, mixing, and writing energy toward a young rapper he found in Detroit called Eminem. This collaboration not only resulted in Eminem's 1999 debut record, *The Slim Shady LP*, and the multiplatinum smash follow-up *The Marshall Mathers LP*, but also a Grammy for their collaboration on 2001's "Forgot About Dre."

"'Forgot About Dre' was actually Marshall's idea," Dre explains. "He said, 'I have an idea for a song, I just need some music to it.' So he sent the chorus to me, and then we went to work on our music. We recorded it at Granny's House Studio in Reno, and then we put the song together in a couple of hours." The collaboration also garnered him a Grammy for Producer of the Year. "That was big," confides Dre. "I love the fact that I didn't have to go onstage and give a thank-you speech. I didn't have anything written down. As it turned out, when they called my name for Producer of the Year, I just stood up. That's going to be the perfect ending of my life story."

Perhaps he should start preparing his acceptance speech for next year now, because an Engineer of the Year Grammy is certainly not out of the question for the technically savvy Dre. He humbly admits that, although he defers to his engineer of choice, Veto, on certain things, he himself is the man behind the board for the majority of the projects he works on. His roots in recording began in a small studio in the back of a club in Compton where he used to DJ. "I would just come in there during the week and try to create my songs, just messing around, seeing if I had it. I would play them in the clubs on the weekend and I would get good responses, so I just kept doing it, and it became my profession." He continues, "I learned how to engineer basically from that club. I also learned a lot from this engineer, Donovan, at Audio Achievements in Torrance. We used to work together a lot, and I eventually started working by myself on mixes. I wanted it to sound a certain way, and I felt nobody was going to be able to dig in my brain and get the sound out that I wanted except me. Every day I would learn something new. I'm actually still learning with all the new technology."

Through the years, as any engineer would, Dre has defined his choices in audio gear. He's candid about his love for any and all Solid State Logic consoles, as well as the Studer A827. He always uses Quantegy 499 tape. His mic of choice is the Sony C800G, which is the only mic he ever uses on vocals. When recording vocals with the Sony mic, he runs it through the SSL compressor and a dbx 160, but he admits to very little EQ on the vocal. Dre explains, "I usually record vocals flat. The only time I put EQ on vocals when recording is if I know for a fact that I'm going to want it to sound like that during the mix. When I want a little more crispness out of the mic, I use the 1073 EQ with just a little high end. I don't use too much compression; maybe 4:1 with the outputs set to zero. I usually do my compression afterwards. I like the compressors on the SSL. I usually have the ratio up to about eight or ten on a lot of things." Dre, a die-hard fan of analog recording, is one of the few producer/engineers left in the world that have not jumped on the Pro Tools bandwagon, and, true to form, he makes no apologies for that.

"I tried digital a couple of times and I don't really like it," he says. "There's just something about it. For me, it's not fast enough just yet. I tried to record into Pro Tools and got one of the best Pro Tools operators down to record the music, and it's just not me. Not yet. We had the Sony 3348 in the studio, and I tried a couple of songs on it, and it didn't give me the sound I wanted. The kick drum started sounding transparent. It wasn't good." When it's time to mix down, Dre makes the unusual choice of mixing straight to DAT, so you can imagine that the DAT machine—his preference is the Panasonic 3800—is a key element in any studio he chooses to work in.

The question on everyone's mind, though, is what gear does Dr. Dre turn to to make his signature beats? Engineer "Veto" confides that there's a laundry list of toys that make a Dre session complete. "The brain of the whole thing is the MIDI sequencer, the Akai MPC3000. We use the Korg Triton keyboard. Usually that's the controller—the [Clavia] Nord Lead and Korg's MS2000. Lately we've been trying out the Alesis Andromeda A6. Someone recommended a Waldorf Q, and we seem to like that one, as well. They let us try it for a day, and we said, 'Yes, we'll keep it!'"

You might also find a nice array of vintage keyboards on hand, including those by Rhodes, Wurlitzer, Moog, and Roland. But aside from synths and electric pianos, Veto admits that other hardware is scarce in Dre sessions.

"We don't use a lot of outboard gear," Dre concurs. "I doctor the vocal as far as de-essing and maybe some low-end EQ for the kicks. We use a lot of EQ on the console and all the limiters. Most of it comes out of the SSL and into the quad compressor. I like the sound of it on the mix bus. That's the SSL quad compressor in the center of the console."

Dr. Dre certainly knows his way around the studio and in and out of a "tool box." This knowledge he credits to once having his own studio, complete with an SSL 4000E/G. "We did a lot of Eminem's first record at my home studio. Actually, the first song we did together, 'My Name Is,' was done there," remembers Dre. Eventually he removed the studio from his home and is now vocal about his love and support of the professional, commercial facility. "I kind of got tired of having a home studio, because you get to the point where you want to feel like you're going to work. Plus, sometimes you have to work with people, and there's just some people you don't want in your house," he laughs.

This love for the commercial recording facility has Dr. Dre hanging out on a regular basis at L.A. recording hotspots like Larrabee West, Encore, and, of course, Record One. "We mix most everything at Larrabee West. I just like a studio that's comfortable, has a lot of space, and, very important, has a lounge with a kitchen," he shares. "The equipment is important, but, to be honest, I'm still working on the same board I've worked on since 1990. The important part is who's pushing the buttons."

One thing that's evident about Dre is that he strives to keep his audience entertained regardless of what he's doing. He wants the records he makes to stand out and intrigue the fans long after they first listen. He ensures this, he says, by putting what he calls his "sprinkles" into the mix. "People come up to me on the street and say, 'I hear something different every time I listen to your record,'" he explains. "That's what I like to hear—that's the sprinkles." Even when he's self-producing, he challenges himself constantly. "I really take a lot of time on each song and make sure it's okay—I'm my worst critic. I want to make sure it's right."

8

Classics

Nick Drake

THE SIMPLE PERFECTION OF *FIVE LEAVES LEFT*, *BRYTER LAYTER*, AND *PINK MOON*

By Jeff Touzeau

This chapter appeared in the March 2008 issue of *EQ* magazine.

Nick Drake's musical career was fraught with tragedy. The enormous community of adoring fans left posthumously exalting his every recorded note—as well as the legions of musicians constantly namedropping Drake as an influence in attempts to quantify their street credibility—are testaments to the notion that the greatest artists are never appreciated during their time. And it's almost too much to bear to think that Drake's lack of commercial success—coupled with a debilitating mental illness—may have led him to ingest a fatal amount of amitriptyline one cold November night in 1974.

In the course of Drake's short life, not a single album he released sold more then 5,000 copies. Toward his death, he was said to be living off of a £20-a-week retainer from Island Records. His music being used in a Volkswagen commercial in 2000 resulted in the selling of more Nick Drake records in one year than the 20-plus that preceded—landing him in Amazon.com's sales chart as a top-five-grossing artist.

Drake's three proper releases (*Five Leaves Left*, *Bryter Layter*, and *Pink Moon*) have stood the test of time and have grown exponentially popular by the day—so much so that, nearly 30 years after his debut, droves of people from across the globe regularly flock to his hometown of Tanworth-in-Arden to pay tribute to a musician who has dramatically affected their lives.

Those pilgrimages are what inspired Drake's estate to assemble his newest release, *Family Tree* [Tsunami Label Group]—a collection of recorded works that span his entire lifetime. It's in the spirit of those who love his music perhaps just a little too late that we journeyed across the globe to talk with producer Joe Boyd and engineer John Wood to get some insights into the recording of Drake's limited discography. What we found out about those legendary sessions was inspiring.

The two of you worked on all of Nick Drake's albums. Can you share some of your recollections of the *Five Leaves Left* sessions?

Wood: For the *Five Leaves Left* sessions, Nick would track live, singing and playing along with the string section. We would split the four tracks by virtue of how we wanted the reverb to be. You needed the natural room reverb first, and if you needed to add artificial reverb, you would do it track by track. For example, you wouldn't put any brass on the same track as the strings, because you wouldn't want the same amount of "space" on a string instrument as you would a brass instrument.

Boyd: The best and most memorable sounds, to me, were on "The River Man." This was done with 12 string instruments set up in a semi-circle in the middle of the room, with Nick on a stool in the middle. There were no over-dubs. There weren't even baffles between the performers—they were just all there together with a conductor. You could do that kind of thing at Sound Techniques studio, because the signal bleed was nice if you were in the right position and if the microphones had the right relationships to each other.

You attribute your ability to record the sonic structure for "The River Man" to the room at Sound Techniques. Can you paint a mental picture of what the studio was like at that time?

Boyd: Sound Techniques was situated in an old dairy in Chelsea. There was a big room, and there was an office on one side and a control room on the other. The control room was deeper. It had a lower floor, and the office had

Nike Drake. (Estate of Keith Morris/Redferns/Getty Images)

quite a low ceiling. The middle of the room went straight up to the original ceiling of the room. You had three different ceiling heights in the same room, so you could move a musician under the office, under the control room, or out in the middle, and get different acoustic atmospheres based on that.

Eventually, they built a vocal booth under the office, which you entered through a sliding door. You could put strings in there, or just something you wanted to record separately. The best sounds were always in the middle of the room, though. That's where we'd put the drum kit, and that's where we set up the musicians for songs like "The River Man."

While recording "The River Man," how were you affected by Drake's performance?

Boyd: With Nick, it was quite simple to keep focus and not be overcome with emotion during the session. What I learned very early on was not to monitor what he was doing, because he was always perfect. We just turned his mics off in the control room and listened to what everyone else was doing. Then you could really concentrate on whether a violin was out of tune, or notice if somebody came in out of order, or be alerted when there was something wrong with one of the sections. You didn't want to be distracted by enjoying Nick's performance.

Wood: The thing about Nick was that he was so good at what he did. People sometimes ask me, "How do you get the Nick Drake guitar sound?" The simple answer is this—we would just stick a microphone in front of him.

You never had to provide him with any guidance in the studio?

Boyd: We pretty much let him do whatever he wanted. That said, there was obviously a lot of discussion around what we were going to do to streamline the session, how we were going to approach capturing the songs for the album, and the positions we were going to set everyone up in to play.

Did you record everything live?

Wood: All Nick's music just went down live, with just a couple of exceptions. To this day, people cannot believe we made those records that way. For *Five Leaves Left*, we knocked off "Way to Blue," "Fruit Tree," and another track I can't remember in three hours.

Was there any specific gear you used to capture his performance?

Wood: I've always believed that recording studios are nothing more than working environments. I've never understood waiting for a Neve to arrive, or going to exotic places to track in hopes of capturing some special feeling in the air. It's the artist that matters. I think worrying about what equipment was used is nonsensical.

Sure. But would you mind sharing what a typical signal chain for recording Drake was?

Wood: We used a Neumann U 67 as the vocal mic, and a Neumann KM 56—a small valve condenser—on his guitar. We chose the KM 56 because it flattered his vocals, as well. As his vocals were recorded live along with his guitar, we had to make sure the mic we were using for each source sounded good on the other source, as there was a fair amount of bleed.

We placed the mics pretty close to Nick's mouth and the sound hole of his guitar. We weren't trying to get a lot of the room in his sound, and we had to get some separation from the instruments that surrounded him in the live room. I'd run the U 67 into a Fairchild 660. His vocal was the only signal that was compressed on those albums. I'd track with the limiter because I was trying to get as much of the final album sound before we mixed. We wouldn't even use much EQ during the mix. And I'd still work that way—even with what digital affords us. You should be able to pretty much put the entire performance to tape and be done with it.

Joe, is John's recording and mixing philosophy similar to your own?

Boyd: I've obviously learned a lot from working with John, and he has informed my approach in the studio. However, I think the biggest influence on my listening—and, therefore, mixing—was my grandmother. She was a pianist, and she taught me a rather arcane, highly conceptual, and slightly dubious idea that piano playing was about "singing by hand." The concept is that a leading melody isn't necessarily meant to be played louder, but you make it sing out in a way so that both hands stay in balance. A melody is important, and it's at the forefront because of texture—not volume. I've always applied that idea to my mixing. The goal is to make the vocal line—the lead melody, and the romantic, emotional part of the music—clear and alluring without being unnecessarily loud or unbalanced. You want to suck in the listener. To achieve this, you could pick out positions in the stereo field from which to pan a source, and thus affect visibility, or you could boost or cut frequencies in the name of changing the listener's perspective on an instrument. You have to keep the elements audible, but you shouldn't prioritize them in a way that is unnatural.

How was the recording process for *Bryter Layter* different from *Five Leaves Left*?

Boyd: In a way, *Bryter Layter* became more complex, because the drum kit changed the nature of the compositions and, therefore, the recording. There was no drum kit on *Five Leaves Left*, just occasional percussion. Once you put a drum kit on, you start doing things with the guitar, bass, and drum track, and Robert Kirby [Drake's string and wood arranger] would write for horns as well as strings, so the whole album got more complicated texturally.

Wood: I spent more time mixing *Bryter Layter* than anything else I've ever spent time on. That's okay, though. Most of the time, you play back an album you've recorded and say, "I wish I would have done this or that." But on *Bryter Layter*, there is nothing I would have changed. We actually mixed it three times. The first time, we had a go in New York at Vanguard Studios because we liked the echo plate they had there. Then we had a go at Sound Techniques—which we didn't like. Then I changed the monitors at Sound Techniques and we had a second go. Those are the mixes that were released.

Tell me a little about the application of plate reverbs on "The Chime of a City Clock."

Wood: Listening to that song, I think this is one of the best mixes I ever did in my life. It also demonstrates everything I hate about current engineering and mixing. It has perspective and depth—two things that you just don't hear people striving to achieve anymore. For this song, we used two echo plates. I would use varying degrees of each plate, plus tape retard depending on what track it was, so there would be two tape delays for the plates. For the vocal, I would use a longer retard than a sax, which has more of a short plate on it. Strings probably have a mixture of long and short, with the high strings having more reverb on them than the low strings.

I'd like to hear your comments on "Poor Boy."

Boyd: That's Pat Arnold and Doris Troy [from Pink Floyd's *The Dark Side of the Moon*] on backing vocals. For this one, I suppose John Simon's recordings on the first Leonard Cohen album inspired me. I loved "So Long Marianne" with those mocking girl backing vocals. When Nick played me "Poor Boy," I said, "We've got to have girls singing the chorus."

Originally, we went in to do a track with guitar, bass, and drums. The morning we did the track, I had been mixing a record with Chris McGregor—a South American jazz pianist—so my head was full of the sound of his piano. When Nick was going through the chords and teaching the bass player and drummer the routine of the song, I kept hearing the sound of McGregor's piano in my head: Chris was hanging around, so I said to him, "Why don't you go down and play it?" And Chris said, "Sure." I just told Nick, "Nick, you've got a piano player." Nick wrote out the chords, they played through a verse and a chorus, and then Nick said, "Okay, he has it." The take on the record is their first take.

Wood: For me, "Poor Boy" is an example of the best sound I ever got out of a piano. We had this piano that, if the person playing it was good, it sounded great. If the person wasn't really good, it sounded like s**t. [*Laughs.*] Thankfully, Chris McGregor was good. Nick plays two guitars on this song. One is an acoustic-electric—a Guild outfitted with a pickup. If you listen in the left side, you'll hear a very jazzy guitar that we had recorded direct. That's the acoustic-electric. On the other side is a very straightforward rhythm guitar. That's his acoustic. I would say that out of all the mixes on the album, "Poor Boy" was by far the hardest one to do. To be able to hear everything when you wanted to hear it required a lot of jumping about with the faders—especially considering there was more than one instrument on each track. The reverb on the background singers would have been a combination of plates and tape retard.

John, you have been involved in Drake's recent posthumous release, *Family Tree*. What are your thoughts on the project?

Wood: I have mixed feelings about it. I think in some ways, Nick would have preferred not to have it released. On the record, there is a sleeve note in the form of Gabrielle [Drake's sister] writing a letter to Nick sort of explaining why it came out. What happened was that, over the years, people had made pilgrimages to his parents' home, and Nick's father was sort of a gadget freak with a tape recorder, so he would give people a compilation cassette of stuff he'd made from tapes that Nick had left. Soon enough, people started making bootlegs of it and making money off it. So, at the end of the day, what this record partly does is that if you're going to have all this stuff bootlegged, you might as well have it done decently.

What technical considerations did you face in creating *Family Tree*?

Wood: We just tried to make it sound as good as we could. I had 170 files to work with, because the same songs would turn up on different tapes. We were getting copies of copies of copies. The only way to do it was in Pro Tools, so we had to transfer it all to Pro Tools, and then line up all the files so we could see which was the best version. This involved a lot of critical listening, and there were instances where we dropped a bit of one track onto another. There wasn't much point in trying to make it all sound unified, because all these things come from different sources and from different times.

How do you feel about the changes that have occurred in the recording process since you worked with Drake?

Wood: The decision-making process has been compromised. Up until the advent of 24 tracks, you had to make decisions as you recorded. You couldn't say, "Oh, we'll do another one of those. We'll dump it on another track in Pro Tools." You

63

had to get on and go with what you recorded, and just build an album from there. I think this is one of the reasons that, for me, Nick's records have massive vitality. Having everybody record at separate times takes a lot of the life out of a recording. There is no longer the sense of performance in albums that there once was. If you have to start resorting to picking apart things with a computer, then I think you need to ask yourself where your music has gone. People spend most of their time trying to control the environment they are recording in, making decisions that really do not have a lot to do with the music itself. I still believe that performance and material are what matters. In the end, you get the sound you deserve.

Joe, how do you feel about the evolution of the DAW?

Boyd: I hate it. It is understandable that musicians take advantage of the possibility to make something perfect. But, cumulatively, these little decisions make for a lifeless record, in my opinion. There is something empowering about working with 4, 8, and 16 tracks that is absent in 128. Limited tracks force you to make decisions. The limitations allow the magic to happen. I've never recorded directly onto 1s and 0s. I've obviously mixed onto ls and 0s, but unless there is something analog in the chain to warm the sound up, I just can't do it. In the digital world, everything is measurable to the minute detail—everything is transparent, and everything is in position, but nothing ever actually mixes together.

What are you most pleased about by your work with Drake?

Wood: One of my best experiences working with Nick was during *Pink Moon*, for no other reason than we just went and did it. Nick literally ran up out of the blue and said, "Let's make another album." Back then, record companies were much more driven by the artist and the product, rather than marketing. Artists had so much more freedom. You didn't submit any demos to the record company, and you didn't argue about any budgets—you just got on with it. I can't remember telling the record company we were going to do *Pink Moon*. We just went and did it. I'm proud of that. Other than that, I suppose I would have been quite supportive as we recorded it, because Nick was very fragile at the time. The only artistic change I noted was that Nick became more belligerent in a way. [*Laughs.*] He really was going to make the record exactly the way he wanted it. He still had a lot of confidence in his playing during *Pink Moon*.

9

Classic
Fleetwood Mac

THE TONE LAYERING AND PERFORMANCE
MIXING OF *RUMOURS*

By Heather Johnson

This chapter appeared in the November 2007 issue of
EQ magazine.

Fleetwood Mac had soldiered through years of midlevel
success as a powerful '60s blues outfit led by guitarist
Peter Green and his "magical" Gibson Les Paul, until hitting ups and downs with various lineups and a tsunami
of drinking, drugs, and mental illness. Although the
band did chart a few bona-fide hits and radio-play favorites ("Black Magic Woman," "Albatross," "The Green
Manalishi," "Hynoptized"), its constant career stalls and
infighting had made it sort of a commercial, ahem, *albatross* by 1975. Few would have expected that a combination of good luck, fortuitous meetings, and renewed
creative energies would not only change the veteran
band's fortunes, but also transform it into one of the
most successful rock acts of all time.

While the big bang was drummer Mick Fleetwood discovering Stevie Nicks and Lindsey Buckingham by sheer chance—and having the insight to invite them to join his band—the event also brought the duo's friend, engineer Richard Dashut, into the fold. Dashut went from mixing live sound for the band's 1975 *Fleetwood Mac* tour to co-producing 1977's *Rumours*—a record that spent six months atop the U.S. record charts, won the Grammy for Album of the Year, and went on to sell 30 million copies worldwide.

You started in this business from ground zero. How did that happen?

I got my first studio job around 1971, at Crystal Sound in Hollywood. I was a janitor, basically. At the time, people like Jackson Browne, Joni Mitchell, Carole King—a lot of really huge stars—were recording there. So here I am—this little punk kid, 20 years old with his eyes wide open—more than happy to answer phones and sweep floors just to be around it. I really wanted to be in the movie business, but after hanging out there, I decided *this* was for me.

I was let go from Crystal—although they tried to hire me back two weeks later. When Dave Devore and Keith Olsen—who I met when they were mastering a record at Crystal—found out I'd been let go, they got me a job at Sound City, which is where they did all of their recording. My first job there was as an assistant maintenance man. But when the head maintenance engineer asked me for a resistor, and I said I didn't burn my draft card, he quickly realized I wasn't suited for electronics. So Keith made me his second engineer, and I got to go into the control room and operate the tape machines. We had Ampex MM1100 and MM1200 tape machines that had to be aligned every day. I had to have the tape heads cleaned, the board cleaned, and the room cleaned and prepared. We were working 18-hour days, doing a lot of commercials—string sessions where I had to set up all the seats and headphone boxes—but, inevitably, one of the string players would plug in their crystal headset and short out the whole system.

We had some great sessions. People like Jerry Wexler worked there. We did Elton John sessions, and we overdubbed the Tower of Power horn section. You could absorb so much. I had to keep myself occupied in those long sessions, so I would listen intently to the music and think like a producer would. If someone made a mistake, would I stop the machine? What would I do? What

Lindsey Buckingham (far left), Christine McVie, Mick Fleetwood (center), John McVie, and Stevie Nicks. (Barry Schultz /Sunshine/Retna)

ideas would I have? I learned that way—as well as by paying attention to what the engineers and producers were doing.

Didn't you meet Lindsey Buckingham at Sound City?

Yes. On my second or third day, I was relegated to painting the control room ceiling in Studio A. There were a few other people helping me—in par-

67

ticular a gentleman and a young lady who was trying to paint the ceiling but kept getting more paint on her hair. I grabbed the paint roller out of her hand and showed her how to do it. That lady turned out to be Stevie Nicks, and the gentleman was her boyfriend, Lindsey Buckingham. Within two hours, we had already decided we were going to get a place together.

They were living with Keith Olsen at the time and were in a band called Fritz. Fritz had broken up, and they had gone on their own as Buckingham Nicks. Lindsey took me into the maintenance room and played me his demos, and the first time I heard them, I fell in love with the music. "Monday Morning" was on there, as was "I'm So Afraid," "Frozen Love"—a bunch of stuff. That's where my real music education started—with Lindsey Buckingham.

When you met Buckingham and Nicks, you were on your way to a good career as a studio engineer, but then you tossed it aside to go on the road with Fleetwood Mac. Why?

The Buckingham Nicks album didn't do so well, and they got dropped from the label. We decided to take matters into our own hands, and [Sound City owners] Joe Godfried and Tom Skeeter offered us studio time to produce our own record—which was very generous of them. We were in the middle of that when Mick Fleetwood came along. Keith was demoing the studio for him as a place to record, and he was using the Buckingham Nicks album to show Mick how great the room sounded. Mick took one listen and basically asked them to join. That was the good news! The bad news was that we had to stop doing the second Buckingham Nicks record. But "I'm So Afraid," "Monday Morning," and "Blue Letter"—which we had started developing—went on the first Fleetwood Mac record they did together.

I had parted with Keith Olsen and had left Sound City by the time they started recording *Fleetwood Mac*. But they were getting ready to go on the road, so Lindsey called and asked if I'd mix the live sound for the tour. Because I was young, and had a tremendous sense of adventure and curiosity at the time—and also because of the girls and the money—I decided to say yes. [*Laughs*].

Was going from studio to stage a difficult transition?

It was not easy. In the studio, you have everything under control and you can spend time getting things perfect. But on the road, you have to deal with the elements—the audience, the room acoustics, the capacity of the room. We didn't have sophisticated equipment back then, either. You just had to work by the seat of your pants, and strictly by ear. It was great, because it taught me the basic sensibilities of layering and mixing. And when you have to get things together in a timely manner—like by the end of the first song—you get very adept at mixing on the fly.

Roadie magazine voted you "Best Live Mixer"—or something to that effect. What would you attribute that to?

My mixing style was different. A lot of people in a live situation would just mix and hold—just get it under control, and then leave it. For me, every song was different. I was a dynamic mixer—but not a proper one. If you want to hear the absolute perfect mix, you can go home and listen to the record. To me, mixing live was an emotional thing. It was about a show—about getting an emotional response out of an audience. I would ride lead guitars and drum parts when I wanted to make a point, and then to drive home the point, I'd mix them a lot louder than most people are used to hearing them. It was a way to get people off their feet and create an emotional experience.

I took a lot of that experience with me into the studio—especially before automation, when the mixing itself was a performance. You had to remember how you had it the time before, you're relying on two or three other people— "hands across the board" as we used to call it—and you would all be riding levels, and what one person did affected the other. That's why we had grease markers. We'd draw a line and didn't dare go above it! But mistakes often made the best mixes. For instance, at the end of "Go Your Own Way," the kick drum was way too loud—to the point where it would start hitting the compression on the radio. If you listen to the guitar solo at the end, the compressor would pump the guitar in rhythm to the kick, and it added to the whole drive of the song. That was a lucky mistake. It wouldn't have happened if we were using automation. The mix was half emotional/half technical, and when you got to the end of a great mix, it was like the ending of a great show.

When the band asked you to produce _Rumours_, you brought out engineer Ken Caillat. How did you meet, and what made you two such a good team?

I had just been on the road with the band for about a year, and we went in after the tour to do a remix at Wally Heider Studios in Los Angeles, where Ken was working. We probably smoked a joint together—who knows. [*Laughs.*] Things went so well with that remix that when it came time to do *Rumours*, I asked him to come work with us. He ended up doing most of the engineering, and I worked more with Lindsey in developing the band's music.

Someone else was supposed to produce *Rumours*, and they wanted to put strings on the record. That turned the band off, so they decided against using him. When we were remixing "Rhiannon," Mick brought me out to the parking lot and said, "Dashut. You're co-producing the next record with us." I was an engineer, not a producer! Who wanted to be *responsible*? I just wanted to get my sounds. [*Laughs.*]

What made Ken and I such a great team was that we had great communication between us, and not much overlap. We both had our specialties. Ken loved fooling with the knobs and tweaking things, and I loved working with the band and the music, and being the interface between the technical and the creative sides. But I did a lot of engineering, too. I even tuned all the drums. But somebody had to be behind the talkback, and somebody had to sit behind the board, and I found myself mostly behind the talkback.

I was way over my head. But living with Lindsey was educational. We'd play Motown, the Beach Boys, the Beatles, the Stones, and other records, and he'd show me what frequencies to listen for and how to layer instruments. We would have a session in front of the record player and then put what we learned into practice at the studio.

Critics praised your—and Ken's—"attention to acoustical detail." What methods did you employ to accomplish such great sounds?

It was the endless pursuit for the perfect sound. Once, we spent ten hours getting kick-drum sounds in the Record Plant's Studio B, and then ended up moving to Studio A and building a special drum platform to get what we wanted. Mick had a very light foot, so we had to try especially hard to get the right kick-drum sounds. We nicknamed him "Featherfoot." [*Laughs.*] He was also known as the shuffle king, because he had one of the most amazing right hands in the business. His talent was in his right hand and snare feel, and the bass drum would follow that.

Anyway, he used his road kit on some songs—which had a very large kick drum—and it was hard to get a good, tight sound out of it. We shoved a Shure SM57 about four inches from where the beater struck the drum head to pick up the attack of the drum head, and then put an Electro-Voice RE20 a foot away from the outside head to get the sound of the kick. Because Mick didn't hit hard, we weren't getting the bottom end from his kick drum. The bottom end on that album came from John McVie's bass. So we opted for the combination of midrange presence and low-midrange punch that those two mics provided.

Still, we had no set technique. We just tried to match the sound of the song. On some songs, we wanted a more ambient-sounding kick—which the RE20 was good for—and other songs needed the drier, deader sound that the SM57 captured. We would record the kick in stereo and then combine the two tracks, mixing one mic louder than the other, depending on the song. We definitely came up with a bigger sound than we would have gotten with just one mic.

Did you apply this recording philosophy to other instruments on _Rumours_?

Oh, yeah. We recorded most of the instruments in stereo and then blended the tracks to get huge sounds. For example, the electric guitar on "Dreams" was composed of four signals: a direct signal, a miked signal, a signal running from the output of the amp head, and another direct signal from a volume pedal. Then we'd pan it all in stereo so parts would sweep from left to right in a very majestic way. It was always about choosing the right mics with the right space for the right song, and that has to be done with one's ear, and with a high degree of sensitivity to the music.

It sounds fun, but it was probably a bit nerve-racking approaching the mix for each song individually, instead of just settling on a basic sonic blueprint for the album.

I remember going through _nine_ pianos at the Record Plant in Sausalito. Of course, we were probably more whacked out than the pianos. [_Laughs._] _Rumours_ took a year to record, and _Tusk_ took about a year and a half. Fleetwood Mac didn't believe in pre-production, and that's good and bad. The bad news is that the album cost a million dollars—which was a ridiculous amount of money back then. The good news is that because we went in with a totally open mind—not preconceived in any way—we came up with things where the sum of the parts were far greater than they could have been if we had worked everything out beforehand. A lot of the songs were written in the studio. A lot of the lyrics were written in the studio. It was a trying but very exhilarating process.

I understand there were some serious issues with the 24-track tape that resulted in many more hours being spent in the studio.

When you drag analog tape across the tape heads, you're basically wearing it out. After about six or eight months, you can really wear the tape out, and it's the high end that goes first. It's subtle, so you don't notice it until the day you listen to your tracks and realize, "My God—these drums are dull. Where are the cymbals?" This is what happened to us, and we were freaking out because we didn't know how to get our high end back. We were starting to see daylight where the tracks were! And we were scared, because Warner Bros. was waiting for the album. Thank God, we had done a set of safety copies after we cut the master track. Even though the safeties were second-generation backups, they still had all the high end, and we overlaid all of the overdubs to those tapes. This was before SMPTE synchronization, so we had to get two 24-track machines and sync the machines by ear. Ken would put on headphones, and we'd pull up the drum overhead tracks on both the original master and the safety master, and then we'd listen to the phasing between the cymbals. Ken would have to turn the VSO control until the phasing would start to go out to time-sync the machines. And, of course, it would go out too far, and then you would have to stop and punch in sections. It was an 18-hour process to do three or four songs. But we pulled it off, and when you listen to *Rumours*, those are the safeties you're hearing!

When you were recording basic tracks, did the band record together?

The guitar solos and drums on "The Chain" were played together. Other than that, I don't think any of the instruments were actually played together. Everything was overdubbed. It took an intense amount of work to get everything to sound natural, but when the parts are right, it's going to sound like they were never overdubbed. When you're working with a group of people as talented as Fleetwood Mac—and you have that kind of time and budget—you have the freedom to experiment and work by your gut instincts.

PERFORMANCE MIXING

Dashut reveals that his experience working the board for Fleetwood Mac's live shows inspired the "performance mixing" approach that he and co-producer/engineer Ken Caillat employed in the studio to energize the sound of *Rumours*. As Dashut details, back in the days before reliable automation, it was the engineer—and as many able hands as he or she could recruit—that moved faders, fiddled with outboard effects, twisted pan knobs, and assembled the mix landscape in real time as the tape was running. The head engineer would often have to command the tangle of hands hovering over the console like a field marshal under fire, yelling things such as, "Mute channel 16 *now*" and "Fade in the second rhythm guitar on the next downbeat."

It was, as Dashut describes, a process of emotion and technique, and it was often as frustrating as it was exhilarating, because there was no "undo" command. If you screwed the last fade, you'd have to start the mix all over again from the top, or mix the fade separately, then cut tape and edit in the desired section.

However, at its best, performance mixing captured sonic and spectral arrangements that were just as inspired and impassioned as a guitarist hitting a transcendent solo, or a vocalist locking into the perfect blend of tone and phrasing. Like all the best musical moments of the pre-digital era, the mix *was* a real-time performance, rather than a DAW operation that can be edited, refined, and saved as countless recallable versions for eons forward. Think about that.

If you feel this type of energy and vitality is missing in your home-studio productions, consider cutting loose the safety nets of the digital age for a mix or two. (Of course, you can still return to DAW mixing if you don't dig the results, so taking a chance isn't really a risk at all.) Tank automation. Completely. Pretend it doesn't exist. And that means for everything—effects, panning, bus assignments, and so on. From now on, every mix move will be done by your own hands in real time—win, lose, or draw.

When you're done, compare your performance mix with a conventional DAW mix that you tweaked, edited, and worried over for days (or weeks). Determine if the "p-mix" delivers a sense of impact, drive, and drama that the "d-mix" lacks. If not, then technological advances have clearly enhanced your production style. But if your p-mix *does* possess more vibe, take the lesson to heart. In the end—as Dashut warns—it's not the method, it's the music.
—Michael Molenda

Considering that you learned your craft before the digital age, how have the new tools changed your approach to recording?

Pro Tools and other computer-based recording systems have changed everything. These systems have really given us the ability to *change* songs after the fact—not just correct them. I find myself relying more on that. You try not to, but you do.

At the same time, you have to be very conscious about getting most of what you need out of the performance. Take the Auto-Tuning of vocals. It used to require 40 takes to get a performance that right. The singer would be so tired, they would just give it up. [*Laughs.*] I feel we miss a lot of that these days. There's no question that technology vastly improves your ability to do things, but in the '70s, we really had to rely on the song. The reason you're recording in the first place is because of the song. Today, the method has become almost as important as the reason for doing it, and that can be dangerous.

10

Foo Fighters

WASTING LIGHT'S LOW-TECH APPROACH
TO HIGH-INTENSITY ROCK

By Ken Micallef

This chapter appeared in the in the May 2011 issue of
Electronic Musician magazine.

"You know that scene in *The Wall* where the faceless
people are falling into the machine that's grinding them
into paste?" asks Dave Grohl from his 606 Studio in Los
Angeles. "Digital editing has robbed drummers of their
identity, just like that. I'm heartbroken by what heavy-
handed producers have done with drummers over the
last 10 years."

"A drummer walks into a studio," he continues, like
he's telling a Borscht Belt joke. "He says, 'This is how I
play the drums,' and the producer says, 'That's not good
enough. I am going to make you sound like a machine.'
That's f**king lame! I am not the greatest drummer in
the world, but when I record drums, it doesn't sound
perfect and I am all over the place and the cymbals
wash a little hard, but that's how I play the drums. If you
don't like it, don't call me back. I wish that every drummer would tell their producer, 'That f**king machine
doesn't make me sound like me. It makes me sound like
you, and you're not the drummer, motherf**ker.' We've

got Taylor Hawkins—who is the greatest f**king rock drummer I've ever played with—why not let Taylor sound like Taylor? So that's why we used tape and no computers."

Wasting Light, Foo Fighters' seventh album, is a messy, often distorted, over-the-top record that pulses with attitude and energy. Every Foo Fighters album is an adrenaline junkie's dream, the twin powers of Dave Grohl and Taylor Hawkins guaranteeing maximum energy like twin turbojets propelling a 747. But *Wasting Light*, recorded analog to tape (API 1608 32-track, two Studer 827s) with no computers, not even to mix or master, is an entirely different beast. You hear guitars clipping, cymbals pushing VU meters into the red, the sound of a live performance: blood, sweat, and tears (literally). What you don't hear is a grid. Or Auto-Tune. Or perfectly lined-up drums.

Deciding to track at Dave Grohl's house with producer Butch Vig and engineer James Brown (veteran producer/engineer Alan Moulder came in to mix), the band (Grohl, Hawkins, Pat Smear, Nate Mendel, and Chris "Shifty" Shiflett, and bassist Krist Novoselic on one track) set up in the garage (drums), the living room (control/live room), and in closets (vocals), with no sound treatment and plenty of bleed. Three baffles were placed behind Hawkins' vintage Ludwig drums, but that was it.

"I am no stranger to tape," Grohl says. "Call me dumb, but the simple signal path of a microphone to a tape machine makes perfect sense to me. There's not too many options, and the performance is what matters most."

But not everyone agreed with Grohl's "analog only" rule. "The first song we recorded, we get a drum take and Butch starts razor-splicing edits to tape," Grohl recalls. "We rewind the tape and it starts shedding oxide. Butch says, 'We should back everything up to digital.' I start screaming: 'If I see one f**king computer hooked up to a piece of gear, you're f**king fired! We're making the record the way we want to make it, and if you can't do it, then f**k you!' Nobody makes us do what we don't want to do. 'What if something happens to the tape?' 'What did we do in 1991, Butch?' You play it again! God forbid you have to play your song one more time."

With that behind them, the team settled into the tracking process: Hawkins recording drums to click, and Grohl's scratch guitar and scratch vocal to a mas-

Foo Fighters in Dave Grohl's garage in Los Angeles. (Courtesy RCA)

ter reel, which was the reel used for edits. Rather than recording numerous drum takes, punch-ins and edited transitions completed the master takes. The master reel and a blank slave reel were striped with SMPTE timecode: "We would lock those two striped reels together and simultaneously bounce down the drums to four tracks (kick, snare, and a stereo mix of all the other drum tracks); Dave's scratch parts would also get bounced over," says Brown. "We would then record all of the overdubs to the slave reel. We never went back to the master reels, due to the fact that we ended up mixing back up at the house. Under normal circumstances, one would lock the master back up with the slave and use the first-generation drum tracks from the master reel (in other words, not the bounced-down drums on the slave reel) when mixing. However, with only 32 channels on the console, that wasn't an option for us. All of the mixes, with the exception of 'Dear Rosemary,' were mixed using the bounced-down drums." Everything was mixed with all eight hands (Grohl, Vig, Brown, and mix engineer Alan Moulder) on deck, riding faders in real time to tape.

"In Pro Tools, you can take a band that's not very good and make them razor-tight," Butch Vig explains from Silverlake, California, where he is working on the forthcoming Garbage album. "But this became more about the band's performances, about what they would have to do in order to make a great record. They wanted a challenge. That was exciting. Somebody would want to do a punch, and I'd say, 'If you go over it, it's gone.' The Foos rehearsed very hard to pull this off, and not many bands could do it."

Vig and the Foos did allow a click track for drums; they're not *insane*. But even then, Vig discovered the joys of free flying and forgetting the grid. "Clicks were used, but it's loose," Vig says. "Sometimes we'd worry about the timing of a snare hit. Then we realized that when everything is off just a few milliseconds, the sound gets wider and thicker. If you zoom in with Pro Tools and put everything exactly on that microscopic downbeat, it's so perfect that it loses a thickness. If everything is off just a little bit, the music just gets wider and thicker.

"It all made our brains switch into a different focus," he adds. "For one thing, everyone is used to looking at a computer screen, so you look at the music, what the timing is, what the waves are like. There was no computer screen at Dave's, so I would look at the meters, which is how I initially learned how to record. We set up this huge HD monitor on the meter bridge of the tape machine so we could see how hard we were hitting the tape. Eventually we started feeding that live to the Net, with no explanation!"

BUNKER DRUMS

Down in the concrete bunker/basement that functioned as a drum booth, engineer James Brown had his work cut out for him. Brown used the same close mics as he would for any date: Yamaha SKRM100 Subkick (with custom API pre) and an AKG D 112 (custom API pre/Inward Connections EQP2/Distressor) on kick; Shure SM57 on snare top and bottom (custom API pre/EQ'd and summed in API 1608/Distressor); AKG 452 (Neve 1073) on hi-hat; Josephson E22S (API 1608 pre) on toms; AKG 452 (Neve 1073) on ride.

But as the concrete floor created mad reflections, Brown experimented with overhead and ambient placement. Grohl demanded more "garage" whenever things became too tidy-sounding, which meant turning up the room mics and turning down the close mics. For overheads, after a shootout, Brown settled on a Violet Designs Stereo Flamingo (Neve 1073) and Shure SM58 "trash" (custom API/UREI 1176, all buttons in, "Brit mode"). Kit ambience (about four feet out) was a Neumann M 49 (Great River/Harrison 32EQ/Retro Instruments Sta-Level); overhead ambience was a Violet Black Finger (Neve 1073/UREI 1176); main ambience, two Soundelux 251s at knee level against the garage door (custom API pres/Dramastic Audio Obsidian). For floor ambience, a pair of Crown PZMs (custom API pres/DBX 160).

"I'd use the same mic placement in that garage, regardless of the mics," Brown explains. "Turning the Soundeluxes away from the drums and pointing them into a corner tempered the top end. The mic choices were more about choosing cymbals and asking Taylor not to hit so hard. That allows more room for the snare and kick to cut through in the ambient mics. That's when you can really hear the garage; the air isn't getting sucked up by cymbals and midrange."

Room mics were placed eight feet out from the kit—basically, against the garage door at the farthest point away from the drums. "It was purely to temper the cymbals," Brown says. "The garage being untreated and literally a concrete box, it was a very harsh, loud environment. So it required an unconventional miking setup. The Crown PZM, whatever you stick it to, it expands its pickup area, so those added a lot of punch in the low/mid area. The Shure 58, I stick it directly behind the drummer's head and compress the living daylights out of it with all the buttons in on the UREI; that adds a trashiness to everything. The Neumann between the garage door closer to the drums is to capture some of the air around the kick drum. There are three mics on kick drum: one inside, aimed at the beater; then the NS10 sub bass; and the kit ambience from the Neumann. The mic pre choices are what I generally use. For tom, kick, and snare, I used my go-to choices."

Grohl sang through his time-tested Bock 251 (Neve 1073/Distressor); Brown used his go-to mics for bass and guitar. Bass choices were an Avalon U5 DI (Neve 1073/Inward Connection EQP2/Distressor) and two close mics on Nate's Ashdown ABM 900 EVO/Ashdown 8X10 cab: Lauten Clarion (FET) and a Blue Mouse. Guitar mics were many: two RCA BX5s, Royer R121, Josephson E22S, Shure SM57, Shure SM7, Sennheiser 421. Guitar pres were "almost exclusively Shadow Hills Quad Gama—occasionally, I would use the API board

79

pres," says Brown. "That would in turn be fed through a Universal Audio LA-3A limiter, just touching the peaks. Nearly everything went through a fader and EQ on the API 1608 console that Butch would manipulate during performance to send as clean a signal to tape. We had to tape a guitar pick to the fader track to stop him burning a hole in the tape!"

After tracking instruments, Grohl cut vocals, typically sitting next to Vig and Brown in the makeshift control room. As with everything he does, Grohl pushed himself to the max.

"Ask Dr. Phil about my headaches!" Grohl says with a laugh. "I like to make vocals feel atmospheric and ethereal. But then I want them to sound like I'm in primal-scream therapy. Some things I am singing I can't make sound pretty. Punk rock is my identity. I am from a little town in Virginia, a high-school drop-out who wanted to play punk rock. So when I am screaming my balls off, it's because I don't feel any different than when I was 15.

"Anyway, I do get headaches. I want a song to have maximum emotional potential when I am singing in the studio. When the mic is picking up every tiny inconsistency, you really strain to make it sound right. And I sit down to sing. That's the only way I know how to do it. Maybe I feel funny 'cause I don't have a guitar on. I project the same; I don't know how else to do it."

RETROSPECTION, INTROSPECTION

"We did a couple songs where Dave sang right next to me," Vig says, "like, 'I Should Have Known.' Lyrically, there are references to Kurt Cobain, but I don't know if Dave would admit to that. We ran Dave's mic into a Space Echo there—it's got this spooky, distorted sound. At the end of that take, the hair on my neck stood up; I couldn't say anything. Dave looked like he was crying, 'cause he was singing so hard. He was obviously channeling something inside. It's one of my favorite songs on the album, and the darkest and weirdest, in a way. I love that song."

Grohl won't confirm that "I Should Have Known" is about Kurt Cobain—only that the doomed legend is in there, somewhere. "There is something to be said for starting over," Grohl says. "To be able to say, if this all ended now, I'd be totally okay with it, and I'd start over again. 'Cause that's what

I've always done. I've always felt like this is temporary, ever since Nirvana became popular. So a song like 'I Should Have Known' is about all the people I've lost, not just Kurt.

"There was a lot of retrospection and introspection going back to the way we used to make records," he continues. "and with someone who started my career 20 years ago: Butch. I wouldn't be doing this if not for Butch Vig. After we were finished, I realized there's a reason why we're here, and why we made the album the way we did, and why we used Butch, and a reason why Krist Novoselic played on a song. I was writing about time. And how much has passed and feeling born again, feeling like a survivor, thinking about mortality and death and life, and how beautiful it is to be surrounded by friends and family and making music."

Ultimately, *Wasting Light* is a life-affirming, uplifting record, like most Foo Fighters records—from the roaring opener, "Burning Bridges," and the guitar shrapnel counterpoint of "Rope," to the Ministry-esque death-metal howl of "White Limo" and the introspective "I Should Have Known." Somewhere in his 40s, Dave Grohl comes to grips with his past by facing his present.

"This band was a f*king fluke," Grohl says. "To think now that we can headline these huge shows and there are these huge expectations, like, 'You better make a f**king hit record!' That kind of s**t. So, okay, I'll go back to my

BIG SOUND ON A SMALL BUDGET

Engineer James Brown's advice for getting past gear limitations:

"If you only have cheap mics and pres on hand, it doesn't mean you can't get good sounds," Brown says. "Understanding mic placement can be the difference between your work sounding like it's made up of a bunch of disparate sounds, as opposed to a cohesive, robust-sounding recording. The main rule of thumb is, if it sounds good in the room, there's a good chance it will sound good recorded. Then if you can add to that an understanding of phase cancellation and how to avoid it, you'll be on your way. The rest of it is all about the way you hear things. But it's hugely important to nurture an understanding or feel for how musical parts and sounds interact and fit together—the alchemy of it, if you will. There's an art to engineering music, so at some point you have to let go of all of that knowledge and start thinking about it in those terms."

garage, 'cause that's what everyone thought we *shouldn't* do. It defused any of that expectation. If we have songs that mean something, and you hear them once and they stick, and they're recorded so it sounds like a beautiful explosion and it feels like human beings making music, then we've accomplished everything that we've wanted to do. It made perfect sense. Why do it the way everybody else does it? I want to sound like *us*, like the Foo Fighters."

11

Imogen Heap

WRITING ABROAD AND RECORDING AT HOME FOR *ELLIPSE*

By Geary Yelton

This chapter features an abridged version of the Imogen Heap article in the October 2009 issue of *Electronic Musician* magazine.

Imogen Heap may not be a household name, but that could soon change with her latest release. *Ellipse* (RCA, 2009) is a stunning album produced in the recording studio she recently built in her home outside of London. Just 31 years old, she is an accomplished singer, songwriter, producer, and multi-instrumentalist who has been nominated for two Grammy Awards, one for Best New Artist in 2007 and another for Best Original Song Written for Film.

Two years ago, Heap bought and moved into the house she grew up in and announced that she would soon start recording her next album there. She began by refurbishing the home and converting what had been her childhood playroom into a recording space built to her specifications. She uploaded the first of 40 video clips to YouTube, detailing her struggles and accomplishments in roughly 10-minute installments. Devoted fans tuned in regularly to check on her progress. Heap expects these clips and some additional material to soon be released as a DVD detailing the making of *Ellipse*.

Her following on the Web is especially impressive, with nearly one million followers on Twitter and more than 350,000 Myspace friends on the day of the album's release. As the songwriting and recording of *Ellipse* progressed, Heap often turned to her fans for advice, soliciting their opinions about whether she should include a song on the album, for example, or which version of a recording they preferred. She streamed live piano performances on Ustream.tv and invited anyone following her Tweets to collaborate on her official biography. She even asked fans to submit samples of their artwork and photography, and then chose the most impressive to contribute to the album art and packaging. All of this group participation gave her audience a sense of ownership and personal investment in *Ellipse*.

I interviewed Heap on the same day that she performed at TEDGlobal (July 21 to 24, 2009; Oxford, England), a gathering of movers and shakers in the worlds of technology, entertainment, and design.

What can you tell me about your studio?

Well, you walk into the room and you'll notice that it's curved. I live in an elliptical-shaped house—hence, the title of the album. [The studio] was my old playroom. I didn't want you to feel like you're in a sterile environment, which I feel when I go to a lot of studios. [That] always baffles me, because music is not about clean lines and flashy silver things. Music, when you get creating it, is kind of messy and a little bit higglety-pigglety.

There's a massive [Digidesign] ICON desk when you walk in that kind of dominates the room, which I don't tend to use very often, but I do like sitting at it because it makes me feel like a professional. On the left of the ICON desk is my Perspex piano, a clear plastic piano I built for my live shows. That's what [holds my computer display], my Nord, and my little looping thing. On the right is the vocal booth, with multiple instruments.

Did you consider other mixing desks before you decided on the ICON?

I've used unautomated mixing desks, a Neve, like when I was 17; that's what I learned from. I've never actually considered having a desk again until I went into Jed Lieber's studio in the Sunset Marquis and he sold me his ICON. I just fell in love because I thought it was so beautiful. It had all these beautiful sparkly lights, and it looks really nice, aesthetically. So I just thought, "If

Imogen Heap in her home studio outside of London. (Jeremy Cowart)

I'm going have a desk, it would be that, because I want to keep it digital." The whole record is all digital, even the mastering. I don't really want to affect the sound using a desk. I like knowing that what goes in, that's what it is and it stays there.

I [record] a lot of acoustic instruments and just process them as audio [data] in [Digidesign] Pro Tools, and manually toy with them like Play-Doh. I don't use much outboard gear at all. You go into some studios and you see racks and racks and racks of gear, but all I actually use is my Avalon 737 for any singular mic stuff, and then if I'm miking up anything else, I use my Focusrite Liquid Channel.

I don't like reverb very much; I much prefer delay. You put loads of reverb on everything and it just fills up the track. I can't get the detail that I like when I'm working with so many tracks. I just try to get the sound right before I put things like reverb on. As far as vocals go, I'll process it if I want really long, backward, messed-up vocals. Then I might use a bit of reverb, but I generally use Waves [SuperTap] 6-Tap delay. I'll make a copy of the lead vocals, and then go in and manually take out every single sibilant, every single t and s and d and anything that will sound like a delay when you hear it in the mix. It basically does what a reverb does, but it has more space and more structure to it.

What microphone did you use for vocals on *Ellipse*?

Always the same one: a Neumann TLM 103.

That's the same mic you've used for your previous albums.

Yeah, exactly. The last three records—the Frou Frou one, this one, and *Speak for Yourself*—all the same mic. And then the same preamp/compressor, the Avalon 737.

What synthesizers do you use?

I don't have that many. I've got my trusty Ensoniq TS-12, which occasionally I might fire up. I've got a little Nord Rack 3 and the [Korg] Electribe MX.

Any software instruments?

I've got Massive and all the Native Instruments stuff, and I like [Apple] Sculpture very much. I like things you can really bend and shift. I love just processing [audio] in Pro Tools. When I really start having fun with sculpting sounds, it's about 6 or 7 or 8 in the evening and everything's settled down and nobody's bugging me. I'll continue through the night if I'm having a good session. I really don't remember how I do things, because I get so lost in it. It's like, if you're driving home from somewhere and you just know your way so well that you get to your front door, you've got the keys in your hand, and you're going, "Oh, how did I get here?" That's what it's like.

You're absorbed in the process.

Yeah, I totally don't remember the process. [I know I must] have some kind of process, but I'm so involved in it that I couldn't really relay it to you.

My friend Justine [Pearsall] has filmed me on and off over the last couple of years, as I've been building the studio and as I've been making the record. That's not going to be available [on DVD] until November, because she's only just started editing it and she's got 350 hours of footage. That won't be like a super-techie, what-plug-ins-type thing. It's more like the building block of an album—[from the] seed of a song to building a studio to then finally staying up late at night and picking out all kinds of random sounds.

[She filmed me] going through the house and recording everything from the tap dripping to the banisters, and using that as my starting point. There are a few songs, like "Canvas," where I really started on the computer, building sounds inside Logic, but then mostly I start with something that's acoustic, like the hang drum or the mbira or the piano or banisters or the light ceiling panels in my studio—which make a very nice timpani sound—and wine glasses at the beginning of "First Train Home." And then it's really the way that I process them, edit them, and mess with them [that] makes it sound not like where it started.

How do you go about writing songs?

With this album, I took a different approach. The last album, I built sounds in [Steinberg] Nuendo and in Pro Tools, and then wrote the song over the tops of tracks I'd built with loops and things. But with this one, I made a conscious decision to write the song first, in the old-school way, because I didn't want to get into the issue of writing a backing track and then spend two months trying to crowbar in a melody over the top of this thing I built that I loved, only to just take it all apart anyway to fit a vocal in. I really tried to get the song first, which is very different from the way I've been working for the last eight years. I wanted to just go and write the songs, which is what I did.

I went on a little writing trip, and I wrote most of the songs. The songwriting, in the beginning spark of the idea, that's really exciting because you're inspired to get in the studio and get working on it. But then there's the slog of writing the lyrics. Sometimes they don't come easy. I wanted to do that side of it in a beautiful place so I wasn't frustrated. I did all the writing away so I could just get to the fun bit of making the music when I got into the house.

That's why you've been traveling so much?

Yeah, well, partly because I needed to get my head emotionally around the fact that I was going to take on the family house. I didn't have a workable studio at the time, and I've never actually traveled, outside of work, on my own and gone to places I've actually wanted to visit. I've done touring—lots of Japan, lots of America, lots of Europe—but it's just the same routes that you go on. I just thought, well, I was 29, and I really haven't been anywhere on my own and just traveled.

It worked out great because I was in quite remote places. I'd have to figure out the language because I was sometimes in the middle of nowhere in, like, the countryside of Japan and trying to find food that I recognized from the local shop. In a way, that was great because it took the pressure off of me just sitting in a room every day, saying, "Right, I've got to write a song." It was like, "Right, I've got to go down and get some breakfast; how am I going to do that?"

The instrumentation on the song "Earth" is absolutely stunning. It sounds as if all the instruments, including the bass and drums, are your voice.

They are indeed, yes. I could have gone the route of really processing the vocals to make them not sound like vocals, but I just thought that defeats the object. I spent quite a bit of time trying to get the best sound out of my voice. And I spent *ages* editing them together. There's over 100 tracks of vocals on it, and it was absolutely completely doing my head in, just hearing the sound of my own voice for, like, three weeks nonstop. But I really had this vision, what I wanted it to be. It was really good fun to write that one.

You orchestrate your vocals in more intricate detail than any singer I've ever heard. Are you more influenced by your knowledge of orchestration than by other singers?

I was never really interested in vocal music as a kid. I learned the piano, so I learned harmony [and] counterpoint through that. And then I learned the clarinet [and] cello, so I understood different parts of the orchestra and how they work with each other. And I studied composition and arrangement, not to a great degree, not even to degree level, just for the love of it.

I like creating something with lots of personality, lots of depth, and lots of things that you can hear over and over—things that you don't notice at all until the 50th listen, that most would say, "Why are you still in the studio working on that damn song?" I want to get the detail that you couldn't possibly take in on your first, second, third, fourth listen. And I'll probably forget that they're there. In five years' time, I'll go, "Ooh, that's a nice sound! How did I do that? I forgot about that." I want to be able to experience music like that, because otherwise people just go, "Okay, I've got that." Well, I would, anyway. I like music I can listen to over and over again. I don't listen to my own music, but that's the kind of stuff I like, with details and lots and lots of parts going on, but at the same time trying to keep a focus.

That's why I always record the vocals first, try to put as little music behind me as possible, record the vocals so they sound amazing, do all the harmonies and make all the parts, even before there's any music—just the bare bones. Then, and only then, start creating the music around it. I spent about a month just doing vocals. I didn't do anything else. I did 10 tracks of vocals when I got into the studio. It was absolutely maddening, but I just wanted to get it out of the way because for me, that's not really the fun bit. The fun bit is making sounds and just getting lost in the audio.

It sounds like you have a very strong sense of balance on *Ellipse*.

Every song is in a different key, and there's six major, six minor. One of them is improvised; six of them were written on the writing trip; six of them were written in the house. Tempos range from 54 to 177 [bpm] because I wanted to get a full sweep of tempos. It's also trying to find spaces to be creative within, because if I just had an empty canvas, it's absolutely impossible to do anything. Where do you start? What color do you use? What kind of brush do you use? It's overwhelming. So I needed to make myself have these bookends to work within, so I'd choose, like, I have to have this kind of tempo and this kind of key, and this type of major-minor whatever because I haven't got it on the record. And sometimes that would be what decided the tempo or key of the beginning of an idea.

With all the work you've been doing wrapping up *Ellipse*, have you found time to get involved with any film projects lately?

No, I haven't had any time at all to do anything. I've had very little sleep. I came straight out of the record, and I got thrown into the album art [and] press images. The only thing I'm doing tomorrow and the day after is TED[Global], and I'm so looking forward to just taking in what's happened for the last two years, because it's been absolutely nonstop. The kind of weight and the pressure of this album, waking up every morning, going, "Oh, I've got to do the record," you know. It still hasn't really sunk in. I still feel like I wake up in the morning, and go, "Oh! No, I don't have to do it." But I've got to do everything else. So I'm really looking forward to these next few days.

Congratulations on making it this far.

Thank you. I didn't think I was going to for a while there.

12

Ladytron

THE EFFECTS-PEDAL EXPLORATIONS
OF *WITCHING HOUR*

By Markkus Rovito

This chapter features an abridged version of the
Ladytron article in the December 2005 issue of *Remix*
magazine.

On Roxy Music's debut album, Bryan Ferry sang of re-
venge enacted upon an unsuspecting object of affec-
tion in a song called "Ladytron." Keyboardist Brian Eno
layered synth drones and strings atop curiously effected
guitars and orchestral instruments. It was a song of
dark emotions wrapped in a seductive groove by turns
relaxed and passionate, and it toyed with sounds and
moods rarely experienced in the pop music of the time.
That time, specifically, was 1972, long before any member of the Liverpool, England, band Ladytron touched
finger to key of any of the group's prized vintage synths,
which were being produced at the same time as Roxy
Music's experimental avant-pop.

Nearly 30 years later, when Ladytron released its
first album, *604* (Emperor Norton, 2001), few listeners
heard a connection between its synth pop and the styl-
ish art rock of fellow Brits Roxy Music. Rather, Ladytron was unceremoniously lumped into the electroclash
movement with acts such as Fischerspooner, Adult., and

Mount Sims, where it would stay through the release of its second album, *Light & Magic* (Emperor Norton, 2002). Although the electroclash label didn't put Ladytron in bad company, it did overlook the breezy sophistication of the band's minimal yet layered synths-and-beats sound and its knack for writing pop hooks and melodies, which stand on their own. What no one could have known for certain was that for its first two albums, Ladytron was gestating in the cocoon of its home studio. The band broke out of this incubator with a yearlong world tour supporting *Light & Magic* and then spread its wings fully when it went into a Liverpool studio with producer Jim Abbiss (Kasabian, U.N.K.L.E.) to record *Witching Hour* (Rykodisc, 2005), an album appropriately enchanting for its title.

SOUND RESOLVE

Witching Hour is all about bending the line between genres, so much so that the ends of the line meet in the middle. In other words, Ladytron has come full circle with its influences, including '70s Krautrock and art rock, '80s electro and synth pop, and the cavalcade of '90s dance styles from which the band draws. Early experimenters such as Can, Neu!, and Roxy Music helped inform Kraftwerk, which in turn inspired the creators of hip-hop, house, and techno but also influenced new-wave bands and the contemporary psychedelics of shoegaze guitar bands. In an artistic progression that may surprise many—yet disappoint few—fans, Ladytron invokes pieces of each of these styles to create an emotional, energetic, catchy, beautiful, intelligent album that is either very challenging to classify specifically or incredibly easy to classify in general as pop music.

"We're not very interested in being a band attached to another band's reputation or sound," says Daniel Hunt (keyboards, production), who wrote the bulk of the material for Ladytron's first two albums. On *Witching Hour*, the other members—Mira Aroyo (vocals, keyboards), Helena Marnie (vocals, keyboards), and Reuben Wu (keyboards, production)—contributed more to the writing.

The result feels more like a stylistically diverse group effort, and it's expertly paced—indicative of a band whose members have all spent the past few

Mira Aroyo (far left), Helen Marnie, Reuben Wu, and Daniel Hunt. (Courtesy of Rykodisc)

years picking up DJ gigs. *Witching Hour* opens with the tension-building drone of "High Rise" and then explodes into the powerfully stoic drive and bounce of "Destroy Everything You Touch," in which Marnie's icily delivered vocals scolding an insensitive friend could be a direct answer to Ferry's "Ladytron" lyrics. The album then ebbs and flows between ethereal, midtempo tunes;

instrumental interludes; and club-ready rockers until it gives way to a gorgeous, synth-pad-drenched conclusion in the last three songs, including the ode to My Bloody Valentine, "White Light Generator," and Ladytron's first certifiable tearjerker, the wistful and climactic "All the Way."

LADY TREKS

For Ladytron's 12-month *Light & Magic* world tour, the group added a live bassist and drummer to the lineup and stopped using sequenced beats and loops onstage in favor of playing all the parts in real time. "We used to play with a laboratory setup onstage," Aroyo says, referring to the nearly 15 vintage analog synths that the band used onstage each night. "It just felt really limiting, like we couldn't go anywhere with it being tied to a loop."

To punch up the live sound, the band added drummer Keith York, formerly of Broadcast, and bassist Andrew Goldsworthy. "We wanted to explore something that was more dynamic," Hunt explains. "The first two albums sound very serene and small compared to how the tracks ended up sounding live, when they became harder and more powerful."

"We got a lot of confidence out of playing as a live band," Aroyo continues. "We're a lot better than we were before." The band started touring to support *Witching Hour* in October (it should cover the U.S. during late winter and spring of 2006) and has kept the six-member format for the gigs. Adapting the album to the stage was much more intuitive this time. "Basically, the way we had done the previous records, we were just a recording band, not a touring band," Aroyo says. "We made the records and then appropriated them live. Whereas with this one, it's still very delicate and precise on the record, but it's punchier. It was quite easy to adapt this one live." That didn't mean that the band simply forsook all of its carefully processed and mixed drum tracks from *Witching Hour* to have them played on a standard drum kit. "We're kind of like a weirdo rock band, but we're not really interested in being a traditional rock band in any way," Aroyo adds. "So the live drum sounds need to fit right in with the rest of the music."

Drummer York plays both sampled sounds from drum pads onstage and a full kit that is miked and effected to capture the essence of *Witching Hour*'s heavily treated beats. It helped that York played drums on about half of the album and contributed to the creation of the drum sounds. "He's very clever with the drum processing," Hunt says. Although York and Goldsworthy are sidemen, they bring a lot to the process. "They're not in the photos and not in the band proper, but they take a lot of responsibility for what they do," Hunt says. "They're an integral part of the way we perform live."

The band has also dropped most of its vintage synths from the stage show to preserve the instruments and ensure better reliability from contemporary digital-modeling synths. Trusty old servants such as the Korg MS-10 and MS-20, the Roland SH-2 and SH-09, the Moog Micromoog, the Sequential Circuits Pro-One, and others are used for recording, but Ladytron replaces them live with models such as the Korg MS2000 and MicroKorg. "A lot of the original sounds were made on [vintage] Korgs," Aroyo says. "The new modeling synths aren't as good as the real thing—they don't have all the natural modulation the MS-10s and MS-20s have—but they're a pretty good approximation."

PREPRODUCTION HOURS

After the *Light & Magic* tour wrapped in the latter half of 2003, members of the band wasted little time in preparing material for the next record. Hunt, Aroyo, Marnie, and Wu wrote material on their own at home, sometimes full songs, or just short sketches of a song. "We write all the songs on guitars and keyboards," Hunt says. "We don't sequence until the last minute." When the group does sequence in parts, it's usually with Steinberg Cubase SX. "We're used to it," Hunt explains. "We've been using it for seven or eight years. A lot of people talk about Logic, especially since Apple bought it. But if you've just come off tour, and you've got to write another record, do you want to work on music, or sit there and learn another application for six months?" Hunt also notes that for the most part, the band eschews software synths because, in the end, they usually prefer the tracks they record on hardware instruments anyway.

After hashing out material individually for a time, the band worked as a group for at least a month piecing ideas into demos for *Witching Hour*. "Because there was such a delay between this album and the last one, people assume it was a creative delay," Hunt says. "It totally wasn't." By January 2004, the *Witching Hour* demos were prepared, and the band took about 24 working song ideas into the studio to work with Londoner Abbiss, who in 15 years of producing has worked with Björk, Sneaker Pimps, Massive Attack, Placebo, DJ Shadow, and many others.

Although Abbiss was a large part of the process, several of the vocal and instrumental tracks from the group's original demos made it to *Witching Hour*. "People assume that because this album sounds a bit different, the producer has changed the sound or that, because we changed labels, the label changed the sound," Hunt says. "This album was headed in the direction it was from the moment it started. Jim brought his skills and a fresh pair of ears and took it to another level altogether."

SONIC SEARCH

A great deal of sonic exploration to find the perfect tones and timbres was key to the studio sessions. "We started doing this six years ago, but now all those sounds we used people can get in any cracked version of Cubase," Hunt says. The band drew upon Abbiss' expert ear and vast collection of rare and exotic instruments and signal processors to diligently create a sonic palette. They spent weeks recording and tweaking sounds, and the band leaned heavily on the producer's collection of effects boxes, especially vintage Electro-Harmonix overdrives, delays, and synth boxes, such as the company's Bass Micro Synthesizer. Unsung heroes also came in the form of old unidentified Russian knockoff pedals, such as the box that mimicked the classic WEM Watkins Copicat tape-delay box. "Some of the sounds were unattainable without these strange boxes we were feeding stuff through," Hunt reveals.

High-maintenance instruments, such as a harmonium (an Indian hand-pumped reed organ) and an ARP 2600 analog modular synth, won over the Ladytron members' hearts in the studio. "One day, we couldn't function at all; we'd been out the night before," Aroyo recalls. "Jim just sat there in the studio all day with a guitar, and he was surrounded by Korg synths with every output going through every pedal he could possibly have and the ARP 2600, as well. All day was spent like that, and we came up with one sound. The ARP 2600 is very tricky."

They treated drums just as meticulously. To record the drums for "amTV," a sassy piece of synth rock with a particularly massive and noisy snare, the team devised a setup that Hunt calls a "freak show." The drums were miked, sent through ring modulators and then into amplifiers, miked again, filtered, and so on. "It was this insane contraption," Hunt boasts. "It ended up producing this drum sound completely by accident, but that was a good experience."

Throughout the recording, the emphasis was on the result, not the method. "A lot of the songs have a mixture of both sampled electronic drums and [acoustic] drums," Aroyo says. "The live drums ended up sounding very tight, crisp, and effected. People might even think that they're sequenced."

Along the same lines, and what's more noticeable on the album, is that guitars and synths are used interchangeably. During the recording, Ladytron often treated synths with guitar overdrive and distortion pedals and sent guitars through Electro-Harmonix synth pedals; on several of the songs, it's tough to determine synth riffs from guitar riffs. For example, the droning lead sound on "High Rise" is ambiguous, but it's actually a guitar played with an EBow. "There's been guitar on all the records, but people are saying on this one, it's more dominant," Aroyo says. "But the guitar is treated so much, it's like the stuff you get in Krautrock or shoegaze records. It's just being used as a sound wave."

BEWITCHING IN CHINA

With *Witching Hour* ostensibly finished in the first half of 2004, the album sat in limbo while the band waited on the logistics of moving to a new record label. While the band considered remixing and DJ gigs, fate intervened when a government organization called the British Council offered Ladytron the rare opportunity to tour China as part of a cross-cultural outreach program. The band couldn't pass it up. "They probably picked us because they saw us as a more interesting proposition than your typical British four-boys-with-guitars band," Hunt says about the mini-tour, which included stops to cosmopolitan cities such as Shanghai as well as obscure locales. "We went to some strange, dilapidated park full of miniature world monuments, and literally no [Western] band had ever been there. The records have never been distributed there, so the only way to get the record was to download it illegally. So the benefits of file sharing are pretty obvious. It's more important for people to be able to get your music."

More significant, China served as the testing grounds for the first live performances of many songs off of *Witching Hour*. "We came back into the studio and mixed having more of a pure idea of what we wanted to do," Aroyo says. Soon after returning, Ladytron secured a deal with Island/Universal in the UK (and Rykodisc in the U.S.)—fittingly, the same label group that reissues Roxy Music discs.

In the interim between releasing *Witching Hour* and touring, Ladytron is demoing for the next album and remixing bands such as Bloc Party and Goldfrapp. The band tends to home-record remixes from scratch using only the original vocal unless another approach is requested. Regarding other artists remixing Ladytron, Hunt gives one strong piece of advice: Be creative. "When we get a remix back and it sounds almost the same as the original," Hunt laments, "it's really disappointing."

13

M83

SATURDAYS = YOUTH'S SONIC TRIBUTE TO JOHN HUGHES

By Justin Kleinfeld

This chapter features an abridged version of the M83 article in the April 2008 issue of *Remix* magazine.

The phrase "If it ain't broke, don't fix it" is usually sound advice for any musician who has achieved a modicum of success in today's tumultuous music industry. It's hard enough to get noticed out there, so why tinker with a winning formula? M83 (aka Frenchman Anthony Gonzalez) has made a career out of going against the grain and by defying logic. Much like Radiohead's evolution throughout the years, Gonzalez has changed his style with each successive album while retaining a certain zeitgeist that makes M83 unique.

In its original incarnation, M83 was a two-man team and included Nicolas Fromageau as Gonzalez's production partner. However, after the success of M83's critically acclaimed sophomore album, the psychedelic rock/electronic *Dead Cities, Red Seas & Lost Ghosts* (Mute, 2004), Fromageau departed M83, making the project a one-man entity. (M83's self-titled debut album was released in 2001.) "I think it was great for me to have Nicolas around for the first two records," Gonzalez says. "The problem was I didn't like to share what I considered to be my child. Even when Nicolas was around, I behaved like I was alone. I'd never let anyone compose for the band because I guess that would have felt like some kind of betrayal. M83 is everything to me. When I write, it is also a part of myself that I reveal. It is how I express my feelings, my fears, my thoughts, myself. Somehow, I think I need to control everything; it makes me feel like I'm alive. It might sound a little selfish, but that's the way it is. I like that feeling of loneliness—just me and my world."

M83's third album, 2005's *Before the Dawn Heals Us* (Mute), progressed from the shoegazer style of its predecessors to a more complete melding of electronic, pop, and rock. However, the fallout from an extensive world tour in support of the album was substantial. Faced with some personal issues after the tour, Gonzalez found it difficult to write music and stopped altogether for several months. Fortunately, Gonzalez awoke from his malaise and garnered enough inspiration to create what some may consider M83's finest and most complete effort to date, *Saturdays = Youth* (Mute, 2008).

HIGH SCHOOL MUSICAL

M83's music has evolved into something that can now be enjoyed by fans of many different musical genres, no longer just a small niche market. Musically, Gonzalez knew he wanted to make something far different from previous records and used his teenage experiences and '80s pop culture as the primary influence. "One of my biggest influences was John Hughes and all the '80s teen movies, such as *Breakfast Club* and *Pretty in Pink*. When I was a teenager, I watched all these Hughes movies and was really influenced by them," Gonzalez says. "As for the title, Saturday is the day of the week that means a lot to me, and it's certainly the most important day for every teenager. The album is a tribute to my teenage years, which are certainly the most important and beautiful years of my life. I learned so much during this period and had such a good time discovering things like drugs, new music, and new movies. This was an experimental period in my life. It was like I was discovering something new and great each day. We can say this is a tribute to our teenage years."

To achieve his goal of creating an album with an '80s vibe, Gonzalez was finicky about the type of the production gear used. While there are a few

M83 in Manchester, England. (Gary Wolstenholme/Redferns/Getty Images)

sounds generated through the computer, a majority of what you hear on *Saturdays = Youth* was created using real instruments and analog gear. His favorite piece of studio gear is by far the Roland Juno-2, which provides Gonzalez with the "John Carpenter" sounds he's looking for. While a vast array of keyboards was on hand to record the album, Gonzalez is also famous for being picky about the sounds he uses from each keyboard. He'll often take the same one or two sounds per synth and recycle them throughout the production.

"It's really just specific for this record that I didn't want to use digital stuff," Gonzalez says. "Sometimes I use [Propellerhead] Reason for sounds, but I wanted to have something different for this album. I'm sure for the next one I'll use a lot of digital stuff. I like to change with each record. Some artists think it's easy to just make music with a computer and that you can release a record by only using the computer. It's not so easy, actually; if you are not talented, it's really hard to work with computers. Software can't make everything, and I'm not good enough to work [only] with computers on this record."

101

STUDIO SESSIONS

Contributors who played a vital role in shaping *Saturdays = Youth* include producer/engineer Ken Thomas, producer Ewan Pearson, singer Morgan Kibby, and drummer Loïc Maurin. Thomas famously worked in a producer/engineer role with some of the biggest names in music, including Queen, David Bowie, Public Image Ltd., the Cocteau Twins, Dave Gahan, and Sigur Rós, among many others. Meanwhile, Pearson is often most associated in the dance-music genre as a DJ and for his popular original productions and remixes. He's currently stepping out from the dance floor and picking up production credit on albums for artists such as Tracey Thorn, Ladytron, and Gwen Stefani.

As for Kibby, she's an actress and musician from Los Angeles whom Gonzalez met through a mutual acquaintance. In addition to providing the female vocals for every track on the album, she assisted in writing some of the lyrics and played various piano parts. And Maurin has been collaborating with Gonzalez for several years and provided production assistance in many areas throughout the recording. Although he had never worked with a producer on earlier albums, Gonzalez was eager to share ideas with both Pearson and Thomas. "I chose to work with the both of them because I wanted this '80s sound," Gonzalez says. "Ken Thomas has worked in the studio for, like, 40 years, and he's so huge. He worked with all these big bands from the '80s. I also wanted a modern sound, which is why I chose Ewan. The combination of the two seemed perfect."

When Gonzalez first approached Thomas and Pearson, he already had fully developed demos for half of the album (recorded in his hometown of Antibes, France). After several meetings and exchanges of ideas, both producers signed on for the production. "I see my job as a producer to help the artist make the record they want to make," Pearson says. "We always talk a lot and play each other records and references, and I try to listen carefully to what they're doing and make certain suggestions but not to change things too much. Not that I really could; Anthony has very strong ideas about what he wants to do—he produced his first two albums himself, remember. Everything he does has a very recognizable signature, and everything on this record is there because he wants it to be."

Gonzalez initially took his demos into Pearson's Berlin studio for preproduction before traveling to Rockfield Studios in South Wales for production
and mixing with Thomas. "I did mostly sound-design stuff and a bit of arranging," Pearson says. "'Couleurs,' for example, was pretty much just an eight-bar
chord loop when Anthony arrived in Berlin, and he wanted to make a dance
track, although it ended up as something else. Maybe I helped open up the
sound palette a bit, added some wonkier analog-synth sound elements and
effects treatments and things. I was a little bewildered at first that Anthony
does all his work with just a couple of keyboards and uses the same patches
repeatedly, but after a while it made sense. The signature sounds that he uses
are part of his identity as an artist, and if you change them too much, you
change what makes him so distinctive and appealing."

With preproduction complete, Gonzalez met with the team at Rockfield
Studios to produce and mix the album. A highly recognizable name, Rockfield Studios has been the birthing place of albums from the likes of Queen,
Black Sabbath, Oasis, and New Order. The recording took approximately three
weeks and ran smoothly, thanks to clearly defined roles. For example, having
worked with Gonzalez in the past, Maurin knew exactly what type of drum fills
he was looking for.

Pearson's primary role in the final production stages was dedicated to
working on "Couleurs" and cutting stuff up with his laptop. "During the actual
production stage, I did more editing and programming and added a few other
ideas along the way," Pearson says. "We wanted to have a percussion battery
[aka marching drumline] on 'Couleurs,' but our drummer, Loïc, didn't have any
percussion and there was none at the studio. So I wandered off for a couple
of hours, had a look around the farm where Rockfield Studios is located, and
came back with a roof slate; a rusty metal cog, which I suspended from a
string; some jars; and a metal gravy boat from the kitchen, which made a
decent-sounding cowbell. I think they thought I was insane as I brought this
stuff into the studio, but we miked it up and it sounded great."

LEGO MANIA

Gonzalez often compares his production style to that of Lego blocks, where instruments and vocals are layered on top of one another to get the signature M83 sound. "We put the vocals into a lot of choruses and reverbs so that it feels distorted, but it's not," he says. "I don't like the sound of my voice when it's all alone, so I just record a lot of layers. It's just the same voice over itself numerous times."

"Anthony's clever and not frightened to do things like repeat vocals," Thomas adds. "He's not shy of repetition and using the same vocal over and over again." The layering effect lends itself to the shoegazer sound often associated with M83, but it also helps with making just about anyone's voice sound good. The album's background vocalists also include Pearson, Maurin, and Thomas' studio assistant.

One of the main reasons *Saturdays = Youth* sounds so polished is because of Thomas' work behind the desk. The album was recorded on a vintage MCI desk and mixed using Genelec 1031 monitors. "The whole thing about mixing with me is that most of it is feeling. You just put stuff on it until it sounds and feels right," Thomas says. "Because Anthony wanted to have an '80s feel, I was using the Roland Dimension D quite a lot because I didn't want to use too much chorus at the beginning. I put Dimension D across a lot of stuff to glue it all together. When I cross the mic, I always have EQ and always have some compression. I'm normally boosting some really high frequencies (16kHz) through a GML preamp, and it gives it the kind of air that makes it feel open. It also seems to tighten up the bass end."

Oddly enough, despite Gonzalez's desire to hire Thomas because of his experience with '80s music, it's far from being the veteran producer's music of choice. "'Kim & Jessie' was a hard song to do," Thomas confesses. "Anthony loves it, but I wasn't really happy with it. It was hard for me to do that stuff because I never connected much with '80s music. I connect most with something that sounds new and it hasn't been done before, which is really hard to find. Sometimes you just say, 'Bloody hell.' [*Laughs.*]"

Massive Attack

3D ON REBUILDING *100TH WINDOW*
ONE PIECE AT A TIME

By Robert Hanson

This chapter features an abridged version of the Massive Attack article in the April 2005 issue of *Remix* magazine.

For any musician, the only thing worse than wallowing away in obscurity is trying to build upon years of unqualified success. For the members of Massive Attack, the pressure became almost too much to bear. From nearly the moment they appeared on the scene, Massive Attack has been heralded as one of the few truly revolutionary forces in modern music: Many credit them with putting the Bristol trip-hop scene on the map and paving the way for artists such as Portishead and Tricky. Massive's sound synthesizes the most important aspects of electronic music, dub, hip-hop, and even guitar-driven modern rock. More important, though, the members have always sought to infuse their music with a human, emotional component that makes their work connect with a far more diverse audience—an approach that has always set them apart from many electronic-music artists. Their dark, ambiguous, almost faceless public persona and careful attention to visual detail have also worked to solidify their reputation as consummate multimedia artists.

Massive Attack's last album, *Mezzanine* (Virgin, 1998), which sold in excess of 3 million copies, catapulted the band from its status as a music-critic buzzword to a worldwide musical enterprise. Through the inclusion of tracks such as "Teardrop"—featuring vocals by Elizabeth Fraser of Cocteau Twins—and "Inertia Creeps" on numerous film soundtracks, and because of heavy media rotation, the hypnotic, processed guitar sound of *Mezzanine* became difficult to escape, and it produced Massive's most tangible level of success here in the States. Success on that level forced the band into a difficult situation: Demanding promotional schedules and the extensive touring eventually forced the members of the band—3D (born Robert Del Naja), Andrew "Mushroom" Vowles, and Grant "Daddy G" Marshall—to come to terms with what the band's future may hold. "We'd all gone off in different ways in our heads," 3D explains. "It was very difficult after *Mezzanine*, because it was a whole year of resolving issues and splitting up effectively."

Although Daddy G used the opportunity to invest time in his personal life and prepare himself to rejoin Massive Attack at a later date, Mushroom's permanent departure from the project centered mostly on conflicting visions of where the band should take its sound. As 3D would reiterate numerous times, the band had always sought to frame each album as a reaction to its predecessor—a way for Massive Attack to distance itself from what was expected of it.

"I wanted to get away from the kind of more soulful elements we were getting into," 3D continues. "I felt that the music I was listening to was all about safety and warmth, and I wanted to do something a bit colder. And it eventually brought around the split between me and Mushroom, because we completely disagreed on that subject." With both Daddy G and Mushroom out of the picture for the time being, 3D and longtime producer Neil Davidge were left with the task of sculpting the next Massive Attack album entirely on their own.

A FLEETING MOMENT

The writing process for what would become the most recent Massive Attack album, *100th Window* (Virgin, 2003), began at a residential studio outside of

3D (left) and Daddy G. (Hamish Brown)

London called Rich Farm. 3D had already spent some time constructing a blueprint for how he wanted the sessions to proceed. Armed with a collection of tiny loops, samples, and odd keyboard and guitar lines, he wanted to build up a pool of sounds and ideas based on live, improvisational jams—a process he likened to classic late-'60s studio experiments. To help the process along, 3D and Davidge brought along members of Lupine Howl (Sean Cook, Mike Mooney, and Damon Reece)—who are better known for their work with Spiritualized—to add live guitars, bass, and drums.

"We spent two weeks of recording just hours and hours of jams," 3D explains. "And we set up lights and strobes. When we felt the track was getting slow, we'd turn up the lights, and everyone would get a bit fucked up and try and get that old '60s or '70s jamming atmosphere. And we got some amazing

107

psychedelic sort of journeys or bits of music, and we had hours and hours of this stuff, which was amazing. We proceeded to reconstruct it in the studio in Bristol, which was a fucking very long-winded process. We sat there with Pro Tools and tried to put the jams back up and sort of tried to tidy them up a bit. We were going back in to pull little bits out—like drums, bass, and guitar parts—and we ended up with lots and lots of quite interesting tracks."

With more than 100 hours of material tracked during those sessions, 3D firmly believed that it was going to be the album's foundation. Much of the impetus behind this approach stemmed from a conscious decision to eschew any use of samples or material that wasn't their own—both for legal and artistic reasons. Unfortunately, through the course of editing the material into usable bits, 3D felt that the essence of the recordings got lost when they were removed from their original context.

"As the year went on," he continues, "what was apparent was that by the very nature of the process, we were destroying the moments we'd created live. And the little parts, individually, didn't have the magic when they weren't working alongside the other parts. When it came to sampling and rebuilding, we thought we'd created a master source of material, a big well to draw from. But it didn't actually quite work out. I think a lot of the things I was feeling was that the bits sounded slightly post-*Mezzanine*, as well: very guitar-driven. And as much as I thought it was great, I wasn't turning us on to write new songs."

Massive Attack spent the better part of 2001 attempting to create a workable foundation from the Rich Farm sessions, which, once edited, yielded an untold amount of material. "We went through a whole period in 2001, after we'd done this, not really coming up with songs and developed tracks, but lots of hapless instrumentals, which were starting to bring us down a little bit," 3D says. It wasn't until the beginning of 2002 that 3D realized he had been heading in the wrong direction all along.

FRESH PERSPECTIVE

"It came to the end of that year, 2001," 3D recalls, "and it was just back over Christmas. We were in the studio, listening to the little bits we'd done. And [we were] floundering a bit and coming to terms with the fact that what we were

doing wasn't very good, which is a pretty difficult place to [
with an idea that you thought was bulletproof. And after Cl
Neil came back into the studio with the guys, and we said,
to start again and write some new things from scratch.'"

Once 3D and Davidge had made the decision to begin rebuilding the album from scratch, they progressed quickly. The group owns their own facility
in Bristol, which houses a full-fledged Digidesign Pro Tools TDM–equipped
studio, as well as a secondary writing room for 3D. The secondary space com-
prises a Mac-based Pro Tools LE system and functions as a simple workspace.
One of the most important aspects of the studio, according to 3D, is the Ether-
net connection that runs throughout the facility. Ideas, sessions, and files can
be quickly shared between the various rooms—an ability that proved to be vital
to the writing process.

"We bought a lot of spare drives, so we constantly keep things backed
up on drives," he explains. "We do a lot of restoring drives to get old sessions
back up, and it gets quite complicated. But we're kind of upgrading things
at the moment because we're always running out of bloody DSP power. It's
always the same story. But everything is on [Pro] Tools, which is quite weird,
because everything ends up going into the same place whether it's vocals or
keyboard parts or live jams; it always ends up in the same place.

"We used everything [on this record]: Moogs, Junos, Roland keyboards—
stuff like that—and basic plug-ins like Absynth inside [Pro] Tools," 3D says.
"And we used things like GRM Tools and Speed and Amp Farm, all the usual
kinds of toys, really. Damon Reece would bring his electronic drums up here,
and we'd sample sounds into that, or we'd use a live kit and mike that."

During the course of just a few short months, the band wrote the majority
of the record. "We took two of the tracks with us from the previous year's work,
which was 'A Prayer for England,' which we recorded with Sinéad O'Connor in
London, and the instrumental for 'What Your Soul Sings,' which we liked too
much to want to discard. We took that with us into last year and basically re-
wrote the album. We started with 'Future Proof' and then went into 'What Your
Soul Sings,' then 'Special Cases,' 'Small Time Shot Away,' 'Everywhen,' 'Antistar,' and then it kinda slowly developed. By February and March, I was booking

udios for June and July because I was confident we were going to finish it."

In direct contrast to the improvisational approach, 3D took the writing process back to a much more familiar place: Many of the tracks on *100th Window* began as simple keyboard or guitar lines, sparse arpeggiator patterns and drumbeats. Although it may not be immediately noticeable, 3D explains that this album is far and away the most complex piece of work the band has ever put out. Where *Mezzanine* showcased more stripped-down arrangements and relied on heavy guitars and drums, the new album is designed to be a more intricate and exacting piece of work.

One such example of this new approach is the closing track, "Antistar." The band booked time at Sony Music Studios in London to record the string parts that build toward the middle of the track. To achieve the Eastern-influenced feel that the group wanted, each discrete track had to be edited, and individual notes had to be pitch-bent to precise quarter tones—an exhausting process that Davidge had to complete entirely by ear. To finish the song, however, the group used a simple breakbeat rhythm that was programmed with a Korg Electribe drum machine.

"We started to work in the way we normally worked, which was to start with very simple ideas rather than lots of ideas," 3D says. "We'd start with a couple of guitar parts with a beat put to it, sound waves or keyboard parts, and then start writing some vocals and writing some lyrics for songs. And that was just how we kind of ended up going, rebuilding everything from scratch but with very minimal moments.

"So now, of course," 3D continues, "it does seem like it was meant to be. It was fated, but at the time, it didn't feel that [way] at all. It felt utterly miserable, and if you look at the album budget, it will testify that. It's going to cost me a lot of money, that whole two years working with 80,000 pieces of music we didn't use."

Following the release of *100th Window*, Massive Attack is gearing up for its first tour in several years. Rejoining 3D on the road is founding member Daddy G. And if their current plans hold up, they plan to release their fifth album sometime inside of the next year.

15

My Morning Jacket

RECORDING *CIRCUITAL* LIVE, SANS COMPUTERS

By Bud Scoppa

This chapter appeared in the July 2011 issue of *Electronic Musician* magazine.

Tucker Martine's two most recent album projects have been all about location, location, location. Last July, the Portland-based producer headed from the rustic Oregon barn where he'd recorded the Decemberists' back-to-basics surprise hit *The King Is Dead*, to a church gymnasium in Louisville, Kentucky, to begin work on My Morning Jacket's *Circuital*. "I went right from one to the next," says Martine, "and there wasn't much of an adjustment for me, because both were such unconventional studio environments."

What's more, both bands were committed to the idea of recording live off the floor, an approach My Morning Jacket would take the whole nine yards, recording to two-inch tape with the five musicians arranged in a circle at half court of the cavernous, high-ceilinged gym. The idea of location recording wasn't new to these guys—they'd recorded their early albums in a Kentucky grain silo.

"In some ways, we've come full circle, though I hate that term," says MMJ frontman Jim James. "I feel we've progressed musically and personally, but just happened to be returning home for this record and making it in a very natural way—just the five of us playing in a circle, going for live, emotional takes from each band member."

"They're a fantastic band," says Martine, "and what does it sound like when they're in a room together and things are spilling into each other? So we purposely painted ourselves into a corner. There's a vitality that comes through when you record that way. It's the sound of people that have to make it work right now and not rely on fixing things later. It also becomes a general feeling of embracing imperfections. There was no computer in the building, so you couldn't get tired or lazy—it was out of the question. No one wanted to do anything reminiscent of the days of old as much as not falling into the traps of modern record making, like not needing to commit early on to arrangement or performance."

"I worked with Tucker doing backup vocals on Decemberists and Laura Veirs records, and we hit it right off," James explains. "We both have the same goofy, f**ked-up, surrealist sense of humor where nothing and everything make sense. I can see a caterpillar on a tree and call it a basketball, and he knows exactly what I mean. Tucker is in a league of his own. His ears are golden and he is a surrealist—which a lot of producers I've met can't fully wrap their heads around. That's why we loved and gravitated to Tucker."

The band had set up in the gym before Martine's arrival. "Our friend Kevin Ratterman, one of the greatest producers and engineers on the planet, had recorded there," James says of the space. "I went to visit and thought it was really special. We also wanted to work with Kevin on this record, so he and I brought all our gear into the wonderful old turn-of-the-century church and we went to town. I gave the guys very simple demos and we began working on them and getting levels." As soon as Martine showed up and familiarized himself with the setup, they started going for takes.

"It really did create a circle amongst everyone's brains and hearts as well as the mics," James says of the resulting experience. "It is so cool to solo a mic and hear bits of everyone else in that mic, as opposed to having it completely

My Morning Jacket: Patrick Hallahan, Carl Broemel, Jim James, Bo Koster, and Tom Blankenship. (Danny Clinch)

isolated and sterile. Obviously, sometimes you need some isolation, but for the most part the bleed was good."

The "let it bleed" approach extended to James' vocals; he chose to sing his lead parts—and play guitar at the same time—surrounded by the rest of the band. "Jim really stepped up and rose to the occasion, because that is such a difficult thing to do," Martine marvels. "That's the biggest challenge of making a record this way—getting the singer to peak at the same time the band's performance is peaking. As a singer, you can always weasel your way out of it and do a scratch vocal, but Jim wouldn't let himself have any outs. I'm sure he felt the pressure to get it quickly, because he knew that everyone else was probably gonna be delivering the goods early on. If the band has played something great several times but the vocals aren't quite there, you hate to ask everyone to keep going even though there's nothing to improve on for them. So they just have to take one for the team."

MMJ had no such problem, thanks to James' inspired singing amid the band's taut playing, resulting in keeper performances in the first few takes once they had the arrangements nailed down. At the same time, they were flexible in achieving their goal, within certain parameters. On some songs, James was sequestered in a room in order to minimize the bleed, while Bo Koster and his piano were also isolated in some instances.

The July sessions lasted nine days, during which the band got four of the songs that wound up on the record, including the epic title track. There was no air-conditioning, with all the windows and doors closed in order to cut down on the sounds of cars passing and birds chirping (some of which can be

CIRCUITAL SIGNAL PATHS

Tucker Martine breaks down the chains for each band member.

Guitars: "All electric guitars were recorded with Royer 121s. Lead guitarist Carl Broemel's amp ended up in the sanctuary, and a Neumann KM 86 captured the room. Acoustic guitars were recorded with either a Neumann M 49 or a pair of Neumann KM 86s, depending on the song."

Bass: "I used a combination of the direct signal through the Evil Twin DI and an EV RE20 on the cabinet."

Piano: "The piano was recorded differently on each song. On 'Circuital,' a Shure SM91 was taped to the back of the little spinet that belonged to the church; this reduced drum bleed a lot and gave it a mid-range presence that helped it cut through the track. That mic was crushed with an 1176. A pair of Shure SM57s were used on 'Freak Out,' and Neumann KM 84s were used on 'Movin' Away.'"

Drums: "A Shure SM57 or a Neumann KM86 was used on the snare, with an AKG D 112 on the kick. The mono overhead kept changing: KM86, M49, Peluso C12, or RCA 44. I always ran at least one drum mic that was distorted, compressed, or both, to be able to dial in attitude and crunch as needed. The Atomasonic Dynoray was helpful for this, as were the Thermionic Culture Vulture and UA 1176. Mic pres were API 212 and 512. I often used a dbx subharmonic synthesizer on the kick, for low end that you feel more than hear."

Vocals: "On some tracks, Jim's lead vocals are the driest and most natural-sounding he's ever recorded (though he broke out his trusty EMT 140 plate reverb recording the backing vocals). His favorite mic on the sessions was an old RCA 77 ribbon mic, on loan from Carl Broemel's dad. All vocals went through an 1176. Sometimes it was hit too hard, because Jim would get excited during a take, and by the time I saw it, it was too late to change it—and we had our keeper take."

heard on the record if you listen closely). But, true to the spirit of the project, the band made the most of the sweatbox conditions. "It added to the sense of urgency and intensity," says Martine. They reconvened for two weeks in November and laid down the remaining six tracks while bundled up in parkas and scarves; the gym had no heat, either.

But the pivotal moment went down back in July when they got that keeper take of "Circuital" and climbed up on the stage at the end of the gym where Martine was positioned to listen through the Proac Studio 100 monitors. "That was a really special moment," the producer recalls. "They were all dancing around the room and bobbing their heads with their eyes closed, and then, when the song was over, they were hugging and high-fiving each other. It was so inspiring to see veteran musicians who were still able to get that much joy out of making music together. It was like we were all going on an expedition together to find something magical, and there it was. We found it, and no one was afraid to have unbridled joy about it. That's how it should be."

It's performances like that one—inspired, synchronous, and tight, like a veteran basketball team kicking it into high gear at crunch time in a tight play-off game—that make *Circuital* such a thrilling, even ecstatic, listening experience. This was one bold experiment that paid off big-time.

16

Nortec Collective

BOSTICH+FUSSIBLE MELD MODULAR SYNTHS AND TRADITIONAL INSTRUMENTS FOR *TIJUANA SOUND MACHINE*

By Ken Micallef

This chapter features an abridged version of the Nortec Collective article in the July 2008 issue of *Remix* magazine.

When Bostich and Fussible (Ramón Amezcua and Pepe Mogt, respectively) were growing up in Tijuana, Mexico, during the 1980s, one thing connected them to kids the world over: ice cream. Where the average American child knew the Mister Softee truck had arrived by its ubiquitous music-box melody, the local Tijuana ice cream *car* played none other than Hot Butter's 1972 smash, "Popcorn," originally recorded by synth pioneer Gershon Kingsley (*Music to Moog By*, 1969, Audio Fidelity). Call that recontextualization marker No. 1.

"I was so inspired by 'Popcorn,'" Mogt recalls from his home in Tijuana. "It was very popular here in Tijuana because it played on the ice cream car. So I used the Future Retro Revolution R2 to re-create the 'Popcorn' sound for our song, 'The Clap.' The Revolution has two knobs, and when you move them it makes a ping-pong sound. I put a sequence similar to 'Popcorn' into the

Revolution, and then by moving the knobs I came up with a totally different thing. But it reminds you of that ping-pong sound in 'Popcorn.'"

Years after chasing the ice cream car, Mogt grew up to become a computer-science engineer, and Amezcua would become an orthodontist before merging disparate sounds as members of the Latin Grammy–nominated Nortec Collective. On its 2001 debut, *Tijuana Sessions, Vol. 1* (Palm Pictures), the group—which also includes Clorofila (Jorge Verdín) and Hiperboreal (PG Beas)—mixed dark, brooding samples of native norteño music against throbbing techno beats, aka Nortec.

STRANGE GEAR, HERE WE COME

Mogt and Amezcua step out on their own to recontextualize even wilder terrain on *Nortec Collective Presents Bostich+Fussible: Tijuana Sound Machine* (2008, Nacional). Beyond simply joining norteño with techno, *Tijuana Sound Machine* is a full-on party riot where myriad cultures get their groove on courtesy of modern and near-ancient technology. Drawing from norteño, banda, ranchera, and other Mexican folk styles, Mogt and Amezcua sample live tuba, mariachi trumpet, upright bass, accordion, and clarinet over madcap oompah beats that would seem to better exist at a German beer hall than a Mexican hacienda.

"We played in Berlin, and they don't know Nortec," Amezcua explains from Chula Vista, California. "They thought we were playing German music. Because of the accordion and polka rhythm and tuba, they asked us where we were from. The same thing happened in France. They hear the accordion and think we are French. This is a fusion that doesn't tell you it's Mexican. It's like Herb Alpert's music. Herb Alpert tells you it's from Tijuana, but you can't say it's Mexican music."

When music has the ability to totally change your perspective, as well as entertain, you call it innovation, and *Tijuana Sound Machine* fulfills every requirement that originality demands. Not only do B+F's culture-clashing tracks surprise listeners the world over, their productions emanate from some truly radical old- and new-school technology. Mogt and Amezcua use a variety of tricked-out and freaky sound machines: EMS VCS3, Analogue Solutions Vostok Matrixsynth, Future Retro Revolution R2 and Mobius sequencer, Orgon Systems Enigiser and Modular synths, Monome 64, and Yamaha Tenori-on, to

Nortec Collective: Bostich (left) and Fussible. (Courtesy of Nacional)

name a few. These modular synths and new touchtone toys bring a sense of hilarity and fun to the native banda, ranchera, and norteño sounds. From the Herb Alpert mariachi romanticism of "Norteña Del Sur" and the Daft Punk-worthy vocoder effects of the title track to the itchy-squeaky brass and banda blowout of "Mama Loves Nortec" (complete with dizzy call-and-response brass and clarinet), Bostich+Fussible mix it up like mad.

BANDA-TECHNO BLOWOUT

Typically, Mogt and Amezcua initiate compositions by creating a sequence on one of their modular synths, looping it, then asking local banda or norteño musicians to jam along with the electronic spew.

"We rehearse with the musicians in our studio in Tijuana," Amezcua says. "We ran the sequence playing the loop for 20 minutes, and the musicians will jam over that [into a Røde mic and Focusrite pre], or maybe a 909. After that, we cut and evaluate takes for the best lines, then we process it in Ableton Live to come up with the most interesting versions. Maybe we'll effect the loops to make weird sounds [using the Triwave Picogenerator, for example]. Then after processing in Ableton, I go back to Pro Tools to finish the tracks."

Using toylike machines such as the Yamaha Tenori-on and the Monome 64 with funky old modular synths like the EMS VCS3, Orgon Systems Modular, EML ElectroComp 101, and Sherman FilterBank QMF filter makes for some

119

fantastically deranged listening. Bostich+Fussible are nothing if not total gearheads. Just hearing them discuss the pieces can be enlightening.

Case in point: The Vostok Modulator Matrixsynth appears on "Rosarito." "Remember that synthesizer that Pink Floyd used, the VSC3?" Mogt asks. "The Vostok is like that, a portable modular synthesizer. We use a lot of modular synthesizers because the sound is not very perfect. When we brought the musicians in and they tried to emulate this belching modular synthesizer, the result was very interesting. I just put a mic into the accordion and then put it into this Vostok synth, and the blending of the two is what gives Nortec this strange ambient sound. When we asked them to play with the Vostok, some of them thought we were joking, or they were scared. They had never heard these types of noises. When they applied the norteño feel to these noises, it became something very different."

Mogt and Amezcua own one of the world's very few Orgon Systems Modular synths, which they use on the tracks "Tijuana Sound Machine" and "Norteña Del Sur." They like the Orgon for both its super-low frequencies and overall warmth. "That was built in the UK. I think there are only 10 of them in the world," Amezcua reveals. "It has plenty of oscillators and LFOs, and the filter on the Orgon is the one we love a lot. This filter has a very fat, very hot and warm sound. We were using a lot of the Moog and Oberheim filters, but the Orgon modular has a very nice-sounding filter. And also the oscillator, the frequency range is a very low sub frequency. Sometimes you are not listening to it but you can still see the speakers moving. We make sequences out of the Orgon, and they are like melodies from outer space. They can sound very microtonal, and that can inspire you to build something from that. You can start putting on top of that some of the acoustic sounds or make a beat out of that. Even though the modular synths are not so practical for a concert or to create a full song, we use them more like an inspirational tool."

Bostich+Fussible are also some of the first musicians to use super-new machines such as the Yamaha Tenori-on, Monome 64, and Future Retro Revolution R2. These small boxes (or UFO-shaped pods, in the R2's case) have an array of illuminated buttons and tiny knobs for tweaking. Pushing the buttons or rotating the knobs generates random displays of twinkling, playful melodies and rhythms.

"The most interesting thing about the Tenori-on is its random mode," Amezcua says. "You can have an idea for a melody and you can change that melody and sing the melody with different notes. You can MIDI it to convert the sequencer and control other equipment. It's only able to sample a one-second note, though; it's like a toy. We use it on tour for quick ideas; it is battery-operated and has speakers. I also use it with a Monome 64. You can touch the buttons and trigger the sounds, and in solo mode you can play melodies in the same tempo as the song. It is very fun and intuitive. Anyone can play it even if you don't know music."

MACHINE TUNES

Bostich+Fussible's unerring skill at upending sounds and destroying expectations is a constant on *Tijuana Sound Machine*. "Mi Casita" merges two-beat polka with farting accordion and looped clarinet, trumpet, and a wacky tuba solo—at least that is what it *sounds* like.

"I use the Triwave Picogenerator there, with a violin forming the loop," Amezcua says. "The drum machine is a TR-606. I filtered the 606 with the Picogenerator and the Sherman Filterbank QMF, which is a big, modular filter. The violin is a country-music style; it repeats the same pattern. Then in the middle I add the EMS VCS3, the weird sound you hear. It sounds like feedback. And then the banda tubas, trumpets, and bass line come in that I recorded live. This is a weird track—the only time where I put more analog synths with live musicians. I cut up and processed the tuba solo in Ableton Live, which allows me to cut and paste different melodies with the original sounds that I record. That is my favorite song."

On the other end of the spectrum, "Jacinto" recalls a blissful siesta. Liquid-sounding accordions loop and delay, and upright bass ascends gracefully with distant children's voices, only to be threatened by nasty guitar distortion and bass drum and cymbal smacks. "The watery sounds are the Oberheim 4-Voice," Mogt says. "The acoustic bass guitar is one I put in the Future Retro R2, a line that one of the norteño musicians played. The vocals are some local kids that I brought into the studio. Those big drum hits are an acoustic drummer who I sampled into the Sherman Filterbank. When the drums are hitting, they might sound like an electric guitar, a distorted guitar, but it's the same rhythm: bass drum, cymbal, and snare, feeding back through the Sherman Filterbank. At the end of the song there are some backing vocals; that is the kids again, arguing about what colors they see in Tijuana."

The rollicking "Mama Loves Nortec" recalls a mad techno boffin mixing a kazoo band, dub rhythms, and a dueling trumpet/tuba chorus with a traditional Russian high-stepping military dance.

"That song is the most acoustic of all the songs," Amezcua explains. "Most of the sounds are processed using only the Sherman Filterbank QMF. One of the samples is from Nortenian banda music, and the drum machine is a 909. It is more acoustic overall, with a traditional trumpet or charcheta playing the harmony and upbeats. I did that entire song in Ableton Live. The call and response between the trumpet and clarinet is hard-panned left and right, cut and pasted in Ableton to create another melody. The breakdown sounds like a string machine, but it's really a reverb effect in Ableton Live 7. It's only a plug-in. There is also sampled timbale, from a live Banda band, cut up in Ableton Live . . . then another clarinet that sounds like a synth, again in Ableton."

By recontextualizing the way we hear Mexican folk music, Bostich+Fussible bring myriad cultures together though *Tijuana Sound Machine*. Germans think the duo's two-beat polkas are all the rage. The French think these two accordion-sampling DJs are as native as François Truffaut's *The 400 Blows*. And as of this writing, U.S. radio and press have caught the Bostich+Fussible bug, too.

"Here in Tijuana we have a lot of hills," Mogt says, "and the antennas from radio stations in San Diego and Los Angeles are here. So we grew up listening to Kraftwerk's 'Autobahn' and disco music like Giorgio Moroder's 'I Feel Love' (recorded by Donna Summer). That music and the funk music like George Clinton, and banda and mariachi—it's all a mixture of different cultures and sounds here."

"The way people think about Tijuana is changing," Amezcua adds. "We are very proud to help change the image of Tijuana. This is a new sound, and we will continue working with this sound. We have other projects, but we will continue to make this Nortec music. For years if you told someone you were from Tijuana, they thought you were a drug dealer. But it's shifting, because there is a cultural movement happening now that is changing how the world sees Tijuana. Now this is our sound, part of our music."

17

Outkast

THE FRIENDLY COMPETITION AND MIXING EXPERIMENTATION BEHIND *SPEAKERBOXXX/THE LOVE BELOW*

By Joe Silva

Portions of this chapter appeared in the August 2003 and August 2004 issues of *Remix* and *Electronic Musician* magazines.

We are rolling in a ridiculously immaculate Land Rover beneath a calm Atlanta skyline just after sunset. All day long, the first real hints of the coming Georgia summer, amped by heavy traffic, have seized the city. But the serene evening cool outside is in direct contrast to the massive sounds pumping through the car's stereo. The music is loud. The music, in fact, is so painfully loud that all of the enamel in my teeth has literally started to throb as we go from track to track. Our pilot for the evening, Andre Benjamin, is 50 percent of hip-hop's most daring duo and co-author of the new Outkast album *Speakerboxxx/The Love Below*: a double CD that, by all indications, sounds like another massive triumph. But below Benjamin's chilled exterior is an undercurrent of mild anxiety.

"Right now, I'm terrified," he says. "Right before *Stankonia* came out, I was terrified. I didn't know what people would think, because it's always so different from what's going on at the time that it could go either way.

Like with *ATLiens* . . . that was like stepping out. Ever since then, every time the album is coming out, you have doubts."

NO MC IS AN ISLAND

Benjamin's massive afro heads skyward, and with the sedate clothing he sports, he seems very much apart from the platinum-blond-wigged persona tagged Andre 3000 that helped Outkast score two Grammy Awards and multi-ple-platinum sales. As we pull into his favorite local vegetarian restaurant, he is the picture of understatement and reserve. The new album has been pushed back twice now, and several things are still not quite ready. Several verses (not mixes, verses) aren't done, but they are still moving toward a fall release. Working separately, he and Antwan "Big Boi" Patton were set to release solo albums, but timing eventually worked against that idea.

"I started to see a theme coming, so I thought, 'Hey, I want to put out a solo album.' And my manager and Big Boi said, 'Nah, you can't do that.' And I was like, 'Why?' And they said that after the Grammys, people will be expect-ing the next Outkast album and that you can't just come with a solo album. I was pissed off and said, 'Well, I'm just going to give all this music away,'" he says, laughing. "I was for real!"

But once he saw his partner steadily at work, Patton also got busy. "Big Boi got on his horse because he saw I was already finished with my album, and he hurried up and did his," Benjamin says. "So Big Boi said, 'I'm gonna come out with my solo album.' And nobody said anything; they were just go-ing to let him do it. He was scheduled to come out in February, and mine was scheduled to come out this summer. But I said that it's so close of a release, why don't we just put them together? And to him, that was really the best thing that I could have said, because no one really wants to go out there and do it by themselves. So it was cool—a double album, two CDs—both of us appearing on each other's album. Hip-hop people just don't do that. Kiss did that! So it's exciting to me. Every album has to be exciting to me . . . like something's going on. To me, a double album is something going on."

The excitement, however, that Benjamin has always required to get on with the business of being Outkast was flagging due to the constant touring

Outkast's Andre 3000 at Stankonia Recording Studios in Atlanta, Georgia, 2003. (Ian Mcfarlane)

the group did in support of *Stankonia* (La Face/Arista, 2000). "It got to a point where I would be onstage going through the motions while performing every night," he explains. "I was totally distant from what I was doing. It was like I was watching myself. There was no passion in it at all. The last show at the University of Georgia was when I knew that I couldn't really keep doing this until I found something that I was passionate about again. I'll just put out the

125

albums until I can feel like, 'Hey, I want to perform!' Because I don't really want to go out there and bulls**t the people."

The rest of the Outkast organization didn't respond too well to Benjamin's decision. "You know a manager gets paid from the [income of the] shows," he says. "And he was like, 'What the f**k you talking about?' So I talked to L. A. Reid [at Arista] about it, and his first response was, 'Oh, well, you're just gonna have to get over that s**t.' [*Laughs.*]

"He was trying to tell me the truth. But after I explained it to him, he understood because he used to play drums in the Deele. You just get to a point where you're not feeding from it, and it's taking away from you. His recommendation was to just tell the people and be up front about it."

ACOUSTIC MANEUVERS

Benjamin took to focusing on playing guitar and inhaling deep quantities of jazz. He hoped not to have to perform again until he was accomplished enough to play an instrument in public. And the origins of the new album began to reflect his change in direction. "A lot of the songs are songs I've had for years," he says. "I just felt that they weren't Outkast songs and that people weren't ready to hear that sort of thing [from us]. Really, I'm only rhyming on this album for two verses. These are songs that I've been writing at home on the guitar. 'Ms. Jackson' was an acoustic song that started on guitar and then became what it is now. A lot of the songs were done years ago, and I just brought them back up, upgraded them, and made them now."

"Now" means the Prince-like sensuality of "Spread," a wickedly high-bpm reworking of the classic "My Favorite Things," and an acoustic duet called "Take Off Your Cool" performed with Norah Jones. Benjamin's side of the album is steeped in the melody that he gravitates to so instinctively. "I'm a melody freak," he says. "I don't consider myself a singer or nothing like that, but I think I'm a melody maker. I find great melodies."

Having initially worked in the Digidesign Pro Tools arena, Benjamin shrugged off that rig once he was introduced to Steinberg's Nuendo package. "When I look at Pro Tools, it looks scientific to me," he says. "Nuendo is set up where you can do things really quick, and I like the graphics, too. I

126

have [Native Instruments] Battery. I have [Propellerhead] Reason and five or six VST keyboards. I love Reason. I love the sounds they have in there. But I haven't really freaked it yet. I have a setup for the road, and I actually did two songs on this album [with that setup] in a hotel room when the heater went out in my house. It's a small MIDI controller, an IBM laptop, some little box that [engineer] John Frye hooked me up with, and Nuendo. That was all I needed. And it's only getting better. That's what's scary: So much stuff comes out every month, it's hard to keep up with it. I just got to find out what really works for me. I jump for new stuff, because one sound could create a whole song. So most of the time, I just do them at home by myself, bring them to the studio, and let Big Boi check them out."

RETURN OF THE PLAYA

In the heart of the Stankonia complex, the group's recording studio, Patton is standing on the polished lid of a Baldwin piano, being photographed and kidding with the steady flow of family, employees, and friends that filters through the ongoing photo session. Between poses, he works on the motions of his bowling technique and occasionally takes a call from a cell phone hidden behind the sheet music. After more than two hours under the hot lamps, he and Benjamin are still as congenial as ever. The large empty space we are standing in is the live room of their studio and is currently populated with props from the last tour; dormant Macintosh peripherals; and bits of classic gear, such as the milk-white Mellotron that sits quietly in a corner.

Much top-shelf music has been etched onto tape in this space. Owned at one time by Bobby Brown, the building has been in the hands of Outkast for several years now. The strings for R.E.M.'s *Automatic for the People* (Warner, 1992) were laid down here, shepherded at the time by none other than Led Zeppelin's John Paul Jones. The Black Crowes have used it as a creative roost, and the ghost of that group's presence is evoked slightly by the herbal cloud that seeps into the studio.

Refreshed by a small measure of green, Patton and the rest of the photoshoot crew move locations. Wearing a jersey from Outkast's own line of clothing that's modeled on the Wendy's burger chain logo, he looks very much the playa. But despite the visually deep contrast to his partner, he and Benjamin share an obvious synchronicity with each other. In the control room, studio engineer Frye is running a new track through a pair of Yamaha NS10s that sit atop a massive SSL 4000 console.

"I'm over it," Frye says about the 80-channel monstrosity. "I've recorded 300 records, and I don't need anything now other than this Mac and Pro Tools. We can work on 8 or 10 projects a night with this [setup], and with that thing, we can do maybe two. It takes me two hours just to get it ready to go."

MIXING MAGIC

Mix engineer Neal Pogue talks to *Electronic Musician* about mixing a track on *Speakerboxxx/The Love Below*.

Tell us about mixing "Hey Ya!"

We mixed it twice in the same night. Dre [Andre Benjamin, aka Andre 3000] knows what he wants, but sometimes he has to hear it a bunch of different ways to be sure. And I'll spend hours mixing until I think it's right. We work hard on everything that we mix, and we try to take it beyond the norm. It can be a tedious process that takes a long time; it's not done until it feels done. We just keep experimenting and going back and forth. After those mixes, I'm usually tired. We exhaust all the possibilities and drain all the energy out of ourselves.

That record was finished down to the last minute. We were up until eight or nine in the morning and had to go to mastering right after that. It was fun, and it paid off, but just thinking about it makes me tired.

How many tracks did you have at the mix?

It couldn't have been more than 40. There were two drum tracks: kick and snare. No hi-hat. It's a clever idea; someone else would have put a hi-hat on, but Dre allowed the track to speak to him when he wrote it. The guitar was the main thing, and then we had these quirky '80s synths going around it and the bass driving it.

What did you do to make the acoustic guitar work?

That took a long time to get right, because it's a big-body kind of guitar, and the bass and guitar got in the way of each other. I had to cut some of the low end on the guitar, so I used the EQ on the console to take some out. I trimmed the frequency a lot at 300Hz—about 12dB. I think that's better than adding EQ to make it brighter, which often adds brittleness.

How many background tracks are there?

Maybe eight for each section. I used very little compression, and I think I

Frye has mixed Patton's side of the album in Pro Tools, and he has been with the Atlanta rappers since before they got their deal with Arista. He was key in acquiring the Stankonia space for the organization, and the studio side of the complex houses separate rooms for mixing and recording vocals, as well as the large open space for full-ensemble work.

"Even though this room is kind of small," Patton says of the control room, "we can have horn players in here, guitars or whatever, and just jam, y'know?" It's a considerable understatement considering that most people's living rooms

boosted at 8kHz by about 2dB. Once again, I cut the low end at 300Hz. I think the [Digidesign] D-Verb plug-in was used on all the vocals—a simple technique for a straight-ahead song.

How many basses are there?

There are two basses. The quirky synth bass that has the resonance on it, and the live bass. I remember Dre not wanting the bass to overpower the track. It was about the acoustic guitar, so it really wasn't about concentrating on the EQ of the bass. The bass had a muddiness that I would usually try to fix, but in this case it was cool so I left it alone. The synth bass had to have more personality; the live bass just rode the track.

What is going on with the tinkly melody keyboard?

It is a key part of the mix, a cool '80s countermelody à la the B-52s, Yello, or maybe even Devo. I just added some high mids to make sure it stuck out through everything else that was going on.

You've said that when you first heard it, you thought it would become a hit. What made you think that?

It was different than everything else that was out; it sliced through all of the cookie-cutter songs. There is nothing better than a fun, feel-good song with a great hook. I read that Prince said he was surprised that, in this day and age, someone recognized "Hey Ya!" was a hit. But I knew. "Hey Ya!" is like Prince's "Little Red Corvette"—an instant hit.

Take a look at the music industry now. People call it cookie cutter, but I call it the General Motors effect: same body, different dashboard, and everything sounds the same. It's a fear factor; nobody wants to be different, because they're afraid they won't sell records. But the industry was built on being different.

Before "Hey Ya!" was released, everybody felt [the potential], but they were doubtful because of industry pressure, because the song was different, and because they just weren't sure. But the public isn't stupid. You've got to give them the benefit of the doubt. They do love music, and if it's a good song, they'll buy it. —Maureen Droney are less than half the size. But sitting back in one of the web-backed chairs that sit in front of the main board, Patton muses on the nature of how Outkast tracks come to be: "I don't even like to think about it. Sometimes, it's just a beat or something I'm humming. As long as we get it down, I don't even want to know where [the inspiration] comes from."

In the case of "The Whole World," the hit single released from Outkast's 2001 greatest hits LP, *Big Boi and Dre Present . . . Outkast* (La Face/Arista), it came from Benjamin's fruitful method of working alone at home and then bringing solid fragments of the track to *Stankonia*. "That started at home with me singing and the beat," he says.

"I brought it to the studio and laid down the melody of the singing first. Then the music came around. I think we did it in about two or three days because we had a deadline."

Outkast is notorious for its continual stream of writing and recording. For the new double album, the word is that they had some 40 tracks a piece to pick from. But despite the muddle of whether Patton and Benjamin would be releasing solo LPs or not, Benjamin is less than concerned that it's still not all there yet. "It's just not ready," he says, smiling. "It's not finished until it's finished."

When it is finished, the record will no doubt be a further illustration of how mature and provocative Outkast's music has grown to be. They are admittedly far from their roots, but Benjamin sees no possibility of it being any other way. "We're way past the original audience," he says. "There's no way we can get back to the original audience, because [back then] we were 17 years old. You just can't go back to doing that. That's like trying to relive a childhood. It's just going to continue to grow if people keep movin' on with it. When I was young, I thought jazz was like something you heard in an elevator. I was never into it. I was never into Hendrix until six or seven years ago. I thought rock music was just noise. But once you get to know it, you think, 'How did he come up with these melodies?'"

The new Outkast equation being what it is at this point, Benjamin plans to possibly investigate taking up formal composition in his spare time. How that will affect his production work is hard to say, but he realizes that most of the magic that Outkast has produced thus far has come from experimentation and deeper investigation.

"During the first album, we just wrote all of our lyrics, and then Organized Noize produced the entire first album," Benjamin says. "When we were on the road for *Southernplayalisticadillacmuzik*, that's when I started to buy equipment like keyboards and beat machines. I started listening to records and finding out, 'Okay, Bootsy played with James Brown and then with Funkadelic, and the Horny Horns were really Fred Wesley.' Seeing the lineage and who played with whom and just getting deeper into it, I started to appreciate it a lot more. And that's going on now. I was never into jazz, but I appreciate it so hard now because I know what it takes to make it. Like even growing up listening to rap music—it was just tunes. It was just something you heard on the radio. But when you make music, you know that somebody had to come up with that. I don't even consider myself a producer. I produce records because that's the title they put on it. I just mess around with sounds and make something that I'm enjoying or filling a void. People always ask, 'What is the Outkast sound?' And I say, 'I just make music that I'm not hearing at the time because someone has to do it.' So anybody really could crank it up."

As it approaches midnight, we part company in the *Stankonia* lot. Benjamin, cranking up a jazzy new Joe Jackson–like vibe that he's been working on, looks thoroughly permeated by the music as he rolls off to his suburban home.

18

Phoenix

WOLFGANG AMADEUS PHOENIX'S HYBRID STUDIO STYLES AND SOUNDS

By Patrick Sisson

This chapter appeared in the July 2009 issue of *EQ* magazine.

Somber French poets and friendly prostitutes sound like fitting inspirations for a raucous, balls-out rock album. While these characters were part of the neighborhood color near the studio where chic French foursome Phoenix—comprising Thomas Mars, Laurent "Branco" Brancowitz, Christian Mazzalai, and Deck D'Arcy—recorded the bulk of *Wolfgang Amadeus Phoenix* [Loyaute/Glassnote], their album wasn't the by-product of wicked indulgence, especially on the inflated rock-and-roll scale of indecent behavior.

A glittering slab of well-crafted electronic pop, the band's follow-up to 2006's *It's Never Been Like That* is a result of the group's perfectionist tendencies (they recorded over 14 hours of music in total), a long recording process, and an attempt to be more abstract. According to guitarist Brancowitz, the group even listened to a soundtrack of modern classical and ambient music to cleanse their auditory palette, and they used Eno's famous Oblique Strategies cards to get through creative roadblocks.

"As a creator, you're always frustrated by your limits," he says. "You want to find strategies to go further. I actually learned Morse code at one point, and I tried to type words rhythmically to see what kind of patterns they would create."

After a search for inspiration that took them to New York and back, the group asked friend Philippe Zdar to co-produce *Wolfgang Amadeus Phoenix*, camping out in his studio in Paris' Montmartre district for nearly a year and a half. Designed in the early '80s by audio guru Tom Hidley—a famed engineer and studio designer—Zdar's studio was an ideal place for the band to challenge its creative process. Half of French house duo Cassius, the producer owns a cache of vintage gear, giving the group plenty of equipment to work with, and his helpful approach kept them focused.

"I think Phoenix has very good taste," Zdar says. "The band members are great producers, and they just needed someone to guide them and keep them on track. It's like directing Marlon Brando. I don't think Brando needed help— he just needed a little guidance."

Zdar felt strongly that the album should sound modern, diverse, and informed by contemporary music and production. His whole approach was to respect the group, give them the time and space to compose and record, and occasionally "make a tackle" in the studio, providing momentary distractions to keep them from getting too caught up in their work.

"He would sometimes come for five minutes a day, and arrive six hours late with a bottle of champagne," Brancowitz says. "He'd say, 'This is great' or 'boring.' He brought the energy. We knew if a song pleased us and pleased him, it was a solid song."

During sessions, the band normally recorded straight to Pro Tools HD, preferring minimal equipment and a very dry sound. Many songs went through multiple versions, so they often needed to add and subtract layers. Plus, Zdar wanted guitars recorded as straight as possible so he wouldn't be hamstrung during the mixing process. "We wanted to record fast and capture the performance, instead of obsessing about the sound," Zdar says.

Much of the charm of Phoenix's tightly constructed songs comes from the clipped, artificial guitar lines. Guitarists Brancowitz and Mazzalai both used

Phoenix: Christian Mazzalai (far left), Laurent Brancowitz, Deck D'Arcy, and Thomas Mars. (Pascal Textiera)

Fender Bullet Stratocasters—cheaper and less popular models of a guitar chosen for its unique sound.

"It's very dry and really plays only one specific style," Mazzalai says. "But they fit perfectly with our style of playing. The sound that comes out is almost plastic."

For "Rome," which opens with a part that Brancowitz compares to the sound of a kid playing alone in his bedroom, the guys recorded their guitar lines through a Telefunken V76 preamp, a Telefunken U73 compressor, and a direct box—standard practice for most of the album. Later, when the tracks were mixed, they were sent through a Helios preamp to add more character, a UREI 1176 compressor, and an AKG BX 20 spring reverb.

As befitting a band that has backed up Air, Phoenix deployed an army of analog synthesizers during the recording process, including a Roland JX-3P, a Korg Trident, a Yamaha CS-80, and a Jen Carousel organ. On "1901," weird, wispy notes from a Yamaha Tenori-on—a step-sequencing synth that was fed through an AMS S-DMX delay—float in the background as big, fuzzy chords from the Korg Trident streak across the song. The group also used a few toy synthesizers, often cranking up the preamp in the recording chain to capture the buzz and hum. It fit the band's philosophy of combining very cheap and very expensive instruments.

"What's good about these instruments is that their beauty lies in their limits," Brancowitz says. "Their utility comes from the mistakes their engineers made."

Zdar normally utilizes a Neve 1073 EQ and a Telefunken V76 preamp to record synths. When mixing, he often sends tracks through a UREI LA-4 compressor—which he feels is especially good for making synths sound tight—and a Massenburg GML 8200 EQ, which helps emphasize bass.

To achieve the modern feel of R&B or techno-style beats, the percussion on *Wolfgang Amadeus Phoenix* required the hybrid approach of blending live and electronic drums. Mars used an Akai MPC sampler to trigger his favorite percussion samples, which were often mixed with live percussion, as well as software samplers such as Native Instruments Battery 3. Signal-chain strategies included feeding the toms, hi-hats, and crash cymbals through an SSL compressor; running sidechains for the snare (a Neve EQ, UREI 1176 compressor, and an AMS reverb) and kick drums (Neve 1073 preamp, Massenburg EQ, and Neve 33609 compressor); and dumping toms into an SPL Transient Designer.

Meanwhile, in the realm of bass, Zdar sometimes aimed for a blend of organic and electronic sounds, as on "Fences." For that song, a Fender Mustang Bass part played through an Ampeg SVT Amp was fused with the synth bass of a Yamaha DX100 synth, and then heavily compressed. "I wanted to blur the real and the synthetic, and make a big, bubbling thing—a real magma of sound," Zdar says.

One of the few sounds on the album that remained relatively straightforward were the vocals, which were recorded with Neumann U 67 and AKG C 12 microphones and sent through a UREI 1176 compressor and an EMT 252 for slight reverb. During mixing, Zdar also applied a Lexicon PCM42 Digital Delay and an EAR 660 compressor.

"We love dry sounds," says Mazzalai. Consequently, Zdar used vocal effects sparingly to heighten their impact. On "Rome," he placed reverb on the verse and first chorus, and then cut it out after the break. He believes this approach made the music more poetic, evoking the feel of walking out of a dark restaurant into the bright sun of the Italian capital.

Ultimately, Zdar took the Pro Tools tracks and mixed them on one of his two SSL 4000 E mixing consoles (he has a spare in case he needs to get one repaired), because he favors the unit's analog sound. He also zeros in on the highs and lows when doing EQ adjustments in order to craft crystal-clear, deep bass and a very tight sound.

"I'll boost highs on a Helios EQ, and, at the same time, I use the filters on the console to take *out* highs," says Zdar. "This gives you the feeling that you have lots of treble, while simultaneously giving you high frequencies that are more rounded and less tiring to listen to. After all, if you want girls to love an album all their life, it's important to mix it well."

19

Classic
Pink Floyd

THE UPS AND DOWNS OF CREATING
THE PIPER AT THE GATES OF DAWN

By Jeff Touzeau

This chapter features an abridged version of the Pink Floyd article in the December 2007 issue of *EQ* magazine.

Forty years ago, a young Englishman named Syd Barrett strolled into Abbey Road's Studio 3 with cohorts Richard Wright, Roger Waters, and Nick Mason in tow. Having just signed with EMI for an astronomical £5,000 advance (and thus all the time necessary to record their debut album), the group set up to track a wildly adventurous release that would alter the canvas of rock music forever.

Barrett's delicate mind was spilling out songs at an unprecedented rate. At just 21 years old, the creative key holder of Pink Floyd had penned a musical narrative that would usher listeners through a previously uncharted world of psychedelia. Swirling guitars, dreamy organ sequences, and a host of celestial sound effects would soon crash head-on with riveting rhythms in a sonic tapestry woven and embroidered with the legend, *The Piper at the Gates of Dawn*.

There was no way for the band to know that their

first full-length endeavor into a hallucinogenic world of melodious mysticism—rife with a cast of mythical literary figures moving in fairy-tale fugues, fully unbounded by the traditional trappings of rock and roll—was going to drastically change the landscape of popular music. Though the band had spent time in the nearby Sound Techniques before entering Abbey Road in that fateful February of 1967, laying down songs such as "Arnold Layne," "See Emily Play," "Candy and a Currant Bun," "Interstellar Overdrive," and "Nick's Boogie"—and the buzz surrounding their live shows was growing at an exponential rate—the young foursome was relatively fresh-faced and green, ignorant to the repercussions of their auditory experiments. No one present knew that the next few moons spent behind Abbey Road's hallowed walls would go down in history as some of the most important studio sessions of the 20th century.

This is the story of those days and of those nights—the story of the creation of one of the most celebrated albums of our time.

Joe Boyd was perhaps Pink Floyd's first friend, helping the group secure funding to develop and track its first single and bringing the band into his London club, UFO, to help cultivate a fan base.

"Onstage, they were quite unusual because they were so anonymous," Boyd recalls. "There was this light show going on, but no spotlight on the individual performers. They didn't even say much—they just played. Syd sort of glowed, but nobody stepped forward as a personality."

Jeff Jarratt—the tape op later assigned to the *Piper* sessions—echoes Boyd's sentiments, relaying his reaction to seeing the band perform prior to entering Abbey Road: "They had a sound I had not heard anyone else do. It was something I had never seen before—the lights, the presence."

Having become familiar with the band's songs, Boyd and the group convened to decide which track would best serve as Pink Floyd's first single. The ruling was unanimous: "Arnold Layne."

Assembling Barrett, Waters, Wright, and Mason in a converted cowshed dubbed Sound Techniques, Boyd began working with co-owners Geoff Frost and John Wood to employ their hand-built equipment to capture the band in its youthful prime. The band was hungry to record, and Sound Techniques was, as luck had it at the time, equipped to handle the group's pensive approach to

Pink Floyd. (Andrew Whittuck/Redferns/Getty Images)

tracking. As Wood points out: "You've got to remember that, at the time, many records would be made on any given day. We might have a two-hour session in the morning for a beer company. Then Joe might come in with the Incredible String Band in the afternoon. Then we might start at 8:00 p.m. on a new album."

But Floyd needed time in order to properly record their abstract compositions, so the team blocked out four nights, from 6 p.m. to 12 a.m., to put "Arnold Layne" and the B-side "Interstellar Overdrive" to tape.

"That was a long haul," Wood assures. "We were used to getting three titles in two hours."

At the time Pink Floyd entered Sound Techniques, the 4-track recorder was the predominant tape machine in high-end facilities. Therefore, decisions had to be made early in regards to track assignments.

"The big rule when you are recording on a 4-track is that you record the whole rhythm section onto one track—a mono mix of bass and drums," says Wood. "Then we would decide how loud we wanted the bass drum, the bass, and the drums—you had to balance the track right when you laid it down. And that isn't a bad thing! If I didn't like the sound, I would change the microphone.

The last resort would be messing about with EQ. I think it's pretty extraordinary how good 'Arnold Layne' sounds in consideration of that."

Track limitations weren't considered prohibitive to getting a great sound. Instead, Wood saw his mission as simply capturing the sound of the band jelling together in a single space.

"People weren't so anal about separation," he says. "We just aimed to get a cohesive sound out of whatever we were recording."

With serious multitracking years away, Boyd arranged the band in Sound Techniques' live room with Barrett, Waters, and Wright circling Mason's kit— which was placed in the center of the room, where the apex of the ceiling was highest from the floor. The band's amps were hidden behind a baffle to minimize bleed into the drum mics.

"That's one of the reasons we got such a great drum sound," observes Wood, noting that the high ceiling in Sound Techniques live room added to Mason's monstrously huge drum sounds. "The room was also very live, and, in fact, we had to deaden it down in the back because we found the reflections were getting a little out of control."

For the "Arnold Layne/Interstellar Overdrive" sessions, Wood employed a miking strategy for Mason's drums that, at the time, was tried and true. The method was a simplistic three-mic approach consisting of a single Neumann KM 56 (or KM 54) as a single overhead, an AKG D 19 on the snare, and a Reslo Ribbon on the kick. Wood also recalls bypassing Waters' and Wright's amps, recording the bass direct into the Sound Techniques custom console, and sending Wright's Farfisa organ patched through a Binson Echorec tube echo unit to get the otherworldly key sounds (particularly noticeable during the organ break prior to the last chorus).

"We didn't spend much time on Syd's vocals," says Wood. "We just put a Neumann U 67 in front of him. He was great to work with. He did those tracks fine. There weren't any problems getting a performance out of any of them."

When it came to Barrett's guitar tracks, however, the group spent a considerable amount of time trying out various mic placements. They finally settled on miking the back of Barrett's Selmer amp—an approach that resulted in a fully developed bottom end that commands attention from the onset of the tune.

Barrett's guitar choice for the sessions, as Boyd remembers, was his famous Danelectro 3021. Also possessing an Echorec unit, Barrett was "entirely in command of his guitar sound." He often used a metal Zippo lighter to scratch his strings—an effect that can be heard at the beginning of the haunting "See Emily Play."

"He was very on top of his gadgets," says Boyd. "I remember him explaining how all this stuff worked to us. His guitar sound was essentially unaltered after it hit the microphone. It was a self-contained thing. Whatever came out of Syd's amp was what we kept."

Having produced a powerful single such as "Arnold Layne," and amply demonstrating a remarkable working rapport with the band, one would have assumed Boyd's fate was sealed as Pink Floyd's producer. However, when EMI's deal went through, the label dropped Boyd from future projects.

"It didn't hurt my self-esteem," he assures. "It made me annoyed. But EMI had a working model of success: George Martin and the Beatles. In-house producer, their studio, their engineer."

Nick Mason reflects positively on his experience working with the Sound Techniques crew, saying, "Those sessions were much more to do with Wood and Boyd coming up with sounds, rather than us. We didn't have the time we had at Abbey Road—we were in there to just get the single made—and Joe Boyd was great for that."

The "Arnold Layne" sessions, however, were not to be Wood's last experience working with Pink Floyd. For reasons still somewhat unknown, newly appointed producer Norman Smith decided to record the second single, "See Emily Play," at Sound Techniques.

"It was quite a shock," says Wood. "Abbey Road was vastly superior to us in equipment and resources. But Pink Floyd wanted to come back for that song. I think 'Emily' is a little bit gimmicky, and that's what you get when you get two bloody recording engineers making a record. There was a lot of fiddling about—the half-speed piano, for example."

Entering Abbey Road to track the remainder of the songs that constitute *The Piper at the Gates of Dawn*, Floyd began working solely with Smith—one of the studio's most experienced engineers, having developed groundbreaking techniques on nearly every Beatles album up until *Rubber Soul*, effectively winning the trust and admiration of his mentor George Martin. As a gifted musician in his own right—and an avid jazz fan to boot—Smith was sensitive to the role that melody played in Floyd's compositions.

"Norman was good news, because he taught us a lot, and he gave us a pretty free hand in the studio," says Mason. "This was a period where producers were expected to control the band, and save money and save time. He was the sort of junior version of George Martin—and that's definitely what he was aiming to be."

Meanwhile, Kevin Ryan, a highly regarded expert on Abbey Road, reveals that Pink Floyd had another ace in the hole during the *Piper* sessions: EMI staff engineer Peter Bown. "Peter Bown was clearly the most daring and experimental engineer at the studio," he says. "He doesn't have that reputation, but studio documentation shows he was experimenting more than anyone else by far. Most of the Abbey Road engineers had a preferred mic setup and approach that they rarely altered, but Peter was constantly changing his mic techniques based on the session, and he was always pulling in various experimental equipment."

Piper tape op Jeff Jarratt speaks further about Bown's innovative streak: "He was completely open to trying any new ideas. If the artist said they were trying to get a particular sound, he might try two or three different mics on something to arrive at what they wanted to hear."

Outfitted with Bown and Jarratt, Smith began working with the band in Abbey Road's Studio 3, encountering behavior from Barrett that was, to say the least, abnormal.

"Syd was an absolute genius," declares Jarratt. "Those sessions were a lot of fun. Syd used to take his shoes off and walk around on his toes. I've never seen anything else like it. He was full of ideas—an incredibly creative person."

Boyd remembers Barrett as "relatively engaged" during the "Arnold Layne" sessions, remarking that he didn't "assert himself much in discussions, but was looked up to as the leader of the band."

"He didn't say, 'This is the way it has to be,'" Boyd says. "Roger would say, 'Okay, we're going to do this,' but then everyone sort of looked over at Syd, who would say, 'Yeah, that's cool.' He was still hands-off in the mixing, though. He would wander off during mixes, returning only to ask, 'How does it sound?'"

Throughout the *Piper* sessions, however, Barrett became increasingly withdrawn—a situation Wood feels may have been symptomatic of a lack of interest in Smith's production techniques. Nonetheless, Barrett was experiencing a creative peak, which shone through during the band's tenure at Abbey Road.

"They were creating this audio image that was exciting in its own way. It was very different than the Beatles," says Jarratt.

Sessions were scheduled to run between 7 p.m. and 10 p.m. but would typically run as late as 3 a.m. This, Jarratt relates, was because the material—while well rehearsed in the live realm—was fluid, due to the band's improvisational nature in the studio. Songs such as the re-tracked "Interstellar Overdrive" and "Astronomy Domine," for example, would vary by multiple minutes in any given take.

Adding to the improvisational approach, the band began adding sound effects that would become integral to the album. Wind and radio sounds, mechanical clocks, and a host of other pre-recorded noises culled from Abbey Road's library added new dimensions to the band's compositions.

"The effects were all logged," recalls Jarratt of the studio's meticulously catalogued stock effect collection. "So if you ever needed a train or a ship noise, it would be fairly easy to find out what selection of tapes was available."

Because of its smaller size, Studio 3 was used for many pop sessions, which required a less critical response than, say, a classical session. The problem was, Pink Floyd was not an average pop band. They needed a large-sounding room.

Given this unfortunate situation, Smith placed Mason's Premier drum set against Studio 3's left wall. "Pretty much everyone used that setup and thought drums sounded best in that part of the room," Ryan observes.

"The bass would typically be put on one side of the drums, and guitar on the other side with a screen around them," adds Abbey Road staff engineer Peter Mew. "You would record three different groups in a day in that era, so you tended to have a pretty fixed setup that you used for everything that you knew worked. If you were going to record four titles in a three-hour session, you needed to know the way you were working was going to turn out right. You usually had just an hour to prepare, and you didn't have much in the way of equipment—you'd have maybe ten mics across the whole lot if you were recording a band."

While the other engineers at the time stuck with their tried-and-true approaches, Bown was anything but predictable. "Most Abbey Road engineers were recording drums with two mics at that time—one on the bass drum, and one overhead," says Ryan. "However, during the *Piper* sessions, Peter expanded his drum setup to five microphones to capture Nick's natural sound in the room. One Neumann KM 56 was used as the overhead and was suspended over the center of the kit. A second KM 56 was placed under the snare, and a third KM 56 was placed on the opposite side of the kit over the cymbal. Sometimes, though, Peter substituted the Sony C38A for the KM 56. A single AKG D 19c was placed in front of each bass drum, a few inches from the skin."

Bown further digressed from the proven miking methods employed by Boyd and Wood at Sound Techniques, opting for a DI/mic approach to Waters' Rickenbacker 4001S and Selmer amp setup, placing an AKG D 19c on the grille of the amp and running a signal direct into Studio 3's EMI REDD.51 12-input/4-output console. Bown also disregarded Wood's direct approach to recording Wright's Farfisa organ, instead miking the instrument's built-in speaker with an AKG C 12. When Wright used Abbey Road's house Hammond organ, Bown switched strategies, placing an STC 4038 a foot away from the rotating Leslie speaker.

Barrett used a Fender Esquire in addition to his Danelectro 3021, running both instruments through a Selmer Treble 'N' Bass 50 amp. A single Neumann U 67 was chosen by Bown to record Barrett's amp—as well as his 1963 Sovereign acoustic (heard on tracks such as "Flaming," "The Gnome," and "Scarecrow")—and a Neumann U 48 was used to record Barrett, Waters, and Wright's vocals, instead of Wood's go-to U 67. It was a total overhaul of the engineering methods used by Wood and Boyd to track Floyd's first single.

In addition to Studio 3's spatial limitations, its control room left a lot to be desired—especially in terms of monitoring. Ryan elaborates: "The monitoring systems were definitely not up to modern standards. They had Altec 605A monitors in the control room, and they were not flat-sounding at all. They rolled off a lot at the top and bottom, and most of the former engineers just laugh now when you ask about them."

Thankfully, Bown and Smith had become deeply familiar with the deficiencies of the 605As and had devised numerous workarounds to ensure the end product didn't suffer due to subpar monitoring.

"They knew exactly how the tape would sound when it would be taken out of the control room," Jarratt says. "Peter and Norman were very aware of what they needed to get out of the sound of the speakers for it to sound right when they were ready to transfer it onto record. The only way to come to that conclusion was through years of trial and error."

"Monitoring and the control room acoustics in those days were a lot different—a lot rougher," adds Mew. "There was severely restricted frequency response in the speakers, and there were also a lot of room reflections. It was very live. Quite often, you get a belief from today's engineers that what's on the tape is exactly what people heard from the speakers in those days, and that is simply not true. They knew what these sounds would sound like in the outside world. All those control rooms in those days were very similar, because they all had the same kind of speakers, and the lack of acoustic treatment. Engineers were moving around from control room to control room, sometimes three times a day. All those guys—Norman, Peter, and the others—they knew the sound of those control rooms intimately from having done it for so long."

Beyond the 605As, Studio 3's control room was fitted with gear that made it almost identical to the Beatles' Studio 2. From the EMI REDD.51 desk (a console with very limited EQ—just a treble and bass control) to the core pieces of outboard (mostly comprised of Fairchild 660 limiters, which added a soft distortion to any source signals they received, and EMI RS124 modified Altec compressors), the group had the best dynamic processors in the business to choose from before dumping their tracks onto Studio 3's dedicated Studer J-37. The butter for the bread, Jarratt says, was the shared echo chamber—located beneath the facility—that made use of EMT plates, which he says are most evident on the beginning of "Flaming."

However, as Ryan points out, Bown was not partial to the now-made-famous-by-the-Beatles Altecs during this period: "Most of the engineers used the Altec compressor on their sessions, but Peter preferred instead to use an experimental EMI unit. It was a prototype solid-state Zener limiter that eventually evolved into EMI's famous TG series. So *Piper* was largely recorded with a combination of this prototype limiter and the Fairchild 660. These units were

147

sometimes inserted into the mic channels on the desk, but mainly they were just on the four outputs which could be sent to any tape track."

At the time, stereo had yet to proliferate the world as the widely accepted format that it is today. Not only were most listeners relying primarily on the radio and small record players to listen to music, but mix engineers also preferred working in mono due to the limitations present in dealing with four tracks.

"There's not a lot you can do to make these recordings stereo—which is why a lot of the early stereo recordings had the rhythm section on one side; they were only meant to be mono, and that's why the stereo field of *Piper* feels so empty in the middle."

Last year, Syd Barrett—known now by neighbors as simply "Roger"—died quietly in his hometown of Cambridge, just one year shy of the 40th anniversary of *The Piper at the Gates of Dawn*. Following his extrication from Pink Floyd just one year after the final mix of *Piper* had been completed, Barrett became increasingly mentally ill, succumbing to a well-documented love affair with LSD, fading into quiet obscurity during the years that followed, and leaving two painfully flawed solo albums—*The Madcap Laughs* and *Barrett*—to document his creative genius.

The rest of the band, however, went on to release a slew of critically acclaimed releases, from the avant-garde *Ummagumma* to the chart-topping *The Dark Side of the Moon*, and from the moody *Meddle* to the smash-hit concept album/film *The Wall*, growing into one of the world's most successful bands before quietly collapsing under the weight of near-constant internal strife.

For all of Floyd's massive legacy pieces—albums that were inarguably more successful than the band's debut—*The Piper at the Gates of Dawn* holds a special place in the hearts of Floyd fanatics, being regarded by many as one of the most influential LPs ever made. The album has been remixed for stereo, repackaged, remastered, and re-released in different forms throughout the years, appearing earlier this year as a special three-disc offering complete with fantastic packaging. But for all the after-the-fact revamping and reworking, nothing could ever quite recapture those moments in time when Piper was dropped by the first slew of listeners onto their turntables—the moments when "Astronomy Domine" or "See Emily Play" first emanated from bedroom speakers and changed the world of rock music.

148

20

The Roots

REFINING LIVE-INSTRUMENT HIP-HOP ON *GAME THEORY*

By Bill Murphy

This chapter features an abridged version of the Roots article in the March 2006 issue of *Remix* magazine.

Rolling down a rain-slogged thruway on the outskirts of Washington, D.C., the Roots' caravan is heading toward the 9:30 Club for one of the group's sold-out, legendary year-end live jams. Behind the wheel of his silver Scion wagon, Ahmir "?uestlove" Thompson scrolls through his prodigious song selection and alights on a string of raw funk tracks from Sly and the Family Stone's classic album *Fresh*, and for a moment, we're transported back to 1973.

"There's definitely a particular sound from that era that I've tried to approximate, and I'm just learning how to find it now," ?uestlove says, referring to the endless studio hours he has logged while coaxing his drum kit into the dirt-encrusted, vintage groovalactics that virtually define the sonic direction of the Roots—hip-hop's baddest (and for all intents, hip-hop's only) full-on live band. But as many of its loyal fans have discovered, the Roots is not just about any one particular style or approach; its eccentricities run the left-of-center gamut, whether it's psychedelic neo-soul, off-kilter jazz-rock fusion, or exotic, dub-streaked production techniques. Like the streets of Philly where they grew up, the members of the Roots embody a musical history that is rich, radical, and wholly unpredictable.

"You remember in the movie *Heat*," ?uestlove asks, "when De Niro was like, 'Can you walk away from everything that you know in 30 seconds?' but he had the itch in him to do that one last killing? We're known for absolutely changing our sound and our direction and totally alienating our fan base and embracing a new fan base with every album. The attraction to all nine of our studio albums is pretty much a different demographic each time, from *Do You Want More?!!!??!* [Geffen, 1995] to *Phrenology* [MCA, 2002]. Part of me still wants to keep that tradition, but another part of me is itching to see if it's time for us to absolutely reintroduce ourselves and start back at square one again. So right now you're catching us at a transitional period, and it could go either way."

ALL FOR ONE, ONE BY ONE

Earlier in the day, back at the loft complex in North Philly that's credited on Roots albums as The Studio (founded in 1996 by cellist, arranger, and MFSB/Salsoul Orchestra alum Larry Gold), executive producer Rich Nichols, who has been with the band since the beginning, is cueing up rough mixes for *Game Theory* (Def Jam Left, 2006) and waxing philosophical about hip-hop in general. Like ?uestlove, he fully understands the complexities of the business and that the unique creative model espoused by the Roots is really unmatched in popular music today.

"We're finding ourselves in the funny place of almost being like an island," Nichols observes. "A lot of things in hip-hop are textural, like an 808 sound or a snare sound—a particular kick sound will change your kick pattern, you know? But when you're playing with live instruments like we do, you almost have to create a particular texture as opposed to just turning on a keyboard or a drum machine or sampling from a record. So we're an island because it's obviously live and because we don't borrow as many of the actual sonic palettes from previous things like other hip-hop artists do—we *create* them, and that in turn influences the musical patterns that come out."

The Roots' ?uestlove. (Jeff Fusco/Getty Images)

?uestlove extrapolates further, going back to the early days when the band was still in search of a unifying sound. "We were blind, and we had to feel our way around," he recalls. "Our main concern was to make sure that sonically we were on point as far as the hip-hop connoisseur is concerned, because before us, I think a lot of people's standard for what was good with live instruments, in 1993, was the Brand New Heavies. And you know, I like their songs, but their instruments had no warmth to them and sounded absolutely clean. So that's when the whole idea came into play of let's sample, loop, and quantize *ourselves* and make it sound perfect. And we found a whole 'nother door of creativity that we never knew about before."

From a songwriting and recording standpoint, the door has since opened onto a couple of different scenarios that have led up to the making of *Game Theory*. One is what ?uestlove calls "the Abbey Road approach" (in deference to the Beatles), where instead of tracking as a group in a series of stream-of-consciousness jams—which is how much of *The Tipping Point* (Geffen, 2004) came together, and which actually still guides *Game Theory* to some extent—each member of the Roots records on his own, gradually building the song into a finished whole.

"There are still occasions when we'll do stuff at the same time," ?uestlove clarifies, "but I prefer, only because I'm very anal about the time and the meter, just to concentrate to a click [track]. I can imagine the song in my head, so it's okay. I know it's hard for some musicians to even fathom tracking a song by themselves without having someone to play with—it's kind of like acting in front of a green screen, doing the CGI thing—but I've absolutely conditioned myself to concentrating that hard."

As acolytes of the '70s funk school and all the analog thickness that emanates from that style, the Roots also took the unusual step of tracking entirely to Digidesign's Pro Tools HD system, without any access to the two-inch tape machines they had used on past albums. "This will also mark the first record in which I'll track my drums in stereo," ?uestlove confides, deferring again to the stripped-down tracking methods of bygone days. "But it was really [mix engineer] Bob Power who showed me—along with Rich [Nichols] and [engineer] Jon [Smeltz]—the potential with Pro Tools that I didn't know before. It's more than just a time-saver; it allows you to try different things out instantly. I've actually become very much addicted to [Line 6] Amp Farm, because as it turns out, it's a great tool for getting an old Studio One sound [after Coxsone Dodd's legendary 8-track studio in Jamaica]. It has a 1985 amp setting that for some reason just gates and compresses the drums; I can put a whole song through it, and it sounds like it's 1972 all over again."

THE SOUND AND THE FURY
On the tour bus outside the 9:30 Club, Roots front man and lead rhyme guru

Tariq "Black Thought" Trotter is staring ahead intently, as if steeling himself for battle before the band hits the stage. Like the other core members of the Roots—?uestlove, bassist Leonard "Hub" Hubbard, and keyboardist James "Kamal" Gray, along with guitarist "Captain" Kirk Douglas and percussionist Frank "Knuckles" Walker—he has devoted much of his life to perfecting his craft in an effort to push the envelope.

Like *The Tipping Point* before it, *Game Theory* is rife with openings for Black Thought to flex his ever-expanding verbal acumen, as well as for the Roots to reassert its standing as a bona fide, studio-savvy rhythm engine with an ear for densely layered beats and melodies. "Long Time," for instance, is a driving, upbeat anthem that surges on the strength of Black Thought's incomparable flow, making it arguably one of the centerpiece cuts on the album. Chicken-picked guitar lines (courtesy of Douglas), sustained bass chords, and a crafty arrangement that bears the stamp of Philadelphia International legend Walter "Bunny" Sigler—whom the Roots recruited for the session—help bring it over the top. "It's a song about Philly," Black Thought explains, "and how rich the musical history of Philly is. I'm referencing South Philly, which is where I'm from, and musically we're kind of paying tribute to all our hometown influences."

Although "Long Time" is the product of one of those rare in-studio Roots jams, "Baby" is a reverb-drenched dub-funk excursion that boasts the results of ?uestlove's solo experiments with drum miking and recording. "In my room at The Studio, I have the privacy to sit there and play with it," he says. "Nowadays, I'm able to track at least 70 percent of the drums myself, and what I've found is that if you want to sound like you're in the '70s, you need to use [Neumann] U 47s and Royer [R-122V] ribbon mics and then experiment with how the signal is processed. When I did the *Voodoo* album with D'Angelo, Russ Elevado explained the difference to me. I always thought it was all in the mixing, and it didn't matter what we recorded the instruments with. That's when I learned from Russ that the [Shure] SM57 mics are your enemy—they're really only good for the snare, and that's about it."

Oddly enough, it was Eminem whom ?uestlove credits as having first turned him on to the fat sonic imaging that ribbon mics can deliver. He also picked up some insight from engineering legend Eddie Kramer—the man be-

ORGANIC MECHANIX

Game Theory marks an evolution in the Roots' exacting and often exhaustive recording method; it's the band's first album to be tracked entirely on a digital platform. For engineer Jon Smeltz, the main challenge was to preserve the fat, gritty, analog-sounding range that fans have come to expect from a Roots project while still taking advantage of the editing and effects-processing capabilities that Pro Tools provides.

When recording the entire band live in the studio, the drums become the main focus. "Ahmir has his own miking scheme when he records alone," Smeltz says, "but the jam-session scheme is a little different—an Electro-Voice RE20 on the kick, with an AKG D 112 on the outside just in case we need something extra. The snare has a Shure SM57 on top and an SM81 on the bottom, with an SM81 on the hi-hat, and then a Sennheiser 421 on the floor tom. For overheads, sometimes we'll use a Neumann U 87 really tight to the top of the drum kit."

Smeltz front ends most of the drum mics through Focusrite ISA 110 mic preamps because "they do very little to color the sound, and they're very musical in their EQ. At times I'll use them for lead vocals, bass, guitar—it's just a personal preference. I mean, I tracked Ahmir's drums for years through Neves. It really boils down to what I have available in my rack, and the Focusrites are my multipurpose preamp."

Another secret to the Roots' staggering low end, especially on "Long Time" and what sounds like a 5-string bass on "Bread and Butter": the Moogerfooger MF-101 Lowpass Filter. "I almost always, without fail, duplicate Hub's bass track in Pro Tools," Smeltz explains. "I'll put the Mooger plug-in on one of them, just to get the sub frequencies or the dominant low frequencies, and set those up against the noneffected track, and that usually becomes a composite of the bass. And the Mooger is really outstanding for other things, as well—on 'Long Time,' I split the kick drum into two tracks and used the Mooger for a little extra kick in the ass."

hind the console for classic sessions by Jimi Hendrix, Led Zeppelin, and, in particular, Stevie Wonder.

"Stevie would play a straight drum track as a metronome," ?uestlove says, "and then he would go on top of what he was doing to make it sound even fatter. So when it came time to do the ride cymbal, he was damn near destroying it. Eddie talked about this Neve compressor that he had that made the cymbals sound like a splash—almost like they were being squeezed. Once he taught us that trick, we used it for Erykah Badu's *Mama's Gun* record and

Common's *Like Water for Chocolate* and *Electric Circus*. I used the vintage Neve compressors on 'Baby' to approximate that 'slow-motion' sound, and I'm stacking snares by duping them in Pro Tools."

DEF, DOPE, AND DAUNTLESS

As with any Roots project, *Game Theory* embraces multiple musical styles. Along with the naked funk of "Long Time" and the spacious dub of "Baby," there's the chaotic big beat (replete with distorted synth lines) of "Here I Come," the bluesy guitar-and-handclaps of "Bread and Butter" (not the track's official title, but one that draws some of its inspiration from the song by Johnny "Guitar" Watson), and the lush, orchestral feel of several as-yet-untitled interludes that are planned to feature string arrangements by Larry Gold.

Fittingly, with the Roots now calling Def Jam home, "False Media" emerges as the album's pivotal appeal to a hip-hop audience that some might say has been lulled to sleep by the ubiquitous winner-take-all, pimp-and-hustler aesthetic still ruling the airwaves today. As a tribute of sorts to Public Enemy's "Don't Believe the Hype," the track captures the feel of a classic Def Jam production, with ?uestlove emulating an 808 beat on live drums while Kamal weighs in with eerie atmospherics on an effects-processed Fender Rhodes.

"That's actually the first song we worked on for the album," ?uestlove recalls. "We were all playing at the same time [live in the studio], so it was a litmus test to see if we could try it out. It's one thing when you're doing a straight-ahead song and playing together; it's totally different when you're trying to do something sonically experimental, but you want to have that band element jelling perfectly. To jell as a unit playing traditional songs is easy, but to jell the other way is a little trickier. It just takes a little more effort."

Long known for its tireless work ethic, the Roots made a career out of harnessing its diverse influences into a fully realized whole—one that blends an uncompromisingly high level of musicianship with an openness to experimentation that most groups, whether in hip-hop or any other musical genre, can't even hope to sustain for just one album, let alone 10. "That's a very important element of our live show, too," ?uestlove says, and it only takes a listen to *The Roots Come Alive* (MCA, 1999) or, more recently, the live suite "The

Seed/Melting Pot/Web" from *Home Grown! Volume Two*–recorded by Gilles Peterson at the BBC's Maida Vale studios and reprised in part on Peterson's excellent *The BBC Sessions* (Ether, 2006)–to get a feel for how hot the Roots can get when the band takes it to the stage.

"There's a meticulous detail that we probably put more into our live show than we do on our albums," ?uestlove observes with a glint of amusement. "We're already anal in terms of the album stuff, but I think live we just take it to another level." And a few hours later, a jam-packed crowd of Roots fans would have to agree.

21

Röyksopp

TURNING PROG-ROCK INSPIRATION INTO AN ELECTRO-POP DREAM ON *THE UNDERSTANDING*

By Justin Kleinfeld

This chapter features an abridged version of the Röyksopp article in the August 2005 issue of *Remix* magazine.

The great thing about electronic dance music is that just about anybody can make it. All you really need is a computer and a bunch of reasonably priced music-production software programs. However, you can't put a price on sheer talent and inspiration—and the use of analog gear. Although the majority of the past decade's dance-music talent came mostly from the UK and the United States, it seems like things have been expanding on a global scale. Relatively young dance scenes in places such as Argentina, Australia, and Norway are injecting the industry with much-needed excitement and inspiration. In particular, Norway has been a place of great excitement during the past few years. This land once known for its black-metal bands is now home to acclaimed electronic acts such as Jaga Jazzist (aka Jaga), Frost, Kings of Convenience (whose Erlend Øye has also achieved solo success), and Ralph Myerz and the Jack Herren Band. However, no other Norwegian act has made as much of an impact on the global dance scene than the mighty Röyksopp.

Escaping from the friendly confines of Tromsø, Norway—far north in the land of the midnight sun—Röyksopp has become what many could consider dance music's most promising crossover act. The duo's debut release, *Melody A.M.* (Wall of Sound, 2001), was a commercial and critical success, selling more than a million copies worldwide while picking up stellar marks in top-notch publications around the world. Some even listed the album among the year's finest releases. It also didn't hurt that the twosome toured the world with Moby and Basement Jaxx. Like dance music's best-known acts (such as the Chemical Brothers and Underworld), it is hard to confine Röyksopp to any one specific sound. With *Melody A.M.*, Röyksopp presented a warm and fuzzy album that challenged listeners with a blend of electronic beats, house rhythms, smooth vocals, folktronica, and frosty Norwegian pop. This was the definitive sound of "cool," yet there was a certain isolated feel about the record that could come only from a place like Norway.

Finding success this quickly can be both a good and bad thing. On the upside, Röyksopp not only sold records like hotcakes, but also became a household name and gained tons of respect. On the bad side, early success brings enormous expectations—often unreasonable. Still, even though the pressure might be overwhelming for some acts, Röyksopp played it cooler than cool when it came time to record its follow-up LP, *The Understanding* (Astralwerks, 2005).

ANALOG HEAVEN

On a spring day at New York City's swank Soho Grand Hotel, Röyksopp's Torbjørn Brundtland and Svein Berge could pass for Calvin Klein models or members of the latest NYC retro band. Getting beyond the pretty faces, it becomes apparent that Brundtland and Berge are, in fact, the real deal. Not only is their knowledge of production nearly encyclopedic, but their studio is also packed with some of the most outrageous toys you'll be able to find anywhere in the world. These two collect keyboards like boys collect baseball cards. But much like a master chef, Röyksopp has a strict policy against revealing its studio setup. Brundtland and Berge prefer to keep their secret ingredients internal. However, they are willing to offer a look into some of the key elements that went into creating their stellar sophomore album, *The Understanding*.

Röyksopp's Torbjørn Brundtland (left) and Svein Berge. (Stian Andersen)

Most of today's respected producers and engineers rely heavily on software synthesizers such as Propellerhead Reason and Native Instruments Reaktor. However, Röyksopp's use of computer programs is merely a supplement to its vast array of analog equipment. That is also a reason that Röyksopp often creates music with such a warm and vintage sound—it is a style that simply cannot be attained solely by the use of the computer. "We use a multitude of sources, and we do not have a formula of how to approach it," Brundtland says. Röyksopp runs much of its media off of a DOS-based sequencer from Voyetra called Sequencer Plus. That software dinosaur was born in 1984, and the last update was in 1991. Although the guys still work with the program, they admit that supplementing the MIDI sequencer with hard-disk recording software—they've used Steinberg Cubase—gives them more creative options. "[Sequencer Plus] is semi-accurate but very easy," Berge says. "We like semi-accurate, though it's a bit of a nightmare with this sequencer because you can never replicate the original piece again. It will never be the same. That's why we use a bit of audio editing."

Brundtland and Berge have also learned that vintage pieces such as analog synths have minds of their own and can't always be counted on. So when sequencing a part with an old MIDI-capable synth, it's rarely going to play back the same way twice. "When you do something in audio, you know that your recording will be there," Brundtland says. "We have these synthesizers that have these 'charming diseases.' [Laughs.] That would be a nightmare if you are working on something, and then you come back the next day and it's a different symptom. If you combine this with digital recording, you'll have a winner."

As for the synthesizers with "charming diseases," Röyksopp did provide a peek into its racks. Chief among all synthesizers in attaining The Understanding's sound are the Korg MS-20 and MS-10 and the Roland Juno-106 (the latter of which has been used in every Röyksopp production in some way) and VP-330; also figuring in are several Roland RE-201 Space Echos and the Korg Synthe-Bass SB-100. "It looks like a little suitcase," Brundtland says of the Synthe-Bass. "It is a suitcase with the smallest keyboard in the world. It only has one sound—the most powerful bass sound you can imagine." Also used prominently on the recording are the Yamaha CS-80 and SY-1 (considered Yamaha's first synthesizer); the Korg PS-3000; and basically the entire Akai sampler series, including the S600 and S950.

With software production, Röyksopp used to run Cubase from an old Atari because of the "funky tightness" that the duo says it gave its beats. However, although Brundtland and Berge do use some audio-editing programs, they offer a word of caution against relying too much on software. "We find it a bit dangerous to use things like Propellerhead Reason, because they are designed to send you off in some [particular] direction," Brundtland says. "Some people find it strange the way we work, like, real eccentric. We just feel that, first and foremost, it is a process where you are not sent in any directions. You have to have your own core ideas in order to move anywhere. Secondly, if you are using unorthodox production methods like us, there is identity added into the music. That is something that's not so commonplace today."

SONGS UNDER THE INFLUENCE

For a record as complex as *The Understanding*, there are many different drawing points for inspiration. The first track on the album, "Triumphant," is a direct tribute to a lot of the progressive rock Brundtland and Berge were listening to at the time. "We just wanted to make a progressive track that could open the album and, at the same point, continue where *Melody A.M.* left off," Brundtland says. "We wanted to make something that had a build to it—a crescendo—in a raw and direct kind of way."

"Triumphant" was in part the product of both an ego and an accident. "It was made on the piano in a drunken haze," Brundtland says. "We were at a party, and there was a group of girls who didn't believe that we made our own music. Sometimes, people just don't believe that you do everything. They think that you are the spokesman and have other people do everything. And we were sort of forced to compose something on the fly to prove it to them. So right there at the party, we came up with these piano chords that floated downwards and upwards again. It ended up being the beginning of 'Triumphant.'"

Next, Röyksopp ran into a bit of a problem when it came to drum programming. The partners tried using a standard kit on the track, but it just didn't sound right on playback. A little searching led to the discovery of a very small and cheap traveler's drum kit. Initially unhappy with the sound of the kit, Brundtland and Berge eventually found the right microphone to make it sound good. They hit the drums as hard as they could to achieve the right sound, sampled them, and programmed them. They used the kit only on "Triumphant," selling it soon afterward.

If there was any doubt that Brundtland and Berge have it together with their production skills, then check out their newest technique: waveform manipulation. They open up an audio-editing program and then use the pencil tool to smooth out a waveform by drawing on it. Drawing over a flat waveform—silence—Röyksopp actually creates the amplitude and frequencies to craft a new sound. The technique was used most on "Beautiful Day Without You," which has a sound reminiscent of a muted guitar. In actuality, the noise came from the inside of a piano. Brundtland and Berge plucked the strings inside the piano and then changed the sound using the pencil tool.

VOCAL TESTING

One thing that immediately jumps out from *The Understanding* is the unique use of vocals, which play two very different roles for Röyksopp. More often than not, vocals are treated like an instrument with an equal part in the final mix; the track "Dead to the World" is a good example of that. However, when working with outstanding vocalists, the duo goes for a more traditional mix to let the vocals stand out. Mics range from a classic Neumann from the '60s to a few less-than-spectacular $100 mics—"49 Percent" is done entirely on a beat-up old Shure. "It looks very '70s Las Vegas–casino style, but it has a different sound," Berge says. "It's not as in-your-face as the Neumann mics."

A majority of the vocals are performed by Brundtland and Berge, but a few interesting guests are also onboard. For "Only This Moment," Norwegian singer Kate Havnevik makes the track truly come to life. Inspired by R&B, the song was originally conceived on an old, out-of-tune Russian piano in Tromsø, but Röyksopp eventually programmed an instrumental piece and began writing repetitive lyrics. The guys knew that the track was going to be a duet, so they began searching for a female vocalist. After hearing her music backstage at the New York Irving Plaza stop of the *Melody A.M.* tour, Brundtland and Berge immediately asked Havnevik to join them in their Bergen, Norway, studio for the recording.

They inserted their own vocals as a placeholder for the female voice, but before recording with Havnevik, they wanted to make sure that the part they wrote for her was going to work. Because their voices were recorded at about two octaves below Havnevik's singing voice, they used a Steinberg VST plug-in called UltraVoice to pitch-shift their own. "It takes the note and changes the texture," Berge says. "It's the same tone, but the formants are different."

"We sang the song and then pitched it up two octaves," Brundtland adds. "It sounded like something out of a cartoon, so we drew down the formants respective to two octaves so it sounded like a girl singing it. We actually tested if this melody and words were going to work."

On the finished "Only This Moment," Röyksopp insist that Havnevik's true voice is represented on the record. "She has this almost divine quality to her voice that is almost ancient singing," Brundtland says. "Everyone asks us what kind of plug-in we used to get her voice that clear—her voice is just like that. It has that quality. When you hit a note without any vibrato, you can get that programmed vibe without actually using it. She's probably one of the few singers we've worked with who sings the most in tune."

Yet another bright vocalist the duo brought in for *The Understanding* is Karin Dreijer, who sings the quirky yet mesmerizing, Björk-reminiscent "What Else Is There." Dreijer is the vocalist for Stockholm, Sweden–based brother-and-sister act the Knife, a charismatic electro-pop act best known for appearing in public sporting SARS masks (aesthetically, think Altern 8). "[The Knife] is from a different background, and we liked that," Brundtland says. "Some people don't want to be virtuosos; they just want to express. The track itself is quite subtle and hidden in some ways, but her voice is quite the opposite. It's a very open and direct expression. Without the vocals, it would be a very down and chilled-out effect."

UNEXPLAINABLE X-FACTOR

The progressive-rock influence on *The Understanding* comes full circle with the masterpiece "Alpha Male," a fierce monster of a rock breaks track sand-wiched between bookends of dreamy, tripped-out psych-rock. Productionwise, the song also stands as the album's most complex. A lot of analog-digital and acoustic-electric juxtaposed properties are layered into one mix, but no single element stands out among the rest. The meaty and over-the-top sound was achieved by not equalizing the mix. "We find that sometimes it has a lot more energy if you sort of mix it bad," Berge says. "You go into the opposite direction of the norm by making one piece, making it all sound like one."

Röyksopp has mastered the ability to add emotion and warmth to electronic music, and that is by no means an accident. Brundtland and Berge prefer to go for the inherent emotion and expression that comes from a spontaneous voice or an instrument rather than the technical perfection that comes with repeated takes. The recordings sound like near perfection even though they might have been technically flawed at one point. "It is about something x, which is undefined," Brundtland says. "Even if your vocal recording doesn't live up to the standards of a proper vocal recording but the expression in the recording is something that you want, always use that recording. Never do a retake for the sake of having it more correct technically. Filters are so strong these days that if there is something wrong with the recording, there are so many ways around it. You can filter it, and if there are pops on the recording, you can restore the waveforms. There is no reason why you cannot use even the crappiest recording."

22

Sharon Jones & the Dap-Kings

CREATING AN ANALOG R&B REVIVAL WITH *100 DAYS, 100 NIGHTS*

By Bill Murphy

This chapter features an abridged version of the Sharon Jones & the Dap-Kings article in the November 2007 issue of *Remix* magazine.

On the corner of Central Avenue and Troutman Street in the Bushwick section of Brooklyn, a busted-up van with its doors flung wide open is cranking Boogie Down Productions' "The Bridge Is Over," the jagged drum machine beats spilling out like shards into the oppressive summer heat. It's an off-kilter 20-year throwback to hip-hop's heyday, but meanwhile, just down the street, a tight-knit group of talented players is dialing back the clock even farther—to a time when sweet soul music ruled the airwaves.

Walking into Daptone Studios is pretty much like walking into any other row house in this rough-and-tumble neighborhood. But what makes this particular house so unique is the full-blown recording studio on the ground floor, a second studio and rehearsal space (with enormous Stocktronics plate reverb) in the basement, and the Daptone Records label offices upstairs. House producer, songwriter, bassist, and Daptone co-founder Gabriel "Bosco Mann" Roth has carefully stocked the studio with a treasure trove of vintage tape machines and analog gear, all in a sincere and dedicated effort to capture a *sound* that he feels has been lost from most recordings today.

"If you listen to Stax or some of the Motown records, or even Beatles records," he explains, his signature dark shades glinting in the late-afternoon light, "they all have this real sense of space to them. I think one of the biggest things is once you pull the drums and the bass out of the middle of a record, it just suddenly opens up that space. Those are the records that make sense to me."

Roth puts his production ideas to the test on *100 Days, 100 Nights* (Daptone, 2007), the third release from the label's flagship act, Sharon Jones & the Dap-Kings. For those not yet in the know, a quick breakdown: the Daps, part of a loose indie collective of musicians that includes Antibalas, the Budos Band, the Sugarman Three, and various other groups on the sweat-inducing Brooklyn soul-funk-afrobeat scene have quickly become a musical lightning rod. As of late, they've attracted the attention of such luminaries as Kanye West (who has sampled the group's wares), the Roots' Ahmir "?uestlove" Thompson (who invited the Daptone Horns to work on a monumental new album with Al Green), Amy Winehouse (as her touring band and on her album *Back to Black*), Mark Ronson (on his second solo album, *Version*), and surely more to come.

Meanwhile, lead singer Sharon Jones has taken off in her own right. Not only did Lou Reed recruit her to join him on his recent "Berlin" tour, but Jones is also slated to appear later this year in the Denzel Washington–directed film *The Great Debaters*.

Charismatic and high-energy to the core, Jones gets to show yet another side of her multifaceted range on *100 Days*, reaching down for some of the southern gospel roots that inspired her as a child.

"Keeping all those spirits alive—that's what a lot of gospel is about," Jones gushes, citing Sam Cooke and Otis Redding as some of her earliest influences and sounding musical even when she's just talking on the phone. "You have to

A Sharon Jones & the Dap-Kings recording session with Ian Hendrickson-Smith, Neal Sugarman, Fernando Velez, Bosco Mann, Homer Steinweiss, Binky Griptite, Sharon Jones, Cochmea Gastelum, Thomas Brenneck, and David Guy. (Jacob Blickenstaff)

listen to these old songs to keep them in your heart. And so I guess by doing that, we've made other people want to bring back that sound and that spirit. Keeping that spirit alive—I think that's what we're doing at Daptone, you know?"

INTO THE SLIPSTREAM

Take a listen to any Daptone production, and the feeling of having discovered a long-lost soul classic in an out-of-the-way used record store might start to creep over you. When Jones and the Daps released a raw and gritty 45 single covering Janet Jackson's "What Have You Done for Me Lately?" for their debut album, *Dap Dippin'* (Daptone, 2002), newbies were left wondering aloud, "So *that's* where Janet got that song?" It wasn't long before word got around that this was a living, breathing soul revue, recording and playing right here, right *now*.

"I first met Gabe when he was running [Daptone's predecessor] Desco Records," recalls Daptone co-founder Neal Sugarman, who doubles as tenor saxophonist for the Dap-Kings and front man for the Sugarman Three. "We had a mutual love for old soul records, so meeting him was amazing, because

167

he had the concept of recording that stuff. I'd been in the studio before, but for him to say, 'Let's record the Sugarman Three on four tracks' had me worried. And it turned out four was perfect, because it was definitely closer to how those records back in the day were made. That's not necessarily our complete motivation, though—we want the music to sound cool first."

While the first two Dap fests often skirted around early '70s funk in terms of the sound they emulated, *100 Days* conjures more of a late-'60s Stax or Muscle Shoals vibe, much of it thanks to Roth's insistence on recording only to tape, as well as his decision to hard-pan the different elements of the rhythm section—drums (Homer Steinweiss) to the left, bass (Roth) to the right, guitars (Tommy "TNT" Brenneck and Binky Griptite) split left and right, horns (Sugarman, Dave Guy on trumpet, and Ian Hendrickson-Smith on baritone sax) spread across one mic and panned right, and congas (Fernando "Bugaloo" Velez) to the right.

"I think what gives a mix character is that *imbalance*," Roth asserts. "When I was doing these mixes, I did try to bring things to the center, and every time I hit it I went back to hard-panning them. One thing about panning real hard like that—and panning consistently—is that it gives a consistent feel to the record, so that when you listen to it from top to bottom, even if you're not really conscious of it, you know that the drummer is sitting over there and the bass player is over there. So I kept it the same for the whole album."

THROAT CLEARING

With such a unique approach to mixing the instruments, Roth's biggest challenge was getting Jones' lead vocal to sit just right—especially because she and the band were cutting most of the songs live, with complete takes and very few overdubs. "Nobody's Baby," for example, with its infectious horns, steady backbeat, and ringing vibraphone line, leaves only just enough headroom for a completely dry vocal take, which Jones uses to advantage by pinning the needles to the max. She almost makes the mic feed back on the chorus, adding a sharpness of emotion that might not have been there if she'd backed off.

"The tape is definitely getting crushed all over the place on that song," Roth admits. "I'm a very strong supporter of never looking at a needle, man. I think something is too distorted when it *sounds* too distorted, so really a lot of things are crushing tape in that—even the drums have a rawness to them, but they're still very open and don't sound distorted or crunchy. They're raw because they're *played* raw and they're hitting the tape raw. That's what we were going for, and that's why I felt the dry vocal made more sense. I was trying to get Sharon's vocals to sit in a way that makes you really feel like she owns the track."

Jones herself would certainly agree. "When I heard the music on that," she recalls, "I was like, '*Aww*—that sounds like something Tina [Turner] would do,' and I came up with that [*sings*] '*Whoo-wee!* She was the queen of rock, and I imagine coming up there was nobody else out there who did stuff like her." With backing vocals on the song by the Dansettes, the nod to Ike and Tina Turner's Ikettes seems a foregone conclusion.

By far Roth's biggest vocal challenge, though, was the album's gospel-inflected closer, "Answer Me." The song was tracked almost in an impromptu manner, with Jones at the piano and singing with the band behind her. Although she wasn't as close to the mic as Roth would have preferred, the take was so inspiring that he knew it was a keeper.

"You can see it in the video [that accompanies *100 Days*]," he says. "Sharon was just amazing on that, but the biggest problem I had was the thickness of the snare drum in her vocal mic—low mids from 200 to 400 [Hz]. When I pulled them out, the drums sounded awesome, but her vocals were just too skinny. And, of course, every time I thickened up her vocals, the band sounded sloppy. So at the end of it, I compromised more toward making her vocals sound right, because really it's her song and she's singing it, and that's the most important thing. The band is kind of secondary, at least on that tune."

LIVE AND DANGEROUS

From the opening horn strains that kick off the mournful title track, it's clear that *100 Days* is a different breed from its predecessors. There's a rawness to Jones' voice, which seems more present and forceful than ever before, and it's clear that the Dap-Kings are going for more subtlety and complexity when it comes to their songwriting, their arrangements, and their sound.

After playing several hundred live shows around the world, they've acquired a tightness that simply can't be faked with any bag of studio tricks.

169

"Gabe and I both agreed that we needed to keep the arrangements far more open in the studio than you would on a live show," Sugarman explains, citing the fact that several of the songs on the album had been performed live on the European festival circuit before they were ever recorded. "Sometimes when you're playing live, with the need to keep the energy at such a high level, it's tough to let that go when you're in the studio with Sharon. After being on the road for six months and then going in to cut this record, the first time through we had to take a step back. It's a really different mindset."

That said, Roth is thoroughly amped about the final results and feels that this is the Dap-Kings' best effort yet. "I mean, this record is mostly live takes," he says. "The band was grooving much harder, and everybody was really locked in. I can really feel it from a producer's standpoint. Listening to the band play, you can feel that they've been on the road just gelling for a few years now. I think Neal said it; we might be a pretty humble bunch, but at the same time we know that collectively when we're playing together, we have something that a lot of bands don't have."

CONVERTING HOUSE TO STUDIO

It wasn't easy converting Daptone's Troutman Street house into a tape-ready recording studio, complete with a soundproofed vocal booth. First, Gabe Roth had to completely rewire the building for the expected increase in power usage—a job that he and Sharon Jones actually undertook themselves. (No injuries were reported.) Next, a wall had to be taken out and the second floor jacked up (using a car jack, no less) to expand the studio's "live room" and create some space for the Hammond B3 organ. Finally, Roth and company used old tires stuffed with cast-off clothing to build a "floating" isolation booth that's completely separated from the rest of the house—thus allowing Jones to wail away to her heart's content at any hour of the night.

"After I moved into the space a few years ago," Roth recalls, "Kenny Dope [Gonzales] chipped in and bought me this one-inch 16-track TEAC tape machine as prepayment for something he wanted me to do for him. That's the first 16-track I ever got. I did a bunch of records on that—the Antibalas' *Who Is This America?* album, the *Naturally* record with Sharon and the Budos Band records. And then just recently, I finally got that Ampex 8-track. So I've been through a lot of tape machines."

23

Smashing Pumpkins

THE SONIC DIARY OF *GISH, MELLON COLLIE AND THE INFINITE SADNESS, SIAMESE DREAM,* AND *ADORE*

By Richard Thomas

This chapter features an abridged version of the Billy Corgan article in the October 2008 issue of *EQ* magazine.

The collective dynamic among Billy Corgan, drummer Jimmy Chamberlin, guitarist James Iha, and bassist D'arcy Wretzky manifested itself in one of the most sonically diverse and emotionally complex bodies of work in rock history. As individuals, they affected one another just as much with their absence as they did with their presence. They are torchbearers of the Alternative Nation, and their music resonates with hippies, shoegazers, Goths, shredders, and e-music experimentalists alike.

The Smashing Pumpkins rose to prominence in the shadows of Wrigley Field on the North Side of Chicago in the late 1980s. Outfitted in cold-weather thrift store threads, they delivered punishing body blows of bombastic, cinematic love-rock, their pop appeal perfectly shaded behind a treacherous wall of sound. Destiny handed them an alternative pedigree, but their cover material—"Sookie

Sookie" (Steppenwolf), "The Joker" (Steve Miller Band), "Venus in Furs" (The Velvet Underground)—exposed deep roots that would inform their future recordings.

"The Pumpkins looked like they were from Mars," says producer Butch Vig. "To see how they looked and hear how they sounded was one of the reasons why people thought they were really special. If you ever saw that band play live, they could absolutely crush people."

GISH

The band had already released a self-produced single for "I am One" in the spring of 1990 before Corgan contacted Vig about producing a Sub Pop seven-inch for the song "Tristessa." The strength of that partnership prompted Vig to sign on for their full-length debut, which was to be recorded at Vig's Smart Studios in Madison, Wisconsin.

"Billy was very ambitious," Vig remembers. "He wanted to make everything sound amazing and see how far he could take it; really spend time on the production and the performances. For me that was a godsend, because I was used to doing records for all the indie labels and we only had budgets for three or four days."

The band loaded into the studio with a modest amount of gear, most of which can be seen in their first few videos. Onstage, the band's signature sound was rooted in Corgan and Iha's mid-'70s Strat/'87 Les Paul combination, but the recording centered around Corgan's rig: an early '80s Marshall JCM 800 2203, known as the "Soul Head," run through Marshall 1960A cabinets, all purchased off "some stoner guy" in Chicago for $800. The KT88 tubes in the JCM produce a round, creamy tone that, when used in conjunction with an ADA MP-1 tube preamp, produced the *Gish* tone. Using the low-input side of the JCM, Corgan would turn the master volume all the way up and then use the preamp's volume to make micro adjustments. A host of effects, from the Fender Blender to the Phase 100, were folded in for extra fuzz and sweep comb filtering. The bass parts were recorded with Wretzky's black Fender P-Bass—dubbed the "Rat Bass" for the scattering of white rat stickers all over the face—and played through a Trace Elliot AH300SM.

The band would collectively hash out the arrangements through exhaustive rehearsals, but when it came time to record, Corgan laid down the majority of the parts. This oft-talked-about procedure became a standard practice.

Billy Corgan. (Paul Bergen/Redferns/Getty Images)

"As good as D'arcy and James are, it was just going to sound better if Billy played it," says Vig. "I think it probably caused some friction, but it was something they dealt with and accepted in the band."

The drums were the one component of the Smashing Pumpkins that Corgan could not reproduce. A jazz drummer by trade, Jimmy Chamberlin paired swing and subtlety with a thunderous intensity reminiscent of legends like Keith Moon and John Bonham. Chamberlin has been a Yamaha endorsee

173

since 1993, but back then his setup was a Pearl DLX Series kit with a 16 x 22-inch kick and a Yamaha steel snare. As Chamberlin remembers, the kit was miked with Sennheiser 421s on the toms, Shure SM57s on the snare, an AKG D 112/Electro-Voice RE20 combo on the kick, and AKG C 414s as overheads.

At the time, Vig didn't have a tremendous amount of money to make significant cosmetic changes to Smart, but the shape of the studio's live room—all odd angles and no parallel walls—made for an incredible sound, inspiring the live feel of the band's studio performance. *Gish* was recorded onto a two-inch, 24-track Otari MX80, but few things were recorded through the studio's newly acquired 56-input customized Harrison console (Vig relied largely on outboard Summit and API preamps), though he says that Harrison's versatile EQ section and exceptional high- and low-pass filters made it easier to quickly carve out pockets in the mix for Corgan's unique tone. When all was said and done, *Gish* cost around $20,000 to produce and took just over 30 days to record.

"For me that was the equivalent of making a Steely Dan record," says Vig, who, two months after wrapping production on *Gish*, traveled to Los Angeles to record Nirvana's *Nevermind*. "Having that luxury to spend hours on a guitar tone or tuning the drums or working on harmonies and textural things . . . I was over the moon to think I had found a comrade-in-arms who wanted to push me, and who really wanted me to push him."

But for all its sonic ambition, *Gish* couldn't hold a candle to what came next.

SIAMESE DREAM

After touring behind their first record, Butch Vig and the Pumpkins spent five months recording their follow-up, *Siamese Dream*, working 14-hour days, six days a week. And toward the end of the recording process, after tours had been booked and a release date established, they worked a full seven days. Alan Moulder, whose history includes dense guitar bands such as Ride and My Bloody Valentine, was asked to mix. He booked two weeks at Rumbo Studios in Los Angeles. The first song took four days. The entire album took 36.

"When we set out to make *Siamese Dream*, we wanted to go way, way over the top," explains Vig. "We didn't care if anybody thought it was overproduced."

Tack a zero onto the *Gish* tab and you come close to matching *Siamese*

Dream's total cost. Through it all, the tenacity of the group's work ethic was eclipsed only by the pressure to succeed. Along the way, Iha and Wretzky ended their relationship, Chamberlin developed what would become an acute substance abuse problem, and Corgan's creative turmoil pushed him to the point of near suicide. His songwriting, as if voiced by a choleric yet optimistic teenager well beyond his years, hinged on defiance, acceptance, family, and alienation. Of the "hundreds of dumb riffs" Corgan says that they would play, the ones that stuck not only sounded good, they felt good to play.

"I'm a person who tends not to repeat technique, which I guess is kind of suicidal in a way," says Corgan. "Most people look at a recording career as a series of conclusions. I've always treated my recording career more like a journey. I think when any artist gets into a comfortable set of choices, that's where the death of creativity lies."

Months of recording meant lots of time for experimentation and tweaking. To help minimize distractions, Vig and the Pumpkins checked into Triclops Studios in Marietta, Georgia, a cozy space that allowed the band a sort of temporary respite. Unlike Smart, Triclops' '70s-style room had high, woody ceilings that made for a modest decay. Vig brought along his API Lunchbox loaded with modular pres for the bass and a few guitar overdubs, but most of the instrumentation was run through the studio's Neve console onto Studer A800s. Corgan's "Soul Head" and Marshall cabinet were still in effect, but he no longer used the MP-1. Instead, Corgan achieved *Siamese Dream*'s highly stylized tone with a litany of DOD pedals and a '70s-era, silver-faced Big Muff Pi. As the guitar he'd used on *Gish* had been stolen, his go-to guitars became '57 Eric Clapton reissue Strats with Lace Sensor pickups.

"We found a secret weapon on that record," says Vig. "A little preamp in a pedal-steel guitar. It wasn't built for a loud guitar. It was built for a low output on a pedal steel, so it had this super high-end white-noise gain that gave the guitar this sonic-jet sound." That pedal-steel preamp—coupled with an old-school tape flanging created by physically speeding up and slowing down the reel by hand—is the sound behind Corgan's otherworldly solo on "Cherub Rock." "Quiet" features hard-panned left and right guitars running through the Big Muff with the tone turned all the way down, while the howling break in the chorus to "Mayonnaise" is nothing but pure feedback created by Corgan's $60 pawn shop "Mayonnaise Guitar."

But Corgan's gear was only part of the equation. The endless overdubs—at least 40 in "Soma"—are well documented, but Vig says that proper mic configuration is what allowed the parts to congeal. Vig's miking technique was as follows: Corgan would crank up his amp to full gain and then set the guitar down. After boosting the headphones send on all the mics, Vig entered the room to move around the mics, using the phase-shifting hiss from Corgan's guitar echo as his guide. According to Vig, an AKG C 414 produced the widest spectrum of sound, a Sennheiser 421 accented the midrange, and ribbon mics were used to obtain a smoother sound with quick, yet mellow, transients.

"You can't have 40 guitars that are all full range," says Vig. "There have to be places for them to fit. You could have low-midrange, or you could have everything scooped out with a high-pass that's cut at 300 or 400kHz."

The miking tactic seemed almost drumlike, which, given Vig's musical expertise, is a fair assumption. "Maybe from me being a drummer, that's an aesthetic I brought to the table that I didn't even really understand at the time," he says.

The army of guitar signals would later make vocal tracking a strenuous procedure for Corgan. Vig didn't much care for the mid-range in Corgan's voice, so to soften that particular timbre he used a Shure SM7 (generally regarded as a more "open"-sounding mic when its rolloff and boost features are engaged simultaneously) through an API preamp and a Summit TLA-100 Tube Limiter, all fed back into Corgan's headphones. Like everything else, vocal takes were abundant, with Corgan sometimes singing for eight hours at a time to make sure his tracks were pitch perfect.

"My voice is really hard to record," says Corgan, smiling. "It's hard to record, it's hard to monitor, and it's hard to mix. I'm Irish—I'm meant to sing sad ballads! My voice isn't really meant for rock, and I'm pretty sure many people out there would agree with me."

MELLON COLLIE AND THE INFINITE SADNESS

Before a single note was recorded, Corgan knew he wanted the next release to be a double album. Flood and Alan Moulder, friends since their early days at the prestigious Trident Studios in London, were tapped to co-produce. The band began rehearsing at Pumpkinland, their Chicago recording space, and Billy began funneling cassette demos to Flood for review. Roughly two-thirds of *Mellon Collie and the Infinite Sadness* was tracked at Pumpkinland on an Otari MTR-90 MKII, while the remaining portion was tracked at the Chicago Recording Company on Studer A820s.

"I love recording at 15 ips NAB, but with Dolby SR, because it just adds a whole different dimension to the sound," says Flood. "Apart from the obvious benefits of Dolby, if you tweak the Dolby unit really, really well, it's a bit like adding an Aphex and a dbx sub-harmonic bass enhancer on every channel. Also, the way that tape changes the sound or modifies the sound, 15 ips is technically not correct, but I find it to be so musical, particularly on the bottom end. This was very much a conscious decision, and very much a part of the album's sound."

Another conscious decision was to change up the manner in which the group recorded. In the past, the band had used only one room to track, which of course meant only one thing could be going on at a time. Hours spent waiting for one person to finish up their part led to frustration. For *Mellon Collie*, Flood would generally work with Corgan in the A room on the Otari and an MCI board, while Moulder worked with Wretzky and Iha in the B room on a Pro Tools rig slaved to both TASCAM DA-88 digital recorders and two-inch tape. The combination of analog and digital opened up a world of recording possibilities and played to the creative strengths of *Mellon Collie*'s adventurous spirit. A track like "Thru the Eyes of Ruby," which contains approximately 70 guitar tracks, would have been nearly impossible to do with tape alone. Likewise, "Porcelina of the Vast Oceans" contains roughly six sections that were all recorded at different times with different instrument and microphone configurations and then fused together—another beneficial by-product of editing in Pro Tools.

Guitar and amplification choices were the key differences between *Siamese* and *Mellon Collie*. For the bass, Wretzky switched up from the P-Bass to a '60s-era Fender Jazz Bass reissue with Ampeg and Mesa Boogie amps. For Corgan, what sounded great about the *Siamese* fuzz pedal setup in the studio made it sound horrible live. He still had his Marshall 1960A cabinets, but Corgan shifted to a Mesa Boogie Strategy 500 and a Marshall JMP-1 preamp (Corgan also notes that he used an Alesis 3630 to drive extra gain into a Marshall). As the ultimate goal for *Mellon Collie* was to capture the band's live, unbridled sound, Billy largely used this touring rig to record.

"Flood felt like the band he would see live wasn't really captured on record," says Corgan. "So a lot of Mellon Collie was tracked by the band at deafening volumes. I mean deafening. There was so much SPL in the room that it was physically uncomfortable. Your ears, your emotional resistance, would wear down."

Flood also discovered that Corgan was a much better singer pitchwise when he didn't use headphones, so he switched Corgan up to a Shure SM58 and had him sing in front of open speakers.

"My experience with U2 taught me that a lot of things you'd expect to become problematic with monitors in the room aren't, and by careful use of screening, by positioning the monitors and what you put in the monitors, you can actually get a lot of benefits," says Flood. "For instance, Jimmy used to love having the kick drum and a bit of snare going through his wedges, which were directly behind him. So if you've got a kit that's lacking a bit of bottom end, you pump the kick and the snare through the wedges and you start to tweak them to get extra weight. We also developed this system whereby we had what was called 'rehearsal mode' and 'tape mode.' In rehearsal mode, everybody was on the floor, the amps were blaring, and you wouldn't have to worry about spills. We had the speakers inside these big coffin flight cases in the back of the room and miked them close up, then miked them about six feet away. Then we'd close the lid. When you were tracking in tape mode, everybody could flick over at the flick of a footswitch and their amps would be quietly purring away in the corner. When you'd give a little bit back to them in their own respective monitors, automatically the sound of the room cut right back and you'd get the vibe of four people playing on top of each other."

For the drums, Chamberlin's core *Mellon Collie* kit was a Yamaha Maple Custom with a 16 x 22–inch kick, a 22-inch ride, 18-inch and 19-inch Zildjian A Custom crashes, 22-inch swish knockers, and 10-inch and 15-inch fast crashes. Because of his big-band background, he frequently changed out his snares, building his kit around the snare and the ride as opposed to the kick. The familiar drumrolls all throughout "Tonight, Tonight" can be attributed to Jimmy's classic $5^{1}/_{2}$ x 14–inch Ludwig Supra-Phonic.

"From there I go to microphones as far as how I want the drums to sit dimensionally in the track," Chamberlin informs. "If I want the drums up front and aggressive, I'll use a lot of AKG C 414s so they sit in front of things dimensionally.

If I want the drums to sit in a rhythm section configuration, I'll lean back towards the 414s and maybe some Shure SM98s. Then maybe go for Shure 12As on the bigger drums."

Mellon Collie debuted at number one on the *Billboard* 200 when it was released in October of 1995. Less than a year later it had crested $6 million in sales, and it was later nominated for seven Grammys. It was the most powerful statement the Smashing Pumpkins had made to date. Unfortunately, much-publicized events that took place during the group's 1996 tour produced an equally powerful effect.

ADORE

Death, divorce, and harsh life realizations "that have only recently probably finished playing out," says Corgan, clouded the two years after *Mellon Collie*'s release. By the time Corgan saddled down to write *Adore*, Iha was focusing on his solo album (*Let It Come Down*), Wretzky was a sporadic presence, and Chamberlin was out of the band. Filter's Matt Walker was brought in to replace Chamberlin for the remainder of their tour, but the hole left by the original drummer's absence would significantly impact the creation of the new record.

"I thought I was going to do this really different album," says Corgan. "So, typical me, I didn't use any of my gear. Like, any. I went out and bought new guitars and strange amps—a Fender Blackface and a Selmer combo, I think. Most of my memories with *Adore* have more to do with programming."

The success of "Eye," an industrial hip-hop crossover track that appeared on the soundtrack to David Lynch's *Lost Highway*, instilled a much-needed confidence in Corgan. It was basic electronic production, but it proved to him that he could press on with more sophisticated fare. Corgan hooked up with Brad Wood (Liz Phair, Placebo) and began recording with the band in Chicago during the summer of 1997. Never one to do anything the easy way, Corgan decided to load into a new studio nearly every week. It was catch-as-catch-can recording. If something wasn't working in a new surrounding or couldn't get set up in time, it wasn't used.

"He was trying to create a different environment, quickly and geographically, and trying to avoid certain things that happen when a band settles into a studio," says Bjorn Thorsrud, who has engineered every Pumpkins record since *Adore*.

Material was recorded on a mix of analog and digital formats. Already familiar with Studio Vision Pro for MIDI and audio editing, Corgan used Re-Cycle to chop up and manipulate drum loops. A Kurzweil K2500 and an Alesis HR-16—the same drum machine used to create the beat for "1979"—were also used for additional rhythmic elements and sequences. Wood's classic EMS VCS3 "Putney" was featured prominently on "Ava Adore." As it was with *Mellon Collie*, experimentation was paramount. Boxes would show up in the post every other day, each one containing a new sample library, vintage synth, or rack module gobbled up from eBay or plucked from the pages of *Keyboard* magazine. Still, the pieces weren't fitting together and, eventually, Corgan and Wood parted ways.

"It was a total crapshoot," says Corgan, who soon relocated to L.A. to refocus his energy. "I was out of depth. There was no process, there was no system, and there was no go-to piece of gear. There was nothing. I learned a tremendous amount, but I couldn't tell you what the hell I did."

Billy reached out to Nitzer Ebb's Bon Harris, who contributed additional programming and sound design with the aid of his Nord Modular, Oberheim Xpander, and massive Roland System 100M. But the songs didn't come into full focus until Corgan reconnected with Flood, whose experience with bands like Depeche Mode and Nine Inch Nails made him the perfect candidate to help actualize *Adore*'s hybrid vision.

The dissonance was evident to Flood upon arrival. The mix of disparate Pro Tools sessions and one-inch tape created a textured canvas that proved difficult to homogenize, and the tension between band members was palpable. The band worked at Sunset Sound until reoccurring technical difficulties with the Neve console forced them to complete the project at the Village Recorder in Santa Monica. To further *Adore*'s maudlin, Goth-tech spirit, Corgan assumed a Max Schreck–like persona, emphasizing his shaved head with lighting and makeup and donning long, flowing garb that accented his 6-foot 4-inch frame.

"I did go around and proclaim rock to be dead," Corgan says, laughing, "which was probably the stupidest thing I ever did. I was in my *Adore* personality saying *Adore*-personality things like, 'F**k the electric guitar!' And of course 12 months later I'm playing [follow-up *Machina/The Machines of God*s] 'The Everlasting Gaze.'"

24

Stereolab

MARGERINE ECLIPSE'S DUAL APPROACH
TO ARRANGING AND MIXING

By Christine Hsieh

This chapter appeared in the February 2004 issue of
Remix magazine.

Once upon a time, Tim Gane was a fresh-faced youth
whose musical aspirations included a collaboration with
peers in the basements of uppity music stores. Rather
than drag an unwilling girlfriend with him into the bowels
of the local guitar emporium to impress her with ama-
teurish tinkering on various high-end guitars, Gane would
assemble a group of friends for impromptu jam sessions,
much to the horror of those in attendance. "What we
would do was turn up randomly at music stores and start
playing the guitar, whatever Led Zeppelin riffs," Gane
says. "Someone would pick up a bass, and someone
would start tapping away on the drums, and all of a sudden, at a set signal, we'd all burst into a song. It sounded
good on paper, but it never amounted to anything."

Some might say that's a good thing, as Gane eventually directed his renegade approach toward bigger
and better things: Stereolab, his musical baby of the
past 13 years, is the revered Channel-crossing indie
troupe whose laid-back pop, retro attitude and elec-

tronic noodling has sent scores of imitators to the studio to churn out pallid versions of the band's distinctively cool, disarmingly unpretentious, and innovative take on modern music. Combining warm, dreamy vocals with rolling rhythms and a smattering of analog-synth effects, Stereolab's latest full-length effort, *Margerine Eclipse* (Elektra, 2003), captures the band's easy charm and spreads it easily across 50-odd minutes of straightforward pop tunes laced with space-age, minimal disco interludes; retro garage-rock riffs; downbeat cocktail-lounge ambience; and stutter-stepped tempos.

A NEW CHAPTER

Produced and mixed with Fulton Dingley, who worked with Stereolab on *Cobra* and *Phases Group Play Voltage in the Milky Night* (Elektra, 1999), *Margerine Eclipse* is an album of firsts. Recorded this past spring in the band's brand-new studio in France, *Eclipse* sees the group adjusting to surroundings that are markedly different from the environs of John McEntire (of Tortoise) and Jim O'Rourke, the Chicago-based producers who've collaborated with the group since its career-defining album, *Emperor Tomato Ketchup* (Elektra, 1996). Stereolab's studio, dubbed Instant O, took 10 months to build but now comfortably houses a good deal of equipment and, according to Gane, an inordinate amount of speakers that he's collected throughout the years.

"It was incredibly stressful to put the studio together in time for the recording," says Laetitia Sadier, the group's vocalist. "And, of course, it was late. It's completely luxurious to have your own studio. But at the same time, a lot of things break down, so you have to find someone to fix it. I don't know anything about how to maintain the studio. It's the job of experts. There are few people who really know, and I know nothing, so it's a bit uncomfortable in that sense. [But] it's really an incredible feeling to just walk 10 meters and be able to record music or rehearse or play loud. It's really great."

This album is also the first that the group has released since the death of keyboardist/vocalist Mary Hansen in December 2002. "The writing process is quite lonely and quite detached—it's always a challenge," Sadier says, speaking in her characteristically subdued manner from her home in France. Sadier, who with Gane forms the creative core of the group, pauses for a second as

Stereolab: Tim Gane, Laetitia Sadier, Dominic Jeffery, and Simon Johns. (Steve Double)

words catch in her throat: "What I really feel is, when I'm onstage and she's not there, that's where I think she will be extremely missed.

"It's dramatic when it comes to writing lyrics," Sadier continues after another pause. "It still feels like a miracle when we have written something. It's not something I work at all year-round and learn to master. It's still really spontaneous. It's not something that's controlled and mastered."

Spontaneity is, after all, Stereolab's calling card during studio sessions. The band does not rehearse beforehand, choosing to build a loose musical structure around Gane's initial sketches and then add Sadier's lyrics and vocals. Gane prefers to cart his ideas to the studio on a basic cassette tape.

Often, he simply records a few bits and pieces strummed on his trusty Ricken-backer 330 guitar before letting the other band members spin off on them in a sort of happy free-for-all. "It's difficult to know who thought of what, actually, because it's all happening at a hectic pace at that certain moment of creativ-ity when you're trying to think of a creative way around a problem," concedes drummer Andy Ramsay. "It goes really quickly, and at the end of it, you're not sure who actually said what, because it can be, at times, quite heated as you're all discussing what you're doing. Sometimes, something will be purely Fully's idea or purely Tim's idea or purely mine, but at the end of it, I can't remember who did what and where, really."

IT TAKES TWO

Given the ease with which the band works in a somewhat frenzied environment, Gane took the *Margerine Eclipse* sessions one step further by laying down an unusual rule: The band had to record everything twice. "On this particular re-cord, about a week before we actually started recording it, I just had a thought," Gane reveals. "I thought, 'Why don't you do two totally separate mixes of the songs, two separate arrangements of the songs, and put one on one speaker and the other arrangement on the other speaker? And then you just put them together and see what they sound like.' In my mind, I imagined it to sound a bit like an early Van Dyke Parks record. It's got that sort of chaotic sound."

Gane suspected that the other band members might be a tad skeptical about the technical difficulties of the idea, not to mention the additional work. But he persisted. "You just get gripped by an idea that you think is quite inter-esting or quite exciting," Gane says. "I know that I can write songs, to a certain level, that are interesting enough, but that is only the first stage. Then it's like trying to explore every possibility of what that can expand to. Sometimes it's fatiguing to always have some sort of concept or some kind of game or trick. The very process of recording [*Margerine Eclipse*] dictated how it was going to sound. It was probably more work, certainly not quicker than what we've done before, but I quite liked that."

Ramsay, though, was hesitant at first. "When initially we heard Tim's idea that we were going to do a separate take on either side, I was slightly horrified," he says with a chuckle. "I was like, 'Oh, my God, what's my drumming going to sound like here?'" For a drummer with a penchant for experimenting with beats and patterns, the pressure to uphold strict, rigid timing might infringe on the creative aspect of the recording process. Fortunately for Stereolab, Digidesign Pro Tools' Beat Detective ended up saving the group a great deal of headache. "For Tim's idea to work, I had to be really tight on the two kits, which is nearly impossible to do," Ramsay says. "Because we had two bass drums playing on each side, they'd have to sound just slightly skewed to really cloud up the low end of the mix. The beauty of Beat Detective is, you can kind of go for it for a bit, and it doesn't matter about your timing so much. So you can play a bit wildly and use Beat Detective to bring you back in time."

With Beat Detective on its side, Stereolab was able to keep a firm grip on the live instrumentation present in the album; indeed, most of the drumming is Ramsay's, with just a Roland TR-77 to fill in the gaps. "We used two drum kits and recorded them in mono: We used one kit on one side and the other kit on the other side," Ramsay says. "I think it's pretty consistent throughout the record. They're similar kits, but I thought about how to make them sound really different. We did the old tricks, like hanging blankets over snares and stuff, and I think we worked through quite a few of Laetitia's tea towels, playing drums on them. All the stuff that sounds like it could be programmed out of an 808 or with a sequencer is all live drums!

"A lot of the credit with that goes to Fulton Dingley. He used mics where I never use them or where I'd never thought to use them before. For instance, he'd use ribbon microphones in the bass drum, and that worked really well. People are normally used to hearing a sort of dynamic microphone, maybe with a condenser outside of it, on a bass drum, but putting a ribbon in it brings a different world of sounds to the table. The sounds tend to have more air in them; they seem to breathe better. You could just have a ribbon mic in front of the drums, and if you compressed it, it would sound almost as good as a whole drum kit."

Ramsay, Gane, and Dingley were constantly thinking of ways to alter their existing equipment's function. "One of the things we would do is record the drums while using the varispeed on the tape machine," Ramsay says. "Or on

Pro Tools, it's got a varispeed just like a two-inch tape machine. So the track would be speeding up and slowing down as I was drumming, which is actually impossible to do, but you can vaguely stay in time with it, even as they're quite big movements in speed. And then you use Beat Detective to put it back in time. But then you have this natural pitch shifting going on in the drums."

BACK IN BRASS

Beyond the drum work that the band put in, organs and synths also posed new challenges. Take, for instance, "Need to Be," a track with a dense mixture of keyboard lines weaving in and out. "It opens with a Roland C-80 digital harpsichord playing three sets of chord inversions and a Vox Continental playing chord pads," Gane says. "The Moog Opus 3 plays the lead line. Into the song proper, a Farfisa Compact Duo Organ is added to the Vox Continental on the left, which is now put through a slap delay. Added to this is a Roland Celeste on the right and a Fender Rhodes on the left."

The various burbles and bleeps punctuating the tune are created by the Studio Electronics ATC-1. "It's a great MIDI-based digital synth," Gane says rapturously. "We wanted to obtain a brasslike timbre with this sound. We knew that we wouldn't have brass or strings, and we didn't want them, either. We could have gone out of our way and done it, but I had the idea of keeping everything limited and using what we had of our own gear—no hired gear, no hired players or anything like that. But I still loved the idea of what brass does, the kind of counterpoints it can do rhythmically in notes and chords; it's their ability to transform the music and have that really beautiful sound. We wanted to explore what it could do and perhaps use a similar timbre and sound, but using other things. And what do you know, it just kind of came out of a synthesizer!"

Another instance in which layering instruments created unexpected, unusual results is the bouncy dance tune "Margerine Melodie." "The bass drum is mixed with backward reverb effect, then filtered and blended together to give the finished sound," Gane says of the warm, spongy kick underpinning the song. "The organ on the right side is a Vox Continental put through an EMS vocoder and vocoded with some triggered drum delays. A second phased and vocoded organ appears a little later. The choirlike reverbed organ that comes in and out is the Moog Opus 3 fed through a delay pedal. All bleeps and bloops are again from the ATC-1 trying to create brass parts."

MUSICAL MELD

Taking full advantage of the resources available to the band is really what made this Stereolab album a bit different from the others. "Often, we'd just try something, not knowing what we're going for," Gane says. "It's more a question of knowing what you don't like."

Working outside of a commercial studio, the band members had to make do with what they had. "With Laetitia, we used two microphones all the time: a Brauner VM1 valve mic and a Sony C48 condenser mic," Dingley says. "We had two microphones going, and we blended the two. One microphone basically had a lack of middle. It had a nice soft top, but because it was weak on the bottom end, it had no real presence. And one microphone had the full range, but the top end wasn't quite as nice, and the bottom wasn't quite as nice, but the middle had a presence. So I rolled the top off of one, the bottom off the other, and it became cohesive, like one microphone."

In the end, integrating the separate takes to sound cohesive, without one overpowering the other, was left primarily to Dingley. In the process of mixing and engineering the album, he had to rely on musical instinct and gut feeling rather than stick to any hard-and-fast rules. "The main places where we had problems were with bottom end," he explains. "It took a lot of patience to work it down until they complemented each other. Often, one drum kit would be brighter, but the other would have more substance to it, so it was a matter of making them sound like one drum.

"For me, generally, it's a sonic sensation," he adds. "When you're blending sounds, you've got to know exactly the sound you want or the sensation you want to feel. And you blend and you tinker until you get that sensation. I listened to the tracks a lot in mono—I know they're very stereo—but I did it to make sure they worked in mono. It's a good way to balance tracks properly. Mono has a great direction, and it softens sounds, as well. What I was trying to do when listening to the tracks in mono was make sure the sounds meshed with each other. I found it easier to listen to them properly in mono separately."

WHAT'S IN A NAME?

After 13 years in the biz, what characterizes Gane and his cohorts is their penchant for unusual combinations, not to mention their tireless devotion to achieving them. In a way, it's slightly difficult to explain exactly what their appeal is, and it's even harder to pin down their recording and production formula. It could just be that it's all in the name: *Margerine Eclipse* is a title that Gane first started to play with while on holiday in Italy, and as one might suspect from Stereolab, it doesn't really mean anything. Still, the genesis of the name is particularly relevant to the group's recording strategy. "I saw a name that said 'Marguerite' or something like that, but I thought it said 'Margerine,'" Gane remembers with a laugh. "I thought it was quite an interesting word, and it made me look at it kind of new. Gradually, weeks went by, and we started thinking about combinations of words that sound interesting; somehow, the word *eclipse* popped into my head. It just conjures up a sort of imagery in my mind that connects itself to the music in a way.

"The music seems to stick itself to the name, and you can never get it apart," Gane continues. "I just like juxtapositions. I like words that are flung together. I used to have this game that I liked playing, which was to make up a sentence that no one has ever said in the history of words before. I always thought that was a great moment—there were just so many disjointed words that you could not possibly put together, and I just find that really interesting."

That is an apt correlation, then, to the way that Stereolab's music is constructed. "I think the most interesting things are when you put the wrong mic onto something," Gane says. "Often, real character and things occur when you just sort of move things around to get things right. On that move from points A and B, there's this point where you say, 'Stop that—that's great.' I think it's important to follow those things that happen. It's not just chance; it's your ear or something in your unconscious that will pick up something that's the right thing to do. Because we don't rehearse as a band, we don't rehearse the songs; we're freer to try anything, really. It's a cross between sort of messing about in the studio and opening up new doorways or pathways where we can enter into and mix the ideas we have in a slightly more known territory."

25

Tegan and Sara

TACKLING 50 SONGS AND HUNDREDS OF LIVE TAKES FOR *SAINTHOOD*

By Kylee Swenson Gordon

This chapter features an abridged version of the Tegan and Sara article in the December 2009 issue of EQ magazine.

For identical twin sisters who have recorded and toured together over the past 10-plus years, Tegan and Sara live awfully far apart. Tegan resides in Vancouver, and Sara is more than 2,000 miles away in Montreal. But it doesn't hold them back.

Although collaboration wasn't always a part of the duo's process, for 2004's *So Jealous*, which spawned the indie hit "Walking with a Ghost," and 2007's *The Con*, featuring the single "Back in Your Head," Tegan and Sara exchanged ideas online. While working on their sixth album, *Sainthood* [Sire/Vapor/Warner Bros.], the twins came together even more, building on each other's ideas via their respective Pro Tools rigs and writing together in person. Tegan also worked with AFI's Hunter Burgan for a few tracks. And in their free time, the sisters collaborated with trance superstar Tiësto on "Feel It in My Bones," from his latest album, *Kaleidoscope*.

Tegan and Sara recorded *Sainthood* at L.A.'s Sound City and Seattle's Two Sticks with producer/engineer Howard Redekopp (the New Pornographers, You Say Party! We Say Die!), guitarist Edward "Ted" Gowans, and one half of Death Cab for Cutie: multi-instrumentalist/producer Chris Walla (who played bass on *Sainthood*) and drummer Jason McGerr. Here, Tegan Quin, Walla, and Redekopp discuss whittling down 50 songs, recording live, doing hours upon hours of takes, and sonic economy.

You had *a lot* of songs to choose from for *Sainthood*. How did you pick the final 13?

Quin: We submitted 50 songs, and a lot of them I wrote in two hours and never went back to again. There was one I wrote when we were in New Orleans that Chris Walla picked on his list of potential songs, and Sara *hated* it. We had a huge fight about it. It's so sad, because one, the way other people perceive your music can really affect how you feel about it. And two, sometimes I write so much that I don't spend the time to complete or rip apart a song and start again. Maybe there is something in that song that if I went back and redid it, it might be the song that changes our band's course in history. But I would rather not go through the rest of my life playing a song with Sara that she doesn't like.

Walla: In a batch of 50 Tegan and Sara demos, there are countless numbers of albums. You can configure those 50 songs in any combination and have 50 completely different listening and emotional experiences. There gets to be real option anxiety at a point. But we set half of them on fire and let them go. And with the [remaining] 23, we just ended up gravitating to whatever worked. It's a beautiful thing to be able to do, because you stop chasing stuff that's not coming together. If we only had 12 songs, then you'd have to make them all go.

Why did you decide to record the bulk of *Sainthood* live? What was the process?

Walla: Modern recording can be so modular and piece-by-piece. There are so many awesome records being made that way, but if you have the time and opportunity to set up and cut something live that has a really organic foundation to it, it seems like it would be crazy not to try and do it.

Quin: When we walked into Sound City, Ted, Sara, and I were playing

Sara Quin and Ted Gowans at Sound City in Los Angeles. (Courtesy Warner Bros.)

with this rhythm section [Walla and McGerr] that hadn't played the songs yet. They're so amazing that magic happened right away, but we spent between 35 and 50 takes honing every little detail. Then there would be that magical take where we would all like laugh and be like, "That was it!"

But it was freaking exhausting to spend the first five hours a day getting sounds and setting up microphones, play until 8 o'clock at night, and then have Howard be like, "Okay, this is take 44. What do you think of this one?" We'd be like, "Oh, *God*." It was just insane when you think of how much we played the songs, and then you'd have to go to bed for six hours and come back and do it all again.

191

Redekopp: The first half of the 40, 50 takes would sound radically different than the second half, because people were still changing things. The song structure, melodies, and chords were there, but it'd be like, "You know what? I'm not going to play guitar. I'm going to play keyboard." And Chris would be trying different basses, and Jason would be like, "I don't think this part works with this drum."

The concept was to just keep hitting tape [Studer A827 two-inch with Dolby SR], and once everyone out on the floor came in and agreed that these were the batch of takes that we liked, we would transfer those into digital [Apple Logic]. Invariably at the end of five, six, seven days, we had to start reusing tape, but by then we'd already transferred all the keeper takes. Some songs I kept maybe four takes, and other songs we kept eight just as insurance. But the principal bed track was coming from one or two takes. And I can count on my hands and toes how many notes actually physically got moved in time on a computer. There's comping involved, but that's really just choosing between takes that worked and takes that didn't work as well.

What were the main instruments used?

Quin: Chris has a crazy collection of Rickenbackers, and Sara is a huge Gretsch fan, so there was a smorgasbord of Rickenbackers and Gretsches. Sara has a couple of Malcolm Youngs, and Chris and I have Duo Jets. There are a few Les Paul and SG moments. We didn't really play acoustic guitar very often on this record. I think the acoustic is the lead instrument on "Arrow," and you can't even really tell. But we both have Art & Lutherie acoustics and a good assortment of Gibson Blues Kings.

Walla: Jesse Quitslund was the Death Cab guitar tech for about three years, and he built amps for Ben [Gibbard], me, and Jason, who owns Two Sticks. We played mostly Jesse's amps—they're small and break up at a really reasonable volume—but we also used my '64 [Fender] Tremolux.

For bass, it was an SVT Classic head and an 8 x 10 cab with one of the ZVex boost pedals for some of it. For the most part, I played a '77 [Fender] P Bass that I love. There are a couple songs that are an old '70 or '71 Fender Mustang. And then there are two songs that are an Epiphone Jack Casady, which is a disaster, but it sounds really cool. It's such a bad best friend, but if you put flatwounds on it, it sounds amazing.

Jason's got so many goddamn drum kits, I can't even keep them straight. But he's a Ludwig devotee through and through. Snare drum–wise, we bounced around between a Ludwig Black Beauty reissue and a couple old Acrolites. The other one that we leaned on a bunch is a WFL kit, which is a pre-Ludwig company. It's just huge and warm and matched the room at Sound City so beautifully.

Redekopp: Jason McGerr brought at least 20 snare drums, three or four full kit setups, and a massive array of cymbals. It was all these different textures: "Hi-hats? You want the 16-inch? The stainless steel?" We'd be 20 takes deep, and all of a sudden one of us would go, "That hi-hat is bugging me." And so he'd change it out. And then I'd be like, "Actually, that really works, but we shouldn't be using the [Neumann] KM 84 anymore. Let's put the SM7 back on the hat."

And there were some tricks, too. One of Chris' tricks is taking an SM57 with an old barrel connector that goes low impedance to high impedance and plugging that into the SansAmp pedal, then into a guitar amp or into a DI, and then into the desk [Sound City has a Neve 8028].

Also, Sound City has this makeshift booth on the floor that the assistants refer to as the "Easy-Bake Oven" because it gets pretty warm in there. Behind it in the corner was this really great low end happening, so we put a U 87 mic there, which we called the Easy-Bake mic. That was always my "glue" mic. But my new one is a Sony C37 as an overhead. Almost every single time you'd turn that one on, and it'd be like, "Oh! There you go."

You recorded vocals and overdubs at Two Sticks. Lots of takes there, too?

Quin: Howard would just be like, "Let's do it again, let's do it again, let's do it again." And I was just like, "Am I terrible?! Either you guys are getting more picky, or I'm getting more terrible." And they were just like, "It's going to be a great vocal record. Just like playing the song 45 times to get the best drum and bass take, you're going to have to sing it 40 times to get the best vocal take." And I was like, "F**k yoooou." It breaks down your spirit. There's no doubt when I finish making records, I never feel elated. I just feel broken.

Walla: There's this weird arc that happens where the first few takes have tons of energy but not a ton of accuracy or detail, and then [the singer] goes into a slump, and then you get to about 15 takes, and it starts to come back. Then the singer and producer get frustrated with one another, take a break, and eat dinner. Then you come back, and it gets to a point where it totally works.

There are a lot of varying philosophies about first take versus last take versus the right take versus chasing something forever and ever, and all the diminishing-returns stuff, but it's just a matter of getting to the point where you can absolutely verify that it feels better than whatever the first or most recent thing is that you did.

What was the signal chain for vocals?

Redekopp: We had a couple Neumann U 87s and a Neumann U 67. There were a couple shout-y background vocals where I had Tegan four feet off of an [AKG C] 414, with just the brightness of the room and the mic. And there was one song where she's spitting out a million words a minute with all that consonance stuff happening. Not wanting to beat the snot out of it with a de-esser, I used a Coles ribbon mic, and it worked great. It features a strong double, so one of them is a Coles, and the other is the 67.

We almost always used a Chandler preamp and Manley Variable Mu [Walla also notes an Empirical Labs Distressor], and a really small amount of de-essing, just grabbing the really fast sibilant stuff. We were trying to encode that, because the vocals went straight into Logic using the Nyquist A/D converters that Chris has. I find particularly when you're encoding vocals straight to digital, just a little bit of de-essing on the way in to take the edge off of the sibilance goes a long way, but nothing heavy, because of course you're not going to get that back once you've destroyed it.

Chris, you mixed "Northshore," "The Ocean," and "Arrow." How'd you approach those?

Walla: I've never mixed in or out of Logic before, and I ended up doing it mostly through the [Quad-Eight Electronics] console. I summed a few things together in Logic and sent them out. But virtually all of the gain reduction, compression, or smashing I did with outboard gear.

I did some pretty dramatic drum-bus compression with the Empirical Labs Fatso and dropped snares and toms back on top after the fact. The gain structure's kind of weird; it's cool to have it on 1 on the way in. It's not broken—it's just kind of strange.

I used the Chandler TG-1 compressor and the Great River EQ-1NV a lot. And then mix-bus-compression-wise, I did a whole bunch of stuff on the back end. I've got a passive Pultec filter—not even an EQ, just a bunch of transformers and inductors. I turned it on but left all the filtering out, so it's basically just running through transformers. From there, it went into a Manley Variable Mu, Smart D2, and GML 8200—where I did a little bit of EQ on the tail end—and then I mixed everything to $^1/_2$-inch at 15 ips.

The album sounds full, but also like you were economical with parts.

Quin: When we started breaking drums, bass, guitars, and keyboards into stems, I was shocked at how little there was. I was like, "Really? There's only two guitars and that one keyboard?" It's so funny that it feels so rich. And I didn't do a lot of double vocals, which has been sort of our sound, to always have 900 of our vocals smacking you on the face. There's something really weird and vulnerable about doing that.

Redekopp: Anybody can keep stacking things up until it sounds cool. But to stay economical puts a huge burden on the performance, and then it sounds more honest in the end. The reason why the record is able to sound that way is because the emphasis was again and again on performance. That goes back to not making a record where the artist is able to look at somebody at the computer and go, "You got what you need, right? Can you tune that? You can fix the timing on that, right? I'm going to go get some food." It's a wonderful tool when you get this great performance and there's one little flaw. But not when it feeds and informs the way people write music. There was *none* of that on this record.

Walla: *Economy* was one of the words that we threw around a lot when we were first starting to talk about this record. I think a lot of songwriters just throw stuff in for varying degrees of insecurity about the song. Like, what makes this one tiny little keyboard part any more or less important than any of the other ones?

Sometimes taking something away is the thing that makes the whole song work. When the bridge went down on the floor for "The Cure," nobody quite knew what to play guitarwise and keyboardwise. So we made a decision on the floor to just leave it as bass and drums. As we got further into the song, it was like, "That's what goes there! Tons of vocals." You do miss the guitars, but when they come in, it's a big breath of fresh air.

How did *Sainthood* compare to past recording experiences?

Quin: *The Con* was a weird record because we didn't do it with a band. Jason flew in and added his drums, and Hunter flew in and did his bass. I didn't even know how to play half of the songs. I'd written them, and then six months had gone by, and there I was trying to record them.

This record was all about the group. Jason would tell me what he thought about my guitar tone. That's never happened before. We've always had amazing musicians play with us, but they felt like drummers that we hired. Because Jason's in a band, he was speaking to me as my equal. Meanwhile, Ted would march over to Chris and say, "I think you should try this bass idea." I'd be sitting there like [*whispers*], "Oh, my God. Ted is talking to Chris about what his bass part should be!" It was fascinating. But we made a band record. We became Death Cab for Tegan and Sara, and it was pretty awesome.

DISORDER TO DESTROYER

Chris Walla on his prized Lexicon Varispeech: "There was a lot of speech-pathology research developed at Lexicon that was cross-purposed into pro audio. The Varispeech was originally intended to help stroke victims and people with speech disorders. The idea was that you could slow down a conversation at regular pitch but keep pitch where it was so that people could practice figuring out how to reconnect their mouth and their brain.

"There was this weird period where [Lexicon was] screwing around with it; I got one that had a feedback knob, which as far as I can tell is completely useless for speech pathology, but it makes everything sound like *Doctor Who*, which is awesome.

"It sounds great under the snare drum, and Tegan's vocals run through it on 'The Cure' when she does the 'Oh, uh oh, uh oh' thing. The Varispeech is a really cool chorus-y, flange-y thing if you set it up that way. But it's a speaker destroyer, too. It's an old ['70s] effect, and Lexicon wasn't worried about being sued by guys who were like, 'You blew up my guitar amp, dude!'"

26

A Tribe Called Quest

THE LIVE AND SAMPLED LAYERS
OF *THE LOW END THEORY*

By Rich Tozzoli

This chapter appeared in the January 2007 issue of *EQ* magazine.

Grammy Award–winning producer Bob Power, whose long list of credits includes the likes of Erykah Badu, the Roots, and Miles Davis, has been behind over 50 charting records and has received more than 20 gold or platinum records—securing his position as one of the leading producers/engineers in the worlds of hip-hop, R&B, jazz, and soul.

Taking Power's résumé into ample consideration, it's virtually impossible to pinpoint the catalyst moment in his rise to the top of the production world. But one of his more career-defining achievements was, inarguably, producing a "then marginally popular" Queens, New York, collective known as A Tribe Called Quest's sophomore release *The Low End Theory*. Simply put, *The Low End Theory* broke new ground for rap in the early '90s. Fusing the talents of Q-Tip, DJ Ali Shaheed Muhammad, and Phife Dawg, the intelligent, sophisticated sound combined elements of jazz, laid-back samples, and smooth lyrics with funky grooves. Critical acclaim followed, establishing the term *alternative rap* and securing Power a seat in the pantheon of great hip-hop producers.

So we caught up with Power late one afternoon to pick his brain about what went into what has become widely regarded as *the* album that ushered in the "second wave of hip-hop." And he delivered—far exceeding our original hopes. So kick off your shoes, turn off the phone, and read on as Power offers a piquant look into the making of what *Rolling Stone* has dubbed album number 154 out of the 500 greatest albums of all time.

The Low End Theory was mostly captured in a variety of New York City studios. Given that you didn't work in any one set location, on what consoles did you do your primary tracking/mixing?

The record was recorded primarily at both Battery and Calliope studios, which were the scene of many innovative things—in terms of recording—happening in hip-hop at that time; though we did a bit of mixing at Soundtrack and Greene Street studios, as well as a few overdubs. The console in Battery K2, which at that time was known as Studio B, was an old Neve 8068 that came over from England and later went to the Battery Studios in Nashville. Everything was tracked through the Neve, from vocals to samples to scratches. We did most of the mixing at Battery, as well—although we did the lion's share of that on an SSL 4064 G. The one or two mixes we took to Soundtrack were done on an SSL 4000 E; and Greene Street had an early, rare, and quick-to-go fully automated Amek APC 1000 that we used, as well. I had a very severe sinus infection during a lot of the mixing of that record—complete with some serious stuffed ears—that led to a lot of balancing problems, but looking back it's like, "Who knew?"

Was it all cut to tape?

Yes, to two-inch 24-track on a Studer A800 [and A]827, and also a slightly modified 3M M79, using Ampex 456 tape—30 ips, no noise reduction. Pro Tools was at a pretty primitive stage at the time, and certainly sounded rough, so it wasn't much of an option. Things didn't really start happening sonically with Pro Tools, for my money, until it went 24 bits.

There are a lot of breaks on the disc—did you have automation?

A Tribe Called Quest's Ali Shaheed Muhammad. (Berry Behrendt/Retna Ltd.)

Yes. Again, we were mostly mixing on the 4064 G, with some 4000 E, which had what I called the "Pacman interface": green type on black—incredibly primitive. I was still in the midst of a big learning phase with SSL automation at that time, and I learned a lot from my assistants. It's funny, though, we actually edited a lot of the interlude material in Pro Tools, though the full songs

199

were all mastered from tape. Prior to that, around the time of the first A Tribe Called Quest album, we were mixing to 1/4-inch—either 15 or 30 ips, depending on the budget. No joke.

Did you actually fly all the samples in manually?

Most of them were sequenced, and the rest either DJ Ali or Q-Tip would cut in directly from the turntables. A lot of the material was sampled from turntables during the sessions, into an Akai S900. My, how far we've come. At that time, I was way into the Atari [computer] and [C-Lab] Notator, which later became Logic. Tip would often come in with a beat sequenced and sampled into an E-mu SP-12, and Ali, bless him, had already started to get into Macs at that point and would bring in tracks sequenced with Vision, as well as samples loaded on the S900. In many cases I would dump those sequences into Notator, go into another room for 45 minutes, and just push the stuff around 'til it felt right. Remember, this was the beginning of the '90s, and reliable sync was still dodgy. Many people used the Roland SBX-80, as Mac interfaces were not terrifically consistent. But one of the nice things about the Atari/Notator combination was that if you had a Unitor [their giant dongle that read timecode], sequencing and sync happened in the same box, which was a big plus.

"Check the Rhime" contains music from the Average White Band's "Love Your Life," as well as some really grooving keys. Were the tracks all sampled, or were performances by Tribe included, as well?

As far as I can recall, it was mostly all samples and loops. I do remember, however, that was around the time where we started supplanting loops with "helpers," playing the same thing to give it a little more dimension, so sometimes we would play the existing bass line an octave down on those wonderful sub-bass sounds on a Roland Juno-106. You didn't hear it as an octave, but it gave the impression of massive bottom end on loops that really didn't have it. If you tried to EQ into that same thing, you mostly ended up with mud. Some of the Rhodes element we doubled, as well, but it was largely samples and loops.

There also seem to be many layers of drums on that tune that cycle in and out. How did that come about?

That happened on a lot of Tip and Ali's beats at the time, though the specifics are a bit hazy. A really large part of that was the fact that even if the sequenced drumbeat stayed the same throughout the tune, the addition of the different loops over the beat made a sort of combinative beat, so the different sections of the song sounded as if the beat elements had changed.

The snare on "Jazz (We've Got)" has serious pop. Did you layer the samples, and if so, how did you then sync them back?

The recording of that album occurred right around the time I really got into layering samples. I'd never heard of the concept, but from time to time I'd think, "Gee, this snare could use some more attack." So I started doing things like layering in the attack portion of a cowbell, for instance, with the snare sample to give it some "hurt." Of course, the sample's tuning also had a lot to do with the overall effect, and I would do this all in the S900. We used a lot of different things—sometimes drumsticks clacked together—and one time I actually had Tip hit a Sennheiser 421 against a tabletop, and we used that behind the snare.

I learned that if you leave a little "airspace" at the beginning of the sample, you can quite precisely slip the timing of the different samples by adjusting the start point, all while the sounds are playing from the sequencer. Also, if you assigned the different samples their own MIDI note, or channel, you could slip them around in Notator. If we recorded another element to the sound after the first was on tape, again, I would move it around on Notator while the track was playing until it felt right. A great trick that I learned from Chris Julian Irwin, who owned Calliope and is a brilliant producer/engineer, was this: If you were using the E-mu SP-12, which a lot of people were, the trick was to offset the SMPTE start time of the song slightly early in the SP-12, and then feed the timecode from tape to the SP-12 through a digital delay—usually a Lexicon PCM 42. Then, as the song was playing, you'd change the value of the delay time, thus "slipping" the feel of the overdub coming from the SP-12 in real time.

Do you remember what you used to record guest bassist Ron Carter on "Verses from the Abstract"?

Yes, very well. It was a funny evening when we recorded him; Tip, Ali, and

I were all slightly terrified. At times, Ron can seem like a very prickly fellow, so, because of his stature, I made sure to converse with him in the booth both about how I was planning to record him and to see what he was comfortable with. I ended up using a Neumann tube U 47 and took his pickup direct, as well. I'm pretty sure I used some stand-alone Neve mic pres that were in an outboard rack and then balanced them on faders on the 4064 G console, bussing the combined signals to one tape track. I had planned on using a Neve 2254e compressor/limiter on him—a piece I was very familiar with. But when I asked him if he was comfortable with that, I got the quickest and most resolute "No" I've ever heard. That said, I learned a valuable lesson that night from Ron about working with "heavy" players in general. If they are serious professionals, and if you speak music with them, they respond in a very "pro" way—quickly . . . and very musically.

What was the overall music climate at that time in the hip-hop world?

I'm probably not the best person to answer that, as I was much older and from a very different background than the artists I was working with. That said, it was what I consider the meat of what I call the "second wave" of hip-hop. Beats made exclusively from 808s, or other drum machines, with their straight eighth-note "tat-tat-tat-tat" hi-hats, were quickly becoming passé, and there were a whole slew of artists coming up who were influenced by many different musical genres, and the atmosphere was one of very open and unfettered creativity. There didn't seem to be the overwhelming need to be "down," just engaging. And Calliope Studio was ground zero for much of that. It's mind-boggling to think of the people coming through there at that time: A Tribe Called Quest, De La Soul, Black Sheep, Stetsasonic.

What was the "must-have" studio gear at that time for recording this "second wave of hip-hop"?

Samplers coming into their own were an absolutely huge fulcrum in the progression of the "second wave": Akai S900, E-mu SP-12, Technics 1200 turntables . . . . You have to remember that this was before hip-hop became the giant money machine that it is today—thus much of the recording took place in whatever way was the least expensive, in terms of both gear and facilities. And, in a way, that was good: One was forced to get creative, rather than just plug in a well-known, high-end piece of gear. At Calliope, mostly due to Chris' vision, we had things fairly early on, including Lexicon PCM-42 digital delays and, slightly later, the PCM-60 digital reverb. Mic-wise, we were using the AKG C414s and C451s for tons of different applications. Personally, I didn't become familiar with some of the "big-studio" staples like the Lexicon 224, EMT plates, UREI 1176, Neumann U 87, and so on until our budgets allowed us to go to the "big" places. But on top of what little we had to work with, we pulled a lot of things out of my personal collection: AKG C24 [and] C12a, Shoeps M221, Neve 2254e—not pieces normally associated with hip-hop, but I loved the way they sounded when put into that context.

Looking back, what do you feel that album left the hip-hop world in terms of recording?

The Low End Theory was the first album, as far as I know, that had samples put together with such detail as to form fairly complex and sophisticated-sounding tracks. The feel was great—it sounded like a bunch of very good players conversing—but because it was so skillfully reconstructed, and the beats were so deep, it actually went places those "real" players never could. Also, arguably, it was the first time, or at least one of the first notable examples, where so much attention was paid to sonics on a hip-hop record, and the world took notice. This record is a testament to the startling creativity of Q-Tip, Ali Shaheed, and Phife Dawg.

But as far as the engineering/mixing goes, why did it come out sounding the way that it did? Part of that was due to the felicity of having a Neve console at our disposal. It was partially due to that album being cut during a very aggressive time of discovery for me as an engineer. Part of it was due to Tip standing over my shoulder at the mixes, saying, "More snare, more kick." But mostly it was due to that intangible confluence of people, the times. It was a record that really took on a life of its own.

Overall, though, it comes down to the same elements that make a good record in any genre: compelling performances of great songs. Although it may be truer in theory than practice, if you have those elements, you can make a great record on an answering machine.

27

TV on the Radio

DAVID ANDREW SITEK REVEALS HIS PLUG-IN
AVERSION ON *RETURN TO COOKIE MOUNTAIN*

By Ken Micallef

This chapter features an abridged version of the TV on the
Radio article in the May 2006 issue of *Remix* magazine.

Production guru and TV on the Radio conspirator David
Andrew Sitek lives in Brooklyn's Williamsburg neighborhood, well known for its budding arts community and
warehouse loft living. The band's Stay Gold studio inhab-
its a dusty Williamsburg industrial block, book-ended by
a gentrified diner and a biker bar. Sitek lives around the
corner from Stay Gold, ever so close to TVOTR's collection of '70s analog synths, '60s rhythm boxes, '40s
Telefunken mics, and a Studer A880 tape machine. Sitek can usually be found at Stay Gold conjuring magical
sounds, but today he is nowhere to be found. The smell
of smoke and racing fire engines reveals why: Sitek's
house is burning to the ground.

"This was actually the second fire I have had in my
life, which is probably why I am a pro," Sitek says a few
hours later. "When I was 21, my house burned down to
the ground, and I lost everything, including 70 two-inch

reels and 3,300 pieces of vinyl. I lived above a restaurant in Baltimore, and some kid threw a cigarette into a trash can and burned down the whole place."

Oddly deadpan, Sitek has the dazed look of someone who has been up all night. And he seems awfully calm considering the glowing embers that were once his home. One week later, ugly reality sets in.

"I am in London for this press tour, and it is a pain in the ass," Sitek barks. "My house burned down; I haven't had any sleep since then. I lost everything. I am in a sh**ty mood. I just need to decompress."

In an eerie case of art imitating life, Sitek admits that TVOTR's latest album, *Return to Cookie Mountain* (Interscope, 2006), is all about apocalyptic events, the end of the world and post-9/11 dread.

"I didn't want to make an apocalyptic album," he says. "It was just hard to shut out everything else that was going on. All the evidence is there that the world could be ending, so while we were making the record, we were constantly reminded of that by what was happening around us."

APOCALYPSE WOW

Return to Cookie Mountain is beautiful and dreadful—gorgeous vocal melodies massaging epic tribal-funk rhythms; clanging percussion drizzled over humongous bass riffs, and, above it all, distorted, thunderous, end-of-days guitar noise that sounds like bombs dropping over Baghdad.

"I watched *Apocalypse Now* seven times while we were making the album," Sitek remembers. "That opening scene where the helicopters come up with the sunrise, that is one of my favorite pieces of film ever. That image wasn't a conscious thing for the record, but I just kept watching that movie over and over for weeks."

Futuristic yet nostalgic, with a pop purity that belies its avant-garde atmosphere, *Return to Cookie Mountain* is the result of bong hits, ancient analog gear, and Sitek's stubborn resistance to plug-ins and software synths. TVOTR's acclaimed LP debut, *Desperate Youth, Blood Thirsty Babes* (Touch and Go, 2004), paired MPC drum programming with the gorgeously stacked vocals of Tunde Adebimpe and the itchy guitar scrabble of Kyp Malone, but with *Cookie Mountain*, Sitek's provocative intention to create "music you will be listening to when the whole world burns

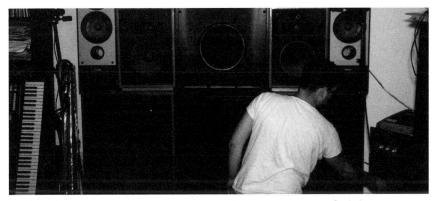

TV on the Radio's David Andrew Sitek in his New York–based Stay Gold studios. (Anthony Gordon)

up" rings with an awful irony. Following the success of his last production, the Yeah Yeah Yeahs' *Fever to Tell* (Interscope, 2003), Sitek is sure of his own vision.

"I wanted things to be more classic than our first album, in the sense of the drums [played by Jaleel Bunton] being recorded traditionally and the vocals being recorded up front," Sitek says. "I tried to stick with old and new technology—the most pure versions of those ideas—like using mic positioning for the drums and the vocals and running everything else pretty much direct. That is either modern or sick."

SONGWRITING HAZE

TVOTR is first of all a live band; therefore, it often approaches recording from a performance—not a studio—construct. Generally, Sitek will write with his Rhythm Ace or Rhythm Master drum machines; the band will play their parts; and he will damage, or rather, effect the results with all manner of outboard tricks and guitar shrapnel.

"I usually lay down a click track with the Rhythm Ace first," he details, "then a rough guitar part and an elaborate MPC part, and then a more elaborate guitar part, and then a scratch vocal. The drums go down midway through the song. We record the bass (played by Gerard Smith) at the very end; that is the sound I am most exacting about. If you record the bass up front, you will rerecord it anyway, because you want it to sit evenly with the rest of the song, and considering how many layers there are in each song, I just have to find the hole for it.

"I am a big adder and subtracter," he continues. "I often put sounds onto 1/4-inch tape and back into Pro Tools, and onto 1/2-inch tape and back into Pro Tools, and on two-inch tape then to Pro Tools. It goes through a million different lives."

A look around Stay Gold studio is like traveling back in time—everything from the Studer A880 to WWII-era Neumann mics and some vintage EMI channel strips—recalling the golden age of studio production. That sense of hardware history informs every move that Sitek makes.

"That is everything to me," he says. "I don't even really look at the equipment when I am changing the settings. I won't care if I am f**king with the attack or the decay; I will just start turning knobs until it sounds right. Even stuff like proximity of microphone and having the singer use different spots to sing for different dynamics, or sing into a corner—that s**t is fascinating to me. Rather than automating volumes, that approach produces different results, especially when you have wooden floors and reflective surfaces."

Another big motivator for Sitek is a copious intake of mother's little helper. Like Jimi Hendrix's *Electric Ladyland*, the Beatles' *Revolver*, and Squarepusher's *Feed Me Weird Things*, *Return to Cookie Mountain* was born out of a dope haze.

"I smoke about three-quarters of a pound of weed a month, and I exceeded that for this record," Sitek says with a laugh. "There were moments, like on 'Tonight,' when I was just lying on the floor, stoned with headphones on, tampering with the Pioneer 1/4-inch reel-to-reel. I took sounds from the Pioneer that we use for slapback and put them back to the mix. I come off the record head, and it is hardwired so the play head goes right to a 1/4-inch jack so we can run it into Pro Tools. Most of the music that I like was made on dope. There is no way I could play a song back to myself 3,000 times unless I was stoned. I don't ever want to repeat myself, so I try to be not too conscious of the process."

PLUG-INS, SHMUG-INS

One part of the process that Sitek is deadly conscious of is plug-ins. Sitek hates the little software buggers with a passion, preferring reamping and knob twiddling to mass-market sound manipulation.

"Plug-ins just gum up the CPU," he proclaims. "I will use the Fairchild plug-in for a kick hit. I will run it through the plug-in and bounce it to disc and put it on my MPC and then replay it. It is not the smartest or easiest way, but I am more concerned with getting the result based on intuition rather than dicking around with a plug-in for six years. When you are using five plug-ins in Pro Tools, they all have a signature way of sculpting the sound. Whereas, if you send [the signal] through 12 different transformers that were made in 12 different time periods, you will never get that sound through a plug-in.

"Instead of using plug-ins, we use reamps," Sitek continues. "Reamping allows you to send stuff out of Pro Tools into an amp or a pedal, then back in; it changes the line level. Reamps are like direct boxes with a dial so you can change the input or output level. I can't even remember what brand we use, but say I record a guitar, and I don't like the sound: I will record the guitar direct, and then I will reamp it. I will send the direct signal out of Pro Tools as if it is someone playing it into a bunch of different amps or pedals to figure out which one is the best. Then I will mic that and record it to another channel."

Another major element on *Return to Cookie Mountain* is a distorted guitar wash that bathes many songs with wide strokes. This guitar shrapnel enters in the most unlikely places to upend convention. From the opening "I Was a Lover" and the grand "Province" (with David Bowie on vocals), to the backward swirls of "Tonight" and the spooky bombast of "Let the Devil In," it's a noise fest for lovers of a more epic approach to sound.

"Most of Kyp's guitar lines are exactly how he plays them," Sitek says, "but the huge, crazy-ass, wall-of-guitar s**t is me playing a '91 Fender Teleplus through an Interstellar Overdriver pedal into the Roland Groove Sampler, running COSM effects, into Pro Tools. For the guitar tracks, I record two different sounds and then combine those two layers to a track and then erase the two originals. Once it goes out of the Groove Sampler, it goes to the Studer A880, where I might slow it down to half speed or speed it up to twice the speed, and I will play along with that."

TRACKING HOURS

"Hours" represents *Cookie Mountain*'s zeitgeist to a T. Stuttering drums introduce a whirring Hammond B3 organ, oozing lavalike bass flows, and a tinkling upright piano outlining a skeletal frame. At one point the drums drop out, and what sounds like a flock of seagulls (not the band) screams through the speakers, followed by the brass flow of the Antibalas Afrobeat Orchestra horns, vocal "oohs" and "ahhs," and a ghostly choir.

"We did a click track first," Sitek explains. "The drums and bass were live, and I used the Korg CX-3 for the Hammond sound. Then we recorded the vocals; all the other instruments were added later. The looping seagulls sound is a Fender Rhodes Seventy-Three going through the octave function of a DigiTech Whammy pedal.

"[As for beats,] It is one continuous drum performance," he continues. "I always record the drums with large-diaphragm condensers, except on the snare, where I use a Sony C37 mic from the '50s. I am not a big fan of room sound; that makes the drums sound separate from the music. We will bang on trash outside the studio, too, using the Earthworks Omni QTC1 microphone. The drums get bigger at one point in the track: There are two room mics that happened to be on; we didn't adjust them. Those tracks just come up at that point to give the song more dynamics. I record cymbals separately. Most of the cymbal tracks I slow down. I initially record them fast, so when I play them back, they are this big *splooshy* sound. It is easier to conceal that sploosh when the cymbals are on a separate track. I record two master tracks of the song with everything but the cymbals onto two-inch tape and then record the cymbals to two-inch tape and then fly them back in so they line up, using the Varispeed on the Studer."

FIRE AND RAIN

If we are nearing the end of the world, *Return to Cookie Mountain* is the perfect soundtrack to the final flameout. Gorgeous vocals, funky beats, and ominous guitars may be the last sound we all hear as trumpets blare and a heavenly host descends. But Sitek is ultimately hopeful regarding music's role in this life and the next one.

"I am not a pessimist," Sitek says, "I just don't believe we are the last species in the food chain. Dr. Emoto [in his book *The Hidden Messages in Water*] was the first to document changes in water crystals. He put the word 'hate' and the word 'love' on two bottles of water, and he took pictures of the molecules. The ones in the hate bottle were deformed. You listen to a song that makes you feel exhilarated; it changes your physical being. [Henryk] Górecki's Symphony No. 3 will change your physical being. We have exhausted all intellectual ways to connect, so it is time to reduce it to something that isn't restricted to the English language. Lack of subtlety is the first sign of a civilization in decline."

28

Classics

The Who

PETE TOWNSHEND ON GENERATING
THE MASSIVE SOUNDS OF *WHO'S NEXT,*
QUADROPHENIA, AND *TOMMY*

By J. J. Blair

This chapter features an abridged version of the Who article in the August 2007 issue of *EQ* magazine.

For the past 40-plus years, Pete Townshend has stood at the epicenter of what is widely regarded by rock fans as one of the greatest, and most influential, acts of all time—the Who. From being named by *Rolling Stone* as "possibly the greatest live band ever" to topping the Guinness World Records listing as "the loudest band in the world," the Who have embodied the spirit of take-no-prisoners, no-holds-barred rock and roll throughout the years—a stance that's seen the group inducted into the Rock and Roll Hall of Fame in 1990 and winning the Freddy Mercury Lifetime Achievement in Live Music Award in 2006, among countless other honors bestowed from musical institutions worldwide.

But this is all well-circulated information, the likes of which can be found just about anywhere. Digging deeper into the world of Pete Townshend, one will first find accounts of his highly regarded literary work, as they relate to the Meher Baba movement, his penchant for charity. But through the media haze of all the ill-fated guitars and extracurricular-activist delving is Pete the Producer—a side of the musical mastermind not often publicized.

Getting onboard long before the home recording revolution hit, Townshend began dabbling as a self-producer even before the Who became a household name, demoing personal projects and tinkering with various technologies all in the name of creating compelling recordings of music that, at the time, didn't appear to be commercially viable. And he never stopped. Through the heyday of the Who and through his career as a solo artist, Townshend has been behind the board for it all—amassing a collection of gear and trying his hand at nearly every technique, every possible recording medium, along the way.

Not many people know this, but you were one of the first recording artists to have a home studio, which makes you the pioneer for the millions of people doing the same thing now. How difficult was that to achieve back then?

I can think of a few people who preceded me. A Dutch fellow called Wout Steenhuis, who lived in Britain and used to appear on European TV, playing along with himself on a guitar and tape machine. Les Paul, of course, may have appeared to have a mainstream studio, but it was certainly designed entirely to support his own creative playing and composing. My friend Andy Newman—founder with John Keane, Jimmy McCulloch, and myself of Thunderclap Newman—used a stereo tape machine to record from track to track, and I first heard his multilayered mono recordings at an event at Ealing Art College in 1963.

My most important entry into the pro technology world happened in 1963 with the recording of my first published song, "It Was You." This was recorded at the TV composer Barry Gray's home studio. He was a family friend of Peter Wilson, the lead guitar player in my first school guitar band. Barry had set aside the entire ground floor of his modest semi-detached suburban home as a fully equipped studio with EMI tape machines, mixers, echo devices, and so on. I asked him a few questions, and it quickly became clear that my modest

Pete Townshend. (Chris Morphet/Redferns/Getty Images)

experience with tape machines, mucking around at home the way we all did in those days—most people used tape recorders to record songs off the radio— could lead to something special.

Later, when I shared this idea with the Who's new manager Kit Lambert in 1964, he immediately told me about the very sophisticated tape machines they used on film sets—Nagras—that were finer even than studio machines and had the advantage of being battery powered. Kit and his business partner Chris Stamp had both worked in films. Kit told me a Nagra costs as much as a car, but there was another cheaper machine often used on studio stages where mains power was available. These were rugged, military-spec machines made by a British electronics company that specialized in public-address systems. They were called Vortexions. My first acquisition was two mono machines; I did not need a mixer, because you could blend the microphone input with the line input. I used old Reslo ribbon mics left over from the Who's career as a pub band. Thus I made my first demos for the Who, trying hard to do as well as Barry Gray had on "It Was You."

My first real Who demo was "Can't Explain," made before I got the Vortexions, on a domestic tape machine, and it was a kind of Bob Dylan–meets–Mose Allison thing, with me whining away with an acoustic guitar. I have lost that tape, sadly, but I later revamped the song as more Kinks-like when I heard their producer Shel Talmy was interested in us. Once I started with the Vortexions, I became more careful about tape logging and archiving and I have almost everything I ever did. A lot of the demos I did were comic in nature, or very lighthearted. I did them for practice, to test a new room, or mic, or whatever. I intended to build a proper soundproofed room at one point; it was a dream of mine. I bought materials and drew up plans, but the Who got very busy on the road, so instead I simply recorded without it and got thrown out of a series of very cool apartments as a result. I moved up from mono machines to two stereo machines, and some of my earliest demos are stereo—bounced from machine to machine. One of the first and the best is "Substitute."

It wasn't until I got to my apartment on Wardour Street in early 1967 that I found a place I could make as much noise as I liked. It was a commercial room, so the buildings around it were empty at night, when I did most of my work. It was here I got my first mixer—a little filmmaker's Uher—and a Grampian spring reverb. A little later in this same room I supplemented my Vortexion machines (that ran at 7.5 ips) with two Revox G37s. These ran at 15 ips, and they sounded superb. I had no idea at the time about aligning them and just experimented with different types of tape to get the best sound.

What helped me make a huge jump was meeting Pepy Rush in SoHo—he lived around the corner to me. He was building pro-quality transformer balanced equipment for various people. He had been employed by the notorious "Magic Alex" of Apple fame at one time to do designs, and he still has the design for what he says was the very first fuzz box he made for John Lennon—though the first I ever saw was the one Jimmy Page used on "Bald Headed Woman," the B-side of the Who's first single, "Can't Explain." Pepy explained to me that I needed to rationalize my crude patch bay with properly balanced 600-ohm inputs and outputs and attempt to insert them into 10kHz bridged tape machines. He provided me with boxes for my Revox machines that allowed this. He also built me a valve limiter. I still have it. I have two today that I still use. This was huge step forward for me. Until then, the sound of modern pop had been a mystery. Few engineers had been willing to divulge that it was the limiter/compressor that made music sound so hot in the pro studio, and not their amazing talent. Later he sold me my first valve mixer, eight channels, stereo with passive Baxandall treble and bass, and a panpot and echo send on each channel. It had a really clean, warm sound. I recorded the Thunderclap Newman record at home using that desk.

What pieces of audio gear from your original setup are still parts of your recording setup? I heard that you still use your Neve BCM-10 and a one-inch 8-track? Do you have any favorite mics?

I'm spoiled. I was around when pro studios were at their peak. I kept quite a lot of my old gear . . . not all of it, sadly. I use 1066 modules in my Neve, via Pepy Rush or Manley compressors. My favorite "cheap" compressor is by Drawmer. But I'd take a brand-new UA LA-4A over anything else if I were confined to a single low-budget compressor. My favorite mic of the moment is the AEA R84. My tape machine is an 8-track Studer A820, 15 ips, no Dolby. I mix down onto an Ampex ATR100 using Dolby SR at 15 ips. I used to really like working on tape at 30 ips, but today I am attracted to the warmth of 15 ips. At 15 ips I get a head bump on the Ampex machine, but my Studer doesn't seem quite so tricky. I listen to the output of the machine in any case, when mixing to the Ampex, so I set the EQ so I am happy with what is coming off the tape, not what is going onto it. My mastering guy usually has me bring in my own machine or comes to me with his Genex.

I have noticed that you spend more time and effort dialing in your guitar sound than just about any artist I've ever seen. Would it be fair to say that your philosophy is to spend the time getting the sound right before you record it? A trend that is emerging these days is to record a direct guitar and then reamp it or use Amp Farm, or even Sound Replacer on the drum sounds rather than starting with a drum sound that's better than a sample. What are your thoughts on this?

I'm constantly struggling with my stage sound, trying to make it sound big when in fact it is small (this is to protect my hearing). In the studio, I just plug an old Telecaster into an old Fender Deluxe, shove a Shure 56A in front of it, straight into a Neve 1066 with a compressor, down to tape. I add nothing, take away nothing. I get a guitar sound in five seconds that blows my socks off. They had this stuff back in 1956. Imagine that! I've never tried the other methods you describe. They sound mad to me, but they might work. They sound like they would work very well on clean lead-line guitar work, maybe not so well on the grungy chordal style I, or people like Angus Young, have.

I've been exposed to my share of drum replacement. Chris Thomas did this on "Face the Face" on my *White City* solo album. He spent hours getting the drums right, then left them isolated, so they have been resampled so many times I hear them everywhere. Great noises. But that was me trying to sound like Prince—probably not a good idea. [*Laughs.*] That guy is so clever. I have now returned to mono drums, recorded with as few mics as possible.

Once we reached the massive, glorious sound of huge drums on early Zeppelin tracks and the Who's *Quadrophenia*, where could you go? Bigger? How? So much incredible work was done, especially by Roy Thomas Baker, but sessions would often be arranged to allow at least a week to get a basic drum sound. Often it was the room the drums were in that mattered the most. Surely even a home studio enthusiast could haul his gear to the local gym one day? Or a church hall? Or a school? Or a river footpath bridge-tunnel? The bathroom can be good, too—just set up the drums in the tub, take out all the soap and towels, and there you go. You may scoff, but I've done it. I'm sure I was not the first.

There are many extremes that you can pursue, I'm sure. I read an interview with Ray Davies where he said they set up corrugated sheet

metal in the hallways of a recording studio and miked the drums from out in the hall.

I've done that, too. But there is only so big you can get. That's my point: If an amateur drummer wants a big sound without having big resources, what I am saying is that they can experiment and get a bigger sound in the ways I suggest.

Speaking of big, you have historically had some of the biggest and most aggressive guitar sounds on records. Can you tell us what your signal path tends to be on electric guitars, i.e., type of guitar, amp, mic, pre, compressor, mic placement, etc.?

On the Who records, I often used my Hiwatt amplifiers—rarely a stack, just a head and a 4 x 12. Whatever guitar I happened to be using sounded good with this rig—Strats, SG Specials, whatever. The mics would usually be a Shure 56A close up, but Glyn Johns often used Neumann U 87 or KM 86 about a foot away. He never combined mics, though, and I don't do that either. It's okay if you stay in mono but can create phase-shift hell in stereo, changing the sound as you combine the mics and when the stereo is mixed down to mono on the radio or TV. I also used, and still use, a rig made for me by Joe Walsh. This is an orange Gretsch Chet Atkins, deeper body, through an Edwards light-diode 110-volt volume pedal (designed for pedal steel), into a 1956 Fender Band-master. It gives that grungy Neil Young sound I use sometimes. You control the distortion with the pedal rather than the guitar or the amp. I do use DI guitar sometimes, too. Danelectros sound so clean on DI that they sound like crystal bells ringing. Those "lipstick" pickups are genius. I also use my current Fender Vibro King stage amps to record. They sound really wonderful, I think, but a little floor compressor of some kind before the amp can help smooth the distortion you choose to dial in.

My guitar tech Alan Rogan replaced Joe Walsh as my guitar mentor and has bought me some great instruments over the years that I wouldn't other-wise have bothered with. The one I like the best is the '56 Telecaster. Orgasmic. Sell your house or your Picasso and buy one. Or steal mine. I would, without a moment's shame. [*Laughs.*] These matters are so crucial, so life-changing, that this is like war. We needed their oil? We went and took it. You want my '56 Telecaster? You need to bring in the paratroopers to claim it back for the

USA. What a great country, the USA. The Telecaster, the Les Paul, the Jumbo Jet. And API, as well. If you do nothing else you have done more for rock 'n' roll and world peace than Mahatma Ghandi. I admit I might be wrong about the oil, though. [*Laughs.*]

And you thank us by smashing our guitars! But back to your guitar sounds, could you tell us about how you record your acoustic?

I used to use a Neumann U 87, about nine inches from the guitar, carefully positioned using headphones, through a Neve 1066 module, just a little 10kHz and 2.4kHz, a little valve compression. Lately I've replaced the Neumann with the R84. This is a ribbon mic, so it hears the back of the mic as well as the front (figure-8). This means you can work the sound of the room into the mix, which is especially attractive in mono.

I'm also a big fan of the R84, particularly on horns and on piano. When you are recording acoustic, are you using the front side or the back, which has the attenuated low end?

I use the front and face the back towards the open studio. Also, I find that if you don't have a great guitar, miking very close can help—but listen with earphones on and move the mic position in clear stages. Give yourself at least 15 seconds of silence between each new experimental mic position. Don't assume that what sounds right in the earphones will need no further work, but every acoustic guitar has its own interesting quality. I like small-body Fylde guitars made in England, but lately I've also taken to Collings guitars from Austin. They are expensive but real emulations of old Martin guitars, I think. I also like the Gibson and Epiphone J200 series. That body shape suits my strident strumming copied from Don Everly and the Flamenco players of the '60s.

In 1970 or 1971, when you were making the demos for *Lifehouse*, which became *Who's Next*, not only did you predict the Internet years ahead of Al Gore, you also did something which was a first, as far as I'm aware of: You used synth filters (with the ARP 2500) and sequenced keyboard arpeggios (with the Lowry organ) as the underlying rhythm track for the band to play over on "Won't Get Fooled Again" and "Baba O'Riley," respectively. Where did you come up with that idea?

My forward-looking notions were all implanted in me at Ealing Art College by Roy Ascott and Harold Cohen. They were able to see that computers were coming and could also see (which is the amazing part) that they would change the way art would work, and language itself. For years I thought nothing about any of this. I had been sidestepped into mysticism and expressed some of that in *Tommy*. I was also involved in rock marketing and image making. By the time the Who hit 1971, the band was about to turn into a cartoon of itself: Roger dressed as a fringe topped with a curly mop; John using his fingers on the bass as though he was eating crab claws' Keith playing drums with his head on fire, laughing until he cried; me wearing a crown and a tie-dye jump suit. Our managers had decided to turn to heavy drugs for amusement.

I decided to move aside and back to academia, and art school inspired experimentation with no boundaries. I was getting steeped in extraordinary ideas by people like Tim Souster, Roger Powell, Karlheinz Stockhausen, and others. I was always trying to come up some new way to process sound that would take me away from the traditional processors used in studios. I quickly found that one of the principles of electronic music was its reproduction through reprocessing systems—"myriad" speaker arrays or swept filters. The first sequencer I worked with was in 1971, the analog one that came with the ARP 2500. Later I tried the digitally clocked sequencer made by EMS in 1973. In fact, the first filtering I did was with the little British EMS synthesizer called the "Putney" VCS3. I persuaded my genius father-in-law, Edwin Astley, to buy a couple, and he became quite adept at using them—great tool for such a gifted orchestral composer.

I just let my imagination go crazy, and people like Tim Souster, in particular, just egged me on. I can remember Tim describing aural head implants for the reception of music and information in 1971. I nodded sagely, knowing he was probably right, and of course he could be proved so any second now. He introduced me to the folk at the BBC Radiophonics Workshop and Karlheinz Stockhausen. Roger Powell and I had some incredible brainstorm sessions over nothing more powerful than a cup of tea. On one occasion we invented a contra-rotating magnetic wheel echo device combined with a moving tape loop that would record individual guitar notes and immediately play them back in reverse.

What stopped me in my tracks soon after the research and the demo recording was the fact that all these effects were impossible to reproduce live. If they had been able to work live, the Who would have turned into Tonto's Expanding Headband. I saw a lecture at Ealing by Malcolm Cecil, one of the founders of Tonto—and he still has the big Moog, I think—and he was an incredible inspiration. That would have been in 1963. Kit Lambert (pre-heroin) had been pretty wacky as our producer, as well. During one session with the Who, he ran around the room holding a microphone to generate interesting phasing and ambience. The Beatles had challenged us all, I think, to try new things.

Also, ever since *Who's Next*, synth pads and sequences have been part of the Who sound, as well as on your solo records. These generally originated on your demos and then wound up on the final record from your existing demos. I can clearly hear this on *Who's Next*, *Quadrophenia*, and even "Eminence Front" (from *It's Hard*). Sequencing and creating synth pads has become infinitely easier to do now, but do you miss any of the ingenuity or artistry that it took to create those parts back then? Do you feel that the soft synths sound as good as your ARP or EMS?

Creating sequenced arpeggiations should not require ingenuity. This is "found" music, like the individual elements in collages in art. One presses some keys, or fiddles around with some software or some setting on a Casio toy, and if what you hear is inspiring, fun, or interesting, you can move ahead with it. It's what you do with it that counts.

The problem with soft synths is never their sound—they often offer superior sound to the originals and terrific extras. But the human interface becomes one you have to construct yourself. For example, the [Arturia] CS80 emulation I use is amazing. But what made the CS80 so incredible was its polyphonic aftertouch pressure keyboard that could be set to change timbre, vibrato, and even pitch both on attack and after-pressure. Each note in a chord could be made to rise or fall in level, or swell with a change in timbre. Just holding a pad could be made interesting and evolving simply by adding pressure to individual keys after you keyed and held the chord.

How come you never got into using the Mellotron? Or did you try it and decide it was something you didn't like?

They had one at IBC as soon as they came out in 1967—the Bee Gees had asked for it. I thought it was horrible. At IBC they also had a wonderful Lowry Lincolnwood organ I used on most Who recordings instead of the Hammond. Hammond is great, but such a stereotyped and hard-to-manipulate sound. I prefer Lowrys, and so does Garth Hudson from The Band.

Finally, I think it's really worth saying again that although I like working analog, I think in some ways I'm just following a current trend, because lots of young musicians I come across seem to want to work that way, too. I really believe that great new music comes from pushing at the envelope of creativity, trying new gadgets, new methods, new ways of doing the same old things. As a composer I think Ableton Live has to be the software that has given me the most immediate way to write new things on a computer rather than tape. At the same time it allows several additional levels of creativity, including that suggestion of mine that "finding" great sounds and loops can inspire new tracks.

You've worked with some of the great producers of all time, like Shel Talmy and Glyn Johns. What did you learn from any of these people, and do you have a preference between working with a producer and producing yourself?

I learned most from Glyn, who engineered our records with Shel. He has a strong personality that allowed him to dominate his own process very precisely. The way he sat, dead-center between the speakers—believe it or not, he was the first to do that so accurately; the equipment he used; the mics he used and where he put them; the reverb he used, always recorded on tape with the source, were all part of a process that he worked with almost intuitively. Many engineers tried to copy him and failed. They simply couldn't hear what he could hear. He built up a sound "picture," I think. When you went in for a playback, you would always be surprised at how solid an image he had created around your playing. Almost like posing for a photo, then seeing yourself in an image that had been Photoshopped. I knew I was gorgeous, but not that gorgeous. [*Laughs.*]

29

Yeah Yeah Yeahs

PUSHING THE SONIC PALETTE INTO SYNTH TERRITORY FOR *IT'S BLITZ*

By Bill Murphy

This chapter features an abridged version of the Yeah Yeah Yeahs article in the June 2009 issue of *EQ* magazine.

We've all heard how a shark has to keep constantly moving forward or it dies, and the same usually goes for a rock band that's banked its reputation on being edgy, engaging, and ahead of the curve. For New York City's Yeah Yeah Yeahs, their "shark moment" came when the trio reconvened in early 2008 to begin work on their latest album. Collectively, they decided not just to leave behind the jagged art-punk sound of their 2006 breakthrough, *Show Your Bones* (and the follow-up EP *Is Is*), but to deconstruct and retool it entirely.

The opening salvo originated with lead singer Karen O, who made the seemingly innocent suggestion to guitarist Nick Zinner that he might consider trying out some new instruments. For anyone even remotely familiar with the YYY sound, that's almost like asking Peter Max to give up his brush, but Zinner didn't flinch.

"There's already been some talk about this album,

with people saying, 'He's putting down the guitar! There's no guitar on the record!'" he says, referring to a recent *Spin* cover story with a dismissive laugh. "The reality is there's still tons of guitar on here, but I'm constantly looking for new sounds anyway. Karen's idea just goes with our band ethos of not repeating ourselves, because we're always trying to evolve."

It's Blitz! [Interscope] marks an evolution on multiple levels. The band enlisted two topflight producers—British expat Nick Launay (known for his work on PiL's legendary *The Flowers of Romance*, and to YYY fans for *Is Is*, as well as recent albums by Nick Cave, Supergrass, and Silverchair) and longtime friend and confidante David Andrew Sitek from TV on the Radio, who has worked closely with YYY since their 2003 debut *Fever to Tell*. What's more, *It's Blitz!* embraces retro new-wave pop, but with a thick low end and deep-space atmospherics worthy of Björk, Massive Attack, or Goldfrapp—all of whom have felt the touch of the album's mix engineer Mark "Spike" Stent.

Meanwhile, Karen O exudes a brighter, sunnier, and more confident mood throughout—a change that might have as much to do with her relocation to L.A. several years ago as it does her rise to maturity. Drummer Brian Chase sounds tighter and drier, giving the music plenty of room to stretch out and breathe. And Zinner flexes his burgeoning chops on an ARP Omni 2 synthesizer and a phalanx of other synths and effects pedals, proving his thirst for new sounds is only just getting started.

"It was really about going in without any plan," Launay says, recalling the first winter sessions he had with the band. "I think the important thing to know about this album is that they went in with maybe one or two tunes, but the majority of the material was written completely in the studio. That was more common back in the '80s when I started making records. It's a very unusual approach these days, and I think the reason they wanted to do that was specifically to come up with something new and fresh."

A total of five studios figured in the making of *It's Blitz!*, but the main venues for tracking were Long View Farm in Massachusetts, Sonic Ranch in Texas (with Launay), and Sitek's former Stay Gold Studio in Brooklyn. "We started in the winter at Long View, and then we went to Sonic Ranch," Launay explains. "The last lot of overdubs were done at The Boat in Silverlake [L.A.], and there

Yeah Yeah Yeahs' Brian Chase (far left), Karen O, and Nick Zinner. (Paul Natkin/WireImage/Getty Images)

were little bits and pieces done at Seedy Underbelly in L.A., which is the studio that I usually work out of, just off Laurel Canyon."

Sitek spent about three weeks in July with the band at Stay Gold, while he and Launay would frequently trade Pro Tools sessions, building tracks and adding to each other's work as time went on. The scope of the project became huge: Each of the album's ten songs went through at least four or five different versions, consisting of sometimes more than 100 tracks per song, and eventually taking up more than a dozen 250GB hard drives.

You don't often hear of two major producers trading licks like this on one album—especially on this scale.

Launay: That's why I think the album works so well, because Dave and I pretty much played what I like to call enthusiastic ping-pong. I would capture the band when they were writing and put all the best elements together with a lot of editing; maybe I'd grab something and put it in backwards, or switch out a chorus for a verse—things like that. Then it would go to Dave, and he might scrap this or that, try something new, and send it back to me and I'd go, "Holy s**t! What happened to all those ideas? This is really good!" There was never any competition—in fact, I found it all quite amusing.

Sitek: It was all pretty open. A lot of it was the band being like, "Okay, let's take it to Nick's world," and then, "Now let's take it to Dave's world."

Launay: We actually had one conversation. I rang Dave to ask him a question about a song. I'd heard that he's a very strong-willed character, but he was totally graceful and nice about it. He even told me, "Man, I'm so glad that you're okay with what I'm doing, because if someone came along and f**ked up my stuff the way I've been f**king up yours, I wouldn't be too happy." [*Laughs.*]

SYNTHESIZE ME

From Nick Zinner's perspective, his approach to getting guitar and synth sounds was equally wide open. Aside from the ARP Omni 2 he picked up on eBay (and which provides the bulk of sounds for the oddly mystical ballad "Skeletons"), he also availed himself of Sitek's huge array of synths, including the Yamaha CS-15—a staple on almost everything Sitek has ever recorded. It, along with a Roland Juno-106, helps drive the arpeggiated bass lines of the uptempo first single "Zero," while an ARP Solina String Ensemble and a Crumar Trilogy provide the strings and pads oscillating in the song's upper reaches.

Then there's the mind-boggling sonic palette that Zinner is able to wrench from his main guitar—an '80s Strat that he's had since childhood—with the help of such exotic pedals as Line 6's DL4 Delay Modeler and MM4 Modulation Modeler, Eventide's TimeFactor and ModFactor, DigiTech's Whammy and Hyper Phase, and a beat-up Roland RE-201 Space Echo, which he uses primarily for distortion filters. With so many choices at hand, Zinner can dial up guitar sounds that can easily be mistaken for synths; for a prime taste, check out the whistling—and Whammy-fied—melody that anchors the catchy "Soft Shock," the only song on the album where Zinner played a vintage Fender Jaguar.

What were the basics of your guitar setup?

Zinner: I like to go through two amps at the same time—a Vox AC30 and a Fender [Hot Rod] DeVille, for example—and then mic those up differently, as well as going direct. We really wanted to get away from the classic big room sound, so I did blends of those different signals. I usually put the guitar into a [Pro Co] RAT first, then the Line 6 Mod, then the Whammy, then the Line 6 Delay, and into the amps.

Launay: We usually had five tracks of Nick's guitar on every song. We'd have two mics on the Vox, which were usually a Beyer M 88 and an AKG 414, with the 414 very flat up against the grille and the 88 at an angle. The combination of them being slightly out of phase with each other is what gives it the basic sound, and then you can manipulate the balance.

On the DeVille, I'd have another 88 and a ribbon mic like a Royer or an old RCA 44. Very often I'd use a combination of any of the four mics—again, I might use two of them and put them out of phase with each other, or sometimes delay one of them, and then all of those would go through a combination of API and Neve preamps.

With the DI, sometimes that would be after all the pedals, so it would be very fuzzy if he was using a [fOXX] fuzz pedal, let's say. And we would replug things constantly—it was like spaghetti junction in there. If we wanted to go back and recreate some of those sounds, it would be almost impossible. We just had to record everything.

On "Zero," how did you "warm up" the signal path of the synths on the way into Pro Tools?

Sitek: For most of that I used the Wunder Audio 1073s and the Retro [Instruments] 176 [Limiting Amplifier]. I'm going direct, so older synths like the Yamaha CS-15 tend to need a little makeup gain on the output. What I like to do is take it to the absolute maximum that I can on the 1073s and then draw it back in by turning the gain down a little bit in the compression stage. That keeps it really bright and frizzly—that's the technical term. [*Laughs.*] By that I mean everything above 2k, where the air starts to distort.

VOCALS WITH ATTITUDE

The lion's share of Karen O's vocals were tracked by Launay at Sonic Ranch using a Neumann M 49, which he also prefers specifically for the way it distorts. "When you get close to it, it cracks up in the same way that a Shure SM57 does," he says. "To me, it's one of the few tube mics that has the mid-range of a dynamic mic, which I think is very important when you're doing rock and roll. If you use a really nice mic on a singer who's gonna give it some attitude, you're not gonna capture that with a delicious-sounding mic. You want something that sounds a little bit more earthy and urban."

How do you use EQ and compression to preserve that attitude that Karen delivers?

Launay: Another thing I like about the M 49 mic is that it gives you this incredible low-mid boost when you get close to it, so when I run Karen's vocal into a Neve 1081, I just leave the midrange alone. I'll boost at about 300Hz to give the sound some thickness, and then a similar amount at 100Hz. I usually boost at 15k, too—I find that the 1081s have the top-end control that's really good for fine-tuning at that frequency.

Then I go into a Tube-Tech CL 1A compressor, which I really like because the attack and release are both very fast. They're very similar to an 1176 in the way they're set up, but they sound a lot warmer and better suited to sibilance than an 1176. Generally, the combination of the M 49 and the Tube-Tech is fantastic. I'll set it at the fastest possible attack and fastest possible release for Karen's voice, and compress so that it's pinning—so the needle is hitting the end stop on the left-hand side when she's at her loudest. It comes very close to sounding like analog tape distortion.

Did you treat her voice with any other effects before the final mixing phase?

Launay: One thing I used on all the monitor mixes that we were doing, and in Karen's headphones generally, was a Roland CE-301 Chorus Echo. I used that as the slapback and reverb because there's a cheap built-in reverb in there that works really well with Karen's vocal. I know that made it onto a few of the songs, and I'm pretty sure Spike may have used it because I told him I thought it sounded great.

DRUMS FOR DAYS

There aren't many rock drummers who will actually tune their drums to the key of a song—in fact, you'd be hard-pressed to find any besides Brian Chase, whose conservatory training at Oberlin College made him somewhat of an anomaly among Brooklyn kit bangers when the Yeah Yeah Yeahs were first coming up. Chase has a number of tuneful moments on *It's Blitz!*, but his tom arrangement on the reverberating album closer "Little Shadow" is probably one of his best.

"The room gives the drums a natural reflective sound on that," he says, "but that's also Nick Launay's touch after the fact. I remember with the kick-drum sound in particular, he would dupe a track and then run it through a SansAmp setting to give it a little fuzz." In fact, aside from the album's two "live" tracks with the full band—"Dull Life" and "Shame and Fortune"—sonic manipulation was the order of the day for capturing and cataloging new drum sounds.

Dave Sitek has mentioned that he recorded different parts of the drum kit separately for the last TV on the Radio album. Is that how you guys worked together, too?

Chase: Yeah. In general for this album, we were essentially going for a very muted kick and snare sound, so a lot of the drums were recorded pieces at a time. We would record a kick and snare track first; because there were no cymbals or toms, it gave us a lot of flexibility to mold the character of those sounds. Then we would layer the tracks from there—usually multiple hi-hat tracks, and then cymbals on top of that.

Was there a basic way you got that muted sound—for example, on "Dragon Queen"?

Chase: I think the kick on that was a 24-inch double-headed kick that was stuffed with blankets. The muting on the snare was just a wallet resting on top, which worked against me a few times because I would end up leaving the studio without it. [*Laughs.*]

The drums on that song almost sound like an old drum machine. How did you record them?

Sitek: Generally, I use the Microtech Gefell M 930 on the snare, but on that particular one I think we actually went way out on a limb and used an SM57. [*Laughs.*] I recorded the kick with a Neumann U 47. You've gotta be

229

JEDI MASTER

Dave Sitek refers to Spike Stent as the "Obi-Wan Kenobi of mixing." Welcome to his inner sanctum. Studio G at L.A.'s Chalice Recording Studios is outfitted with an SSL 4080 G console, and for a while now it's been the main base of operations for Mark "Spike" Stent. More than just a mix engineer, Stent has built a sterling reputation over the years for truly shaping and crafting a mix, using filters and effects largely at his discretion once he gets creative input from an artist. The approach must be working; his client list includes everyone from U2 to Radiohead, and he has more on the horizon.

"I love the SSL Gs," Stent raves. "I don't particularly like mixing on any other console. I basically use a mixture of the console and plug-ins and automation on Pro Tools or Logic; for the Yeah Yeah Yeahs album, it was Pro Tools. I was brought up old-school, so I like the analog sound because it has a certain toughness, and I find it a lot easier to get what I want quickly out of that."

From the layered guitar and synth atmospherics that coat the tail-out section of "Dragon Queen" to the subtle variations in texture of Karen O's vocal on "Hysteric," Stent folds himself seamlessly into some of the finishing aspects of *It's Blitz!* He favors a number of SoundToys effects plug-ins, including EchoBoy and FilterFreak, but uses them judiciously in conjunction with the console, accessing automation controls in the box as well as on the desk itself.

"Karen had tracked up 'Hysteric' quite a lot," Stent observes, "but where she sings the actual word in the background, I stuck it through EchoBoy. I also time-adjusted her vocals in places, so one side would go left and one would go right with a very short delay; that makes it sound wider, phase-y, and a bit more 3D. I also have a dual chain that I tend to use where I'll split the vocal up to two channels and EQ them differently. One goes through an LA-2A, and the other goes through this blue-stripe, black reissue special edition 1176, which I use on everything."

In the end, Stent had options galore; not only were the Pro Tools sessions delivered to him in all their multitracked (and color-coded) glory, but producers Launay and Sitek also included loads of extra "grayed-out" tracks that Stent could activate if he was looking for something different.

"Dave and Nick did amazing jobs," he says, "and the soundscapes that they created for me to work from were incredible. And nothing should be taken away from Nick Zinner. He's an incredible guitarist, and I feel he completely reinvented himself on this record. There are traditional fans who are gonna go, 'What's happened?' but I think it's important for bands to try new things, and not just do the same record all over again."

real careful in terms of wind with that, so I doubled up the kick shell with another empty shell in front of it, and then put the mic in that shell and carpeted the whole thing. That gives it a little more space between the head and the microphone, but you don't really sacrifice distance, because it's all in its own chamber.

You must have done something on the way into Pro Tools.

Sitek: Everyone asks me what I use on the drums, and I'm like, "Well, who's the drummer? Is he on acid?" [*Laughs.*] One thing I will say is that I'm big about low cuts. I cut the lows out of almost everything, so that when I finally do the bass, you can hear every aspect of it. The kick and the human voice are my priorities in every song that I work on.

Can you give us a hint, though?

Sitek: Well, I mod those Dolby A-Type [Model] 361s to compress just the high end and disregard the low end. Those are my favorite things on earth. I'll put Karen's vocal through those things, too. If you want the crispy tippy top to stand out and you don't want to deal with an EQ or a mix issue, the 361s are great for that.

Dwight Yoakam

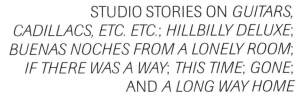

STUDIO STORIES ON *GUITARS,
CADILLACS, ETC. ETC.*; *HILLBILLY DELUXE*;
BUENAS NOCHES FROM A LONELY ROOM;
IF THERE WAS A WAY; *THIS TIME*; *GONE*;
AND *A LONG WAY HOME*

By Dusty Wakeman

This chapter features an abridged version of the Dwight Yoakam article in the May 2006 issue of *EQ* magazine.

In 1985, I had the honor of being asked to record tracks for Dwight Yoakam's first album, *Guitars, Cadillacs, Etc., Etc.*, by Pete Anderson, Dwight's producer, guitar slinger, and general partner in crime. By way of background, I first met Pete when we worked together on a record called *A Town South of Bakersfield, Vol. I*, which he was producing for Enigma Records. We were working at my studio—Mad Dog—which was in Venice, California, from 1980 until we moved to Burbank in 1995. The studio had been booked out every Monday through Friday by Enigma, and I had been recording a lot of punk and metal with an Enigma staff producer/A&R guy named Ron Goudie. We recorded everything from TSOL and Channel 3 to Stryper. The "cowpunk" scene was flourishing in L.A. at that time, with bands like Lone Justice, Rank and File, the Screaming Sirens, and the Long Ryders.

Ron told me of plans to record a country and cowpunk compilation and asked if I wanted to be the engineer, which, being Texas born-'n'-bred, I jumped on. Pete Anderson walked in the door, and we really hit it off. Dwight was in the process of getting signed, and had already released the EP version of *Guitars . . .*, which was creating quite a buzz. They were opening for bands like X, Los Lobos, and the Blasters, and really connecting with those crowds. The plan was to go in and cut four more tracks to complete the album. There was some controversy with the label, Warner Nashville, who wanted Dwight to go to Nashville and work with "the establishment" there. There have been scores of great records recorded there that we all love, but this was the tail end of the Urban Cowboy era, and most everything coming out of Nashville at that moment was pretty wimpy and formulaic. Pete liked me because I was coming from a rock background but knew and loved classic country. He had Dwight drop by Mad Dog to meet me while working on *Town South of Bakersfield*. I remember Dwight and Pete looking at the 2-track and being impressed with how hot the recording levels were.

GUITARS, CADILLACS, ETC. ETC.

We were booked into Capitol Studio B for something like three days, as I recall, to cut four tracks: "Honky Tonk Man," "Guitars, Cadillacs," "Bury Me" (a duet with Maria McKee), and "Heartaches by the Number." We were like kids in a candy store—we kept waiting for some adult to come and stop the fun. Dwight and Pete had spent a lot of time thinking about what they wanted to sound like, listening to records and really analyzing what they heard. This is what got us to Studio B at Capitol; many of the great California country artists had recorded there—Buck Owens, Merle Haggard, and so on. Capitol has eight live echo chambers under the parking lot that were poured when they built the studios and that were a distinctive part of the sound we were going for. Capitol was, and is, a true world-class studio complex, and Studio B remains my ideal of what a great room should be. When we built Mad Dog in Burbank, our Studio A was modeled after Capitol Studio B, which featured a Neve 8068, a Studer A800s, a great-sounding large room the size of a basketball court (it actually has a hoop in it), and two large iso booths stacked on top of each other.

Dwight Yoakam. (Kip Lott)

I'd come up outside of the "studio system" and had learned things largely by trial and error (making s**t up), so I was both elated and terrified when I sat at the console and the assistant, Steve Himelfarb, asked me what microphones I wanted to use. I think I replied that I was open to anything he cared to recommend. I did know, though, that we had to have one of Capitol's great U 47s on Dwight's voice, which I had coming through the 8068s 31102 modules into an LA-2A, and then straight to tape.

We built a little "hut" in the center of the room—with the U 47 facing toward it—in order to control the amount of room getting into the vocal, giving us a more focused sound. The band was totally well prepared, every overdub was planned, and Dwight never did more than a couple of takes in those days. We moved across the hall to Studio C to mix on the Neve 8108 with Necam 1 automation, taking advantage of the echo chambers and EMT plate . . . still the best I've ever heard. Studio C had a rack of Pultec EQP-1A3 EQs, one of which ended up on Dwight's vocal, along with a dbx 160x compressor. The 8108, though a maintenance nightmare, was a nice-sounding mix board—great EQs! We spent a lot of time referring to albums and A/B-ing our mixes for overall sonics with some classic country albums, really trying to achieve that classic sound for our record, yet still having it have the dynamic impact of a rock record.

HILLBILLY DELUXE

We recorded and mixed *Hillbilly Deluxe* in late 1985, with pretty much the same setup as on *Guitars . . .*, the big difference being that we were coming off a hit record. They had toured in an RV non-stop for about ten months, and by the time they came home, Dwight was a star, part of the "New Traditionalists" movement in country, along with Steve Earle and Randy Travis. Once again Pete had everything completely planned out. The band was well rehearsed, and Dwight would walk out and give us one to three great takes.

I think we may have done some very light comping, but big sections, not words. The signal path for Dwight's vocals stayed the same. One great change on this album was the addition of Charlie Paakkari to the team. Charlie was officially my second engineer, which was kind of a joke to me, because he was so much more knowledgeable than I was. He was a staff engineer at Capitol—one day an assistant, the next day a first—working with a lot of the great masters. It was an amazing education. The one smart thing I did was to let him really contribute to the project and share his knowledge of that studio with me. Again we mixed across the hall in Studio C. I was really proud of my tom sound on "Little Ways," which I had running through a Pultec and the Fairchild 670, with a lot of live chamber on it.

BUENAS NOCHES FROM A LONELY ROOM

Enter the technology: Once again we were firmly ensconced in Studio B, this time with another hit record under our belts and a bigger budget to work with. Unlike the first two albums, which we raced through, we actually had some time to stretch out and try some things. We cut the basic tracks on the Studer A800 with 16-track heads and then bounced to Mitsubishi 32-track digital machine for all the overdubs. Charlie Paakkari was once again working with us, and we had some fun. We spent half a day figuring out a way to sync the tremolo in one of Pete's Fender Twin Reverbs to our drum track. Pete's two Twins had been modded to allow one tremolo to drive the other, so we figured there must be some way to control it from an external source. We listened to the sound that was coming from the "master" tremolo—it was basically a low-frequency pulse. We hooked up a signal generator with an audio trigger input to an oscillator and filtered the sound to match the control that the Twin generated, then fed a mix of the drums into it, and plugged that into the slave tremolo. Amazingly, it worked.

The track is "What I Don't Know." I was amazed by how many people actually noticed that the tremolo was locked to the drums and asked how we did it, which had been a secret until now. One of the great things about Capitol, besides the great rooms, is the amazing level of support available from the staff, especially the tech staff—very handy when you're in experimental mode.

By now, we had gotten into full-on vocal comp mode and I had purchased an Emulator EIII, which we used for tweaking and flying. It was a great machine for pitch correction in those pre–Pro Tools days, although you had to take it apart and reseat the cards every time you moved it. Dwight had been touring nonstop since the last album and was barraged by promotional duties, so getting the vocals took a little longer. Dwight's voice is so clear when he's in good shape that it would be obvious right away if there was any hoarseness present. Thankfully, we had the time to spend to get the great takes.

This album also features Buck Owens on "Streets of Bakersfield," which went on to become DY's first number-one single. We were just putting together Dwight's vocal comp when Buck showed up to sing, and it wasn't sounding right. I discovered that somehow the console tapes' take numbers didn't line up with the actual take numbers, so I discreetly pulled Pete aside and told him what happened. He said, "fix it—I'll stall for time." He went out and kept those guys busy while Charlie and I frantically rebuilt the comp. That song also features Flaco Jimenez on accordion, which was recorded in the iso booth in Studio C using the same U 47 and a Focusrite mic pre we'd been using for some overdubs. Once again we mixed in Studio C.

IF THERE WAS A WAY

I consider the first three albums to be part of the "phase I" of DY's recording career—most of those songs were written and performed live before *Guitars . . .* was recorded. *If There Was a Way* marked the beginning of "phase II." All of the material was new, some of it co-written with other writers, and we had lots of time to make the records. We used more outside musicians for overdubs—to his and Pete's credit, Dwight's band always played on the records, even venturing into strings and background singers. The parameters that had been set on the first three records were definitely being pushed.

Another big change for me was the change from Charlie Paakkari to Pete Doell as my "assistant engineer." I consider both these guys to be two of the finest engineers anywhere, and I learned so much from working with both of them. Charlie was unavailable, and we knew and respected Pete Doell from working across the hall from him at Capitol for years.

Now, Dwight is an amazing singer who on any given day is capable of walking out and giving you a couple of perfect or near-perfect takes, but getting his vocals got more difficult in this era for several reasons—he hadn't been performing these songs live for years, and, on many days, by the time he'd get to the studio (usually early evening), he'd have been on the phone all day taking care of business. Aside from his music career, he was starting to get active in film, which requires lots of Hollywood lunches, meetings, and long phone conversations. The upside was the string of beautiful actresses and models that would drop by for a visit. In fact, sometimes the presence of a couple of babes would be the catalyst for that great performance we were looking for. But by now, we were deep into vocal comping and tweaking, which Pete Doell brought a lot to—he has perfect pitch. Although I had good relative pitch, I really learned to hear pitch from working with him, especially sharpness. The slightest bit of "pitchiness" would provoke a physical reaction in Pete Doell. This also was the first record to be mixed by David Leonard, who is a brilliant mixer best known for his work with Prince and John Mellencamp. At first I wasn't thrilled with the idea of someone else mixing "my record." But he totally blew my mind—another great engineer that I learned volumes from.

THIS TIME

In many ways, *This Time* was a career peak for DY. It's been his biggest-selling album to date and yielded a Grammy award for Best Country Vocal Performance for the song "Ain't That Lonely Yet." Pete's guitar solo on "A Thousand Miles from Nowhere" was another blazing classic. We'd usually do Pete's solos at night after DY would sing—lights down low, monitors cranked. Those were some magical moments, sometimes after a day of routine "work"—the kind of moments that keep you coming back. DY, too, would give you those moments, when he was rested and not distracted by all the BS he had to deal with. We were experimenting with Pro Tools by now; we had Scott Humphreys and Paul D'Carli there helping us—two of the pioneers of the medium. We really had fun with it on the track "This Time"—we were more interested in using it to make things greasier as opposed to tighter. We were back to analog, cutting basics on the A800 with 16-track heads and doing overdubs on a second 24-track A800. When we used Pro Tools, we would bounce it from the 16-track and back to a new spot on the tape, building the track from there. Once again, the U 47 was employed, either through the Neve 8068 or through my John Hardy M1 pres, which I still use. Pete Doell had found a Fairchild 660 compressor in a storage room at Capitol, and retubed it, and we used it on everything—Dwight's vocals, Pete's guitar, Tara's bass, everything.

GONE

Gone was an interesting, artistic album to make. *This Time* had been a huge record for Dwight, with the never-ending touring a success like that requires. It was recorded in much the same way as the previous two, with even more experimentation with Pro Tools, and musically the walls were pretty much blown out. The writing was eclectic, very much a statement of Dwight's influences. Stylistically, it ranged from straight-up country to British Invasion power pop to the huge orchestral "Nothing," with the gospel background vocals. I loved it, but I think it might have left some of his core audience behind. We used the same vocal setup as on *This Time*.

A LONG WAY HOME

Long Way Home turned out to be the last album that was made with this team, and in some ways, it's one of my favorites. The writing is really good, especially the song "A Long Way Home," which seemed somehow to sum up where Dwight was—and, by extension, where all of us were at that time in our collective and individual journeys. Dwight's relationship with his label had somewhat soured by this time, and he was doing very well in the movie biz, but he was more focused on this record than he'd been in a long time and was very creatively engaged in the making of it. This time, it was Pete's turn to be distracted—being a label head can be time-consuming. I think he was comfortable knowing that the team he had assembled over the years was quite capable. Once again, Michael Dumas co-engineered, and I'd been credited as engineer and associate producer (whatever that means) for quite a few records by this time, which meant I was doing more musically than just recording. A lot of these labels tend to blur when you've worked with the same people for a long time. For me, I enjoyed working so closely with Dwight on *A Long Way Home*. Technically, we were using the same combination of analog and Pro Tools that we'd been using for quite a while. Michael quickly became a Pro Tools whiz, and we were bouncing tracks back and forth between us. *A Long Way Home* wasn't well promoted and didn't sell like some of Dwight's bigger records, but a lot of the more astute critics realized what a gem it was, and I still enjoy revisiting it.

OTHER GREAT TITLES FROM NEW BAY MEDIA